D1631289

D

Chronicling
Trauma

THE HISTORY OF COMMUNICATION

Robert W. McChesney
and John C. Nerone, editors

*A list of books in the series
appears at the end of this book.*

Chronicling Trauma

Journalists and Writers on Violence and Loss

DOUG UNDERWOOD

UNIVERSITY OF ILLINOIS PRESS

Urbana, Chicago, and Springfield

© 2011 by the Board of Trustees
of the University of Illinois
All rights reserved
Manufactured in the United States of America
C 5 4 3 2 1
∞ This book is printed on acid-free paper.

Library of Congress Cataloging-in-Publication Data
Underwood, Doug.
Chronicling trauma : journalists and writers
on violence and loss / Doug Underwood.
p.   cm. — (The history of communication)
Includes bibliographical references and index.
ISBN 978-0-252-03640-8 (cloth)
1. Violence—Press coverage. 2. Psychic trauma—Press coverage.
3. War correspondents—Mental health. 4. Authors, American—
Psychology. 5. Violence in literature. 6. Psychic trauma in
literature. 7. Journalists—United States—Biography.
8. Journalists—Great Britain—Biography. 9. Journalism and
literature—United States. 10. Journalism and literature—
Great Britain.
I. Title.
PN4784.V56U76   2011
820.9'3552—dc22   2011012406

To my wife, Susanne
Whose work in the corridors
of loss and grief has shown me
how love, faith, and listening
can ease the pain of
traumatic experience.

Contents

Trauma, News, and Narrative

The Study of Violence and Loss in Journalism and Fiction

> "We are all bitched from the start
> and you especially have to be hurt
> like hell before you can write seriously."
>
> —Ernest Hemingway

Ernest Hemingway has meant many things to many people, but one that he was not comfortable with was his standing as the monumental example of how traumatic experience can shape the life of a journalist-turned-novelist. When Hemingway once said that he would never write about his growing-up years in Oak Park, Illinois, because he "did not want to hurt living people," he was being disingenuous at best. Hemingway—who did not mind hurting people in myriad ways throughout his career—knew that there were dark shadows and family skeletons looming in his youthful past.[1] In an adult life where he became a notorious alcoholic, struggled with depression, volunteered for war and covered most of the major military conflicts of his lifetime, and ultimately committed suicide, Hemingway demonstrated on a mythic scale how the pursuit of a journalistic career and its expansion into a drive for artistic success can be connected to a history of family and personal dysfunction and a lifetime of traumatic experiences that grew out of his risk-taking philosophy of life.

Kay Redfield Jamison in her study of the relationship of manic depression to artistic temperament features Hemingway and his family background of suicides (his father, sister, and brother also committed suicide) and emotional illness (one son was manic-depressive; another son suffered from posttrauma psychosis). Hemingway was at the front of a group of journalists-turned-novelists and other journalist-literary figures (Samuel Johnson, James

Boswell, Mary Wollstonecraft, Samuel Taylor Coleridge, Charles Lamb, Charles Dickens, Edgar Allan Poe, Walt Whitman, James Russell Lowell, J. M. Barrie, John Ruskin, Mark Twain, Eugene O'Neill, Virginia Woolf, Dylan Thomas, Hart Crane, and Graham Greene) that Jamison identifies (along with an index of other writers, painters, and musicians) as suffering from various degrees of emotional imbalance that were major factors in their creative ambition.[2] Although the cultural archetype of the psychologically tortured and emotionally unstable artist has been around since the romantic period of the early 1800s, there has been a spate of contemporary studies—in addition to Jamison's—that have found evidence of an association between creativity and predisposition to mental illness.[3] At the same time, researchers have begun to pay close attention to the impact of trauma and coverage of violence on journalists, the subjects of their coverage, and the secondary effects on their audience—including examining the possibility that journalists who have suffered early life stress (such as unhappy childhoods and distorted family relationships) may gravitate toward high-risk assignments, such as war reporting.[4]

Journalism and fiction built on a journalistic foundation are natural fields for the study of trauma—both because of the nature of the events covered by working journalists and because so many of the literary figures who have been the focus of scholars interested in trauma began their careers in or were associated with the journalism profession. Journalism has long trafficked in the subjects of trauma—crime, violence, accounts of war, as well as psychological profiling of deviant and disturbed personalities. Novelists, in turn, have explored these same subjects in the course of developing their imaginative characters and by borrowing from their own traumatic life stories to shape the themes of their fiction. It may be no surprise then to find that journalists who have become novelists and literary figures would turn out to be intensely involved in investigating and demonstrating the impact of trauma on literary writing and the literary personality. This study draws on the appeal that stories of trauma and psychological stress have had for writers and their audiences and builds its analytical framework on the research that has examined the role of traumatic events and youthful traumatic family experiences in the literary accounts of and the mental health issues dealt with by authors and artists. In examining the nature of these experiences in the lives of important journalist-literary figures in the United States and the British Isles dating from the early 1700s to today, I will be exploring the role that dealing with trauma has played in the shaping of their journalistic and literary value system and its incorporation into their literary works. In doing this, I will be contending that the intersection of journalism and fiction writing is a particularly valuable place to gain insights about trauma's role in literary expression.

Journalism is perhaps the only profession outside the military in which involvement in war has been romanticized, and where drinking, profligate behavior, and itinerant and unstable career paths—as well as the "toughness" to deal with the traumatizing topics of news coverage—are celebrated in the profession's lore and myth. From the emergence of the modern newspaper in the 1600s, the focus of journalistic coverage often has included events with traumatic overtones—murders, executions, fires, military battles, bizarre births, the consequences of madness, claims of sightings of monsters and ghosts, and such. This fit with the recognition by early editors that readers would buy written accounts of occurrences that were presented as strange, violent, mysterious, or threatening, all of which in prenewspaper days were the material of folk tales, legends, ballads, and other devices that humans have used to communicate their fascination with the frightening and the aberrational in life. In the early days of newspapers, when they had small circulations, were irregularly published, and often were written anonymously by an editor using a wide array of literary devices, a publication could contain accounts of hangings, freezing bodies for later resuscitation, rebellions against the monarchy, and advice for how to manage depression and melancholy (all of which the eighteenth-century journalist and biographer Boswell produced for the periodicals of his era). However, as journalism professionalized with the coming of the industrialized newspaper of the early nineteenth century, the parameters of journalistic expression grew more restrictive and the techniques for covering the news more formulaic and predictable. Particularly as news organizations took on the pretense of covering matters in an "objective" and scientifically detached fashion, the profession of the "reporter"—hired starting in the early 1800s to cover the "beats" (the courts, the jails, the police stations) where newspapers found their stories of crime and human waywardness—meant a person who was expected to frame the events of the world through the commercial goals and organizational dictates of his or her employer.[5]

In the meantime, the genre of the novel—which became a popular success with the imaginative and innovative writings of the journalists-novelists Daniel Defoe, Jonathan Swift, and Henry Fielding in the 1700s and reached a level of respectability with educated readers in the era of the Victorian journalists-turned-serial-novelists, Dickens and William Thackeray—offered a new avenue of expression for journalists and ex-journalists who had grown frustrated with the limits on "honest" dialogue in the commercial publications of their day. As a novelist, Dickens discovered that—unlike in his newspaper journalism, where he was required to write within the framework of dry, early-nineteenth-century political reporting—he was able to develop fictional themes that were connected to his own childhood traumas, and he came to believe that fiction writing was the way to personalize and humanize issues of human suffering and touch readers' hearts with scenarios that pointed the way to political reform. Twain rebelled against the ponderous content of his brother's small town newspapers in Missouri and Iowa by trying to get more humor, parody, and satire into their columns; his reporting career came to an end in 1864, in part because the *San Francisco Morning Call* would not print his account of the stoning of a Chinese immigrant by a gang of Irish youths. When Twain was let go by the newspaper, his editor tried to ease the blow by telling him he had a greater calling in literature, thus setting the tone for generations of journalists who would turn to fiction writing as newspapers became less hospitable to candid and creative expression.[6]

In particular, the culture of the newsroom and the posture of the typical urban journalist took on a cynical, hard-shelled tone by the late nineteenth century that fit with an opportunistic system of "scoop" seeking and news formulas that were exploitative of human tragedy. This meant that news writers were expected to deal with human pain only within the conventions of industrialized news reporting and where the ability to "handle" traumatic experience became one of the measures of the successful news professional. This often made fiction writing—with its greater opportunity for subjective expression and its freedom from the legal and commercial restraints built into conventional news accounts with identifiable subjects—a liberating option for journalists who wrestled with psychic difficulties, hungered to convey their personal vision of life, and found imaginative writing a more expansive place to explore their own emotional terrain and the challenges of the external world.

Much contemporary medical and psychological research has focused on the connection between early childhood and later psychological stress, traumatic experience, and the adoption of unhealthy habits and lifestyles as coping mechanisms for dealing with troubled emotional lives. This examination applies this research to the world of the journalist, the profession of journalism, and the role that psychological stress may have played in journalists' ambitions to succeed in fictional and other literary pursuits. In addition, I draw on recent scholarship that examines the relationship of trauma and literary writing, and I owe a debt to the scholars—including Anthony Storr, David Aberbach, Kirby Farrell, Janice Haaken, E. Ann Kaplan, Mark Heberle, Cathy Caruth,

Ruth Leys, Laurie Vickroy, Leigh Gilmore, Kali Tal, and others—who have studied the influence of trauma and human loss on novelists, poets, and other literary figures, including a number who began their careers as journalists.

This study focuses on 150 journalist-literary figures in American and British history and the traumatic events in their lives that can be viewed as contributing to their emotional struggles, the vicissitudes of their journalism careers, and their development as artists. (See table 1 in the appendix.) Although some of these figures are best known as novelists, poets, or playwrights, all had important experiences as journalists, and many have been studied by journalism as well as literary historians. In more than two-thirds of the cases, these journalist-literary figures suffered some form of employment trauma while working in journalism, including being fired from a job, having their writings censored or suppressed, covering military conflicts or other stories in dangerous circumstances, or having an emotional breakdown while in a journalism job. (See table 2 in appendix.) In a number of cases, the extent of these traumatic experiences was only made clear when they left commercial journalism and were able to write about them in more intimate and subjective terms in their literary works.

Thus it is in their fictional writings and autobiographical accounts—along with biographies and critical studies of their work—that one can gain some of the best insights into how early life stress and adult emotional distress may have influenced journalists with literary ambitions. Journalists at work in their professional environments seldom write openly or directly about the influence of stress and trauma in their own lives—and certainly not so when they are performing their regular journalism tasks. A host of conventions— the macho professional culture of the typical newsroom, the pose of "objectivity" and detachment in standard news writing, the assumption that risk-taking in the name of newsgathering should be undertaken without complaint, the pressures of a deadline-oriented work environment that leaves little room for introspection—means that journalists rarely discuss their inner lives in ways that reveal emotional vulnerability. Even among newspaper columnists and magazine writers, who are given some latitude to express themselves in personal ways, there are few who will discuss their own psychological condition in any but the most guarded manner. As a result, it is in the accounts of some of the most famous journalists in history—namely those who have gone on to establish a reputation as novelists and/or writers of literature—that the few honest insights about the inner conflicts of the journalistic personality often can be found. A key point in this study is its suggestion that the examination of journalists who have left the profession to take up novel writing or other literary activities offers important opportunities to analyze trauma's effects in ways that the study of practicing journalists alone may not, and that the interplay of these two fields (fiction and journalism) is a fruitful avenue for examining the impact of trauma in writers who have found the freedom to explore its consequences outside of the constraints of the newsroom.

Contemporary psychology and family systems theories postulate that many psychic disorders, addictions, and emotional dependencies result from a complex of causes usually rooted in brain chemistry, genetic inheritance, the difficulties of early life and family training, and proclivities ingrained in the personality. These studies also suggest that the effects of trauma are greatest when they operate as part of an aggregate of influences that work together to undermine psychological health. Psychologists point out that these individual and family attributes, life stresses, and personal habits tend to work in combination with each other, and that commonly a disturbed personality will share one or more of these traits and/or circumstances and embrace one or more problematic life responses in dealing with emotional disequilibrium. This schematic is mirrored in an extensive literature that has grown out of literary and psychological studies. In it, scholars—often influenced by Freudian, feminist, and cultural studies theories—have pointed to the effects of traumatic experiences, personal losses, childhood stresses, family disturbances, and inherited characteristics and connected them to artistic activity. By noting these patterns in the lives of many journalist-literary figures, this study suggests that these points of psychological and emotional stress—working in single and in multiple fashions—have played an important role in shaping their personalities and in driving them to artistic accomplishment. It also suggests that in some cases a journalism career may have compounded psychic tensions and added to the mental health stresses identified with artistic ambition, as well as serving as the catalyst for drawing unstable personalities into journalism as a pathway to the fulfillment of literary and fictional ambition.

This work builds on my earlier volume, *Journalism and the Novel: Truth and Fiction, 1700–2000*, which explores the relationship of journalism to literary and fictional writing since the emergence of modern journalism and the modern novel. In that analysis, the intertwined nature of the journalistic and the literary-fictional traditions is examined, as are the important contributions that journalist-literary figures and journalists-turned-novelists have made to the literary canon. The volume includes a discussion of what is meant by the term *journalist-literary figure,* which is defined as a writer of fiction and/or nonfiction who had an important career in journalism and built his or her literary work on a foundation of journalistic research, reporting, and professional experience. The methodology for determining how writers were classified as journalist-literary figures, including most of the 150 figures who are the focus of this study, is explained there, and there is an appendix that describes their backgrounds in journalism and some of their most important literary works.[7]

It was in doing this earlier research that I first noticed how often issues of trauma, emotional instability, and substance abuse have played a role in the lives and the careers of these journalistic writers. In selecting the 150 journalist-literary figures for this study, I focused on writers who have had significant-enough journalistic and literary careers that there is detailed biographical information from which to draw. I made an effort to pick writers who had meaningful experiences as journalists, including many who suffered at least one traumatic event in their journalistic career. In assembling the list, I followed the practice of Jamison in finding examples of writers whose lives and careers allowed for the most telling examination of the relationship between trauma, journalism, and literature. Although this list is selective and should not be viewed as statistically or scientifically representative of all the journalists who have engaged in fictional or literary writing, it does include many of the most prominent British and American journalist-literary figures that I focused on in my discussion in *Journalism and the Novel*.

Finally, my work with the Dart Center for Journalism and Trauma has given me greater insight into the way issues of trauma and stress work within the journalistic profession, and I am appreciative of the opportunities to interact with the researchers and journalists who are connected to the center. In particular, the contribution of Roger Simpson, my University of Washington colleague, in taking over the Dart Center and moving it to the UW in 1999, and the efforts of Bruce Shapiro, Roger's successor as Dart Center director, associate director Meg Spratt, who runs the Dart Center West at the UW after the main operation's move to Columbia University in 2009, research director Elana Newman, and Dart Center founding figure, Frank Ochberg, have been helpful influences. It was those interactions, as well as the encouragement I received from my then department chair, Jerry Baldasty, that led me to move my research about journalist-literary figures in the direction of trauma studies.

The work of Newman and Anthony Feinstein, who has done pioneering research in association with the Dart Center about the impact of trauma on journalists, has developed out of the studies of combatants from the Vietnam War and other recent military conflicts, as well as the establishment of the formal diagnosis of post-traumatic stress disorder (PTSD) in the 1980s that led to the examination of how these issues affect journalists involved in combat reporting or other coverage of violent and traumatic events. These studies, which are grounded in the behavioral and quantitative methods of social science and medical and psychological research, draw many of their conclusions from surveys and interviews of journalists and others who have experienced traumatic events. In this area of research, traumatic experience has tended to be defined in dramatic terms and associated with the experiences of people who have been witness to or victims of events and circumstances (warfare, terrorist attacks, violent crime, and natural disasters) that fall outside the realm of normal, day-to-day human experience.[8]

The studies of Jamison and Storr, in turn, tend to be more qualitative in nature and draw for their conceptual foundation on interpretive readings informed by psychological theory of the biographical and literary record of writers and artists. Jamison and Storr, both psychologists by training, have been influenced by Freudian, Jungian, and later psychological concepts and Sigmund Freud's own romantic notions of the powerful role of childhood events in determining adult psychological health. Jamison and Storr put a strong emphasis on family history—both in terms of the transmission of psychological proclivities from generation to generation, as well as the experiences of children growing up in psychologically stressful or dysfunctional family circumstances. Although they do not discuss journalism or journalism's influence on the artistic tradition specifically, implicit in their analysis is the notion that many literary pursuits are methods for people to "write out" their psychological distress, and particularly so in eras before writers and artists had psychological theories and therapies available to help them understand what was happening in their emotional lives. Within this field of study, I also draw on other psychological theorists—most notably, Alice Miller, and her book, *Prisoners of Childhood*—to help better comprehend the psychological patterns that are identifiable in a number of journalist-literary figures whose grandiosity, narcissism, and frozen emotional lives can be viewed as connected to unmet childhood needs and the necessity of developing a false self in order to satisfy parents who looked to their children to address their own "narcissistic wounding."[9]

Jamison and Storr point to a variety of opportunities that art and literary production offer to the person with a distressed psyche. Manic-depressive personalities, for example, can find in the intensity of art an activity to match their manic drives and compulsions, as well as a means to explore and chronicle the meaning of their depressive episodes. Literary themes also offer a way to work out and try to make sense of family and personal strife, as well as to provide writers with the feeling that they are in control of a story that in life might otherwise seem chaotic, confusing, or abusive. Finally, society tolerates and even expects the expression of aberrational feelings and themes in fictional literature, and writers with psychological issues have found it an acceptable place to express emotions, ideas, and story lines that would otherwise be deemed outside the pale of what is allowable in normal social intercourse or in nonfictional journalistic writing.

Storr cites research that indicates that the lack of a warm parental relationship can leave people predisposed to the development of depression; that children with depressed parents or who lose a parent early in life are more likely to become depressed themselves; and that writing and other creative activities can be effective ways of coping with loss. He sees this dynamic at work in the careers of a number of journalist-literary figures—including Rudyard Kipling, H. H. Munro (who wrote as "Saki"), and P. G. Wodehouse—who came to use imagination as a refuge from the world. Storr says Kipling—who at age five was left in England with a retired naval captain and his wife who punished Kipling and his sister with beatings and enforced isolation—described the five years before his parents returned from India as "The House of Desolation." As an adult, Kipling remained elusive and shunned publicity; he was at his best and most relaxed around children; and he identified with others and empathetically experienced their lives, which Storr sees as growing out of the watchful and wary concern of a child living in an abusive situation. The early life traumas of Munro, who lost his mother at the age of two and was left to be raised by relatives, including an irrationally punitive aunt, and P. G. Wodehouse, who as a child was put under the care of a stranger and moved around to different schools, help to explain, Storr says, why as an adult Wodehouse dreaded individual contact and tended to retreat into a world of fantasy and Munro concealed his feelings beneath a protective mask of cynicism and exhibited a sadistic streak (a trait he shared with Kipling).[10]

The final stream of research that influences this study grows out of literary studies and involves the work of literary scholars who also have become highly influenced by Freudian and psychological theory in examining the role of trauma, childhood distress, and sexual and psychological abuse on literary production. Edmund Wilson, the prominent literary critic, was one of the first to probe this phenomenon in his 1929 work, *The Bow and the Wound*. Wilson's interest in early life trauma—which grew out of his own unhappy childhood growing up with two harsh and emotionally withdrawn parents—led him to apply the insights of Freud to the impact of childhood trauma on the personalities of fellow journalist-literary figures Dickens, Kipling, and Hemingway (among other artists). The contemporary writings of Aberbach, Heberle, and Farrell have carried on this line of inquiry by examining the effects of trauma and loss on an even greater range of literary writers and novelists, including some of the journalist-literary figures identified in this study.[11]

A key element in the work of literary scholars in this area has been their expansion of the meaning of trauma beyond catastrophic events (or physical occurrences that cause acute injury or wounds, as the translation from the Greek implies) into the realm of psychological issues that can be connected to childhood stress and emotionally disabling experiences. This study follows their lead in using an expanded definition of *trauma* to encompass "memory that is imbedded in the neurophysiology of pain and fear," including childhood events and emotional losses, and their interactions with inherited psychological attributes and temperamental proclivities that can have a powerful and often lifetime impact on the individual. The study of depression and its causes is of particular importance within the scope of this volume because so many of the journalist-literary figures examined here suffered from its effects and behaviors that are seen as connected to depression (suicidal tendencies, substance abuse, philandering, and destructive lifestyles).[12]

Given the broad scope of my use of the term, I have adopted for this study the definition of *trauma* used by Janice Haaken in her 1998 work, *Pillar of Salt*, which she defines as an acute subjective distress response to an unbearable reality and/or an overwhelming external event. Psychic trauma, she adds, is "any developmental event or crisis that overwhelms the ego's integrative capacities, compromising subsequent adaptive structures. Trauma may take the form of a discrete event, such as the loss of a parent or birth of a sibling, or chronic strains and stresses, such as neglect and abuse. What is crucial is not simply the magnitude of any 'shock' to the system but the availability of psychological structures—particularly object relational (self in relation to other) representations derived from early attachments—that permit a relatively nonpathological integration of disturbing experiences." Haaken's definition of trauma has the virtue of both being expansive in nature and encompassing of a wide range of potential "triggers" of psychic stress. It also takes into account the fact that psychological response to traumatic events is not necessarily deterministic in nature, and that different people—depending on their early life experiences, their genetic and temperamental make-up, and their adaptive capacities—may respond differently to similar life events and circumstances.[13]

In my usage of the term, *trauma* can have a closed loop influence on the human psyche; it can be caused by both the experience of a shocking event and/or sustained abuse to the nervous system, as well as by the stresses growing out of a person's basic psychological underpinnings and/or the impact of internally generated emotional distress. For many of the figures in this study, their experiences of anxiety, depression, morbidity, and despair could be traumatic events in the same way that upsetting experiences generated by outside factors could be. In coming out of family backgrounds where emotional weakness was not acceptable and/or in working within a professional environment in which people were expected to be tough and self-contained, a number of these writers found it traumatic to discover that their internal psychological workings did not support this approach to life and that they could be overwhelmed by feelings that they could not understand or control. In this respect, *trauma* is treated here as a broad and holistic term that encompasses the totality of emotional pressure on the human nervous system as it manifests itself in feelings whose sources are not always transparent to the person undergoing the experience.[14]

The early life traumas experienced by the figures in this study range from deeply shocking ones—Lamb pulling away the knife from his mentally ill sister after she had stabbed their mother to death at the dinner table, the schoolgirl Mary McCarthy dealing with her younger siblings after the death of both her parents in the flu epidemic of 1918, the eleven-year-old Conrad Aiken finding his parents' bodies after his father murdered his mother and then committed suicide, the young Elie Wiesel surviving the Nazi death camps but losing his mother and father and sister in the process—to what some might view as more commonplace experiences of chronic family dysfunction. Although much of the psychological research defines *trauma* as a single horrific experience that produces a shock to the human organism, Freud believed that the adult reaction to trauma may operate on a sliding scale and can connect to childhood history through a progression of symptoms that develop into psychological dysfunction. One can presume, for example, that Lamb's growing up with a manic-depressive sister, a progressively senile father, and a bedridden mother, plus his own history of being institutionalized during an emotional breakdown, created great psychological tension for him, but that his witnessing his sister killing his mother was a traumatic experience. Still, the connection between the event and the nexus of psychological "stressors" suffered by Lamb—episodes of deep depression, often triggered by his responsibilities as caretaker for his mentally ill sister, a life in which he did not feel he could marry because of his family duties, drinking to excess, and searching for self-expression and psychological relief in art and writing—may be seen within a pattern of related syndromes, inherited attributes, and nervous system responses of a person with both genetic and life experience links to the sources of psychological turbulence.

In this discussion, it must be remembered that there is a long history dating back to the observations of Aristotle ("all men who have attained excellence in philosophy, in poetry, in art and in politics . . . had melancholic habitus") and Charles Darwin (it is sadness that can "lead an animal to pursue that course of action which is most beneficial") that points to evidence that depression, despite its pain, can have a positive effect on human problem-solving and adaptive capacities. The prevalence of depression among writers and artists has led some scientists to speculate that the "ruminative" tendency and obsessive thinking patterns of the depressed person can lead to more intense focus and greater accomplishment that can be advantageous to certain individuals. Although there is much debate about the value of psychological suffering within human evolution, artistic achievement is often held up as one of the strongest cases that can be made for "depression's upside," as Jonah Lehrer has put it, as do studies that show that "expressive writing" about one's condition can lead to significantly shorter depressive cycles. However, there are other researchers who view depression—as well as trauma's role in serving as a source of psychological scarring—as a double-edged sword in that it may be useful up to a point but can become debilitating if it is overwhelming or spirals out of control. Among the journalist-literary figures studied here, this pattern can be seen in the way that traumatic events and psychological suffering often helped to catalyze their journalistic and their artistic accomplishments but also to undermine their capacity to live healthy and integrated lives.[15]

From Freud's time forward, there has been debate within the medical and research community as to how extensively the definition of *trauma* should be extended beyond the "shell-shock" of soldiers and whether adult traumas from war and violent events should be treated in the context of childhood background. *Trauma* meant a physical or physiological wound until some time between 1874 and 1886 in France when it came to designate a spiritual, psychic, or mental injury, or what Ian Hacking calls a "wound to the soul," and was linked to memory as the activating factor in the emergence of later symptoms of emotional distress. This growing awareness of the psychological consequences of trauma grew out of Jean-Martin Charcot's studies of shell shock in soldiers in the late 1870s in France that eventually were connected to Freud's study of "hysteria" in Victorian women in the 1890s. Freud himself felt that the adult responses to war trauma may lie in the sources of narcissistic libido and traumatic childhood events, but he acknowledged that he did not have the evidence to prove it. However, it is not going too far to infer from Freud that the difference in how soldiers react to trauma may depend at least to some degree on how the combat situation triggered prior psychic conflicts and earlier traumatic happenings.[16]

As part of what Caruth has called the "unclaimed" or unprocessed experience that is carried in the body, she notes that—in large part, because of the healing effects of writing autobiography and life stories—there has been a surge of interest in both composing and studying literary memoir. Gilmore cites a number of works by figures in this study—including Whitman's *Leaves of Grass*, Frederick Douglass's *Narrative*, and McCarthy's *Memories of a Catholic Girlhood*—as examples of autobiographical narratives that were written to deal with trauma. War experience, in particular, taps into humans' "natural" storytelling function, says Nigel C. Hunt, and the use of memory to develop a narrative can be a critical feature in a person gaining an emotional framework and some sense of control over a tragic event.[17]

The study of trauma also has been pulled into the contemporary controversies that have surrounded the recovered memory movement, the scandals about child sexual abuse in schools, day-care centers, and the priesthood, the battles fought between prosecutors, psychologists, and scholars over how much to believe about allegations by children of parental and caretaker sexual abuse, the expanded focus on women's experiences and spousal abuse, and the role of trauma in minority communities and among people who have suffered from tragic global events. Laura S. Brown, for example, insists that the boundaries of trauma should be extended to cover vulnerable populations, and she blames white, middle-class definitions for tending to minimize the effects of constant stress and humiliation on people of color, gays, women, and people of low socioeconomic status. Haaken blames gender politics for trauma in male soldiers and trauma in women being treated as separate fields of study for so long (that way traumatized soldiers would not have to be treated as hysterics). But this changed in the 1980s when cases of repressed sexual and child abuse came dramatically to public attention, and traumatic memory as a field of study spread to other disciplines, including history and ethnic, literary, and women's studies.[18]

I hope to sidestep many of these controversies by making no claims for the diagnostic "truths" about the behavior and the life circumstances that I describe among the journalist-literary figures studied here. My own intuition tells me that the reaction to and recovery from traumatic events is complex and likely requires factoring in family history, childhood experiences, and genetic predisposition. However, I recognize that I am not a trained psychologist (as are few biographers and literary scholars); at the same time, because many of the journalists-writers in this study are historical figures, it is impossible to apply contemporary forms of psychological testing and examination to their situations. As a result, my approach here is descriptive and interpretive where the biographical evidence allows it, but I leave it to the reader to draw his or her own conclusions. I see this work—which in scholarly papers I have called an "historical-conceptual analysis"—as the foundation for a meaningful hypothesis for quantitative researchers who might want to test it on contemporary subjects who can be examined using today's psychological and social science testing methods.[19]

The contemporary study of trauma owes much to the psychologist Robert J. Lifton and his work with returning American veterans of the Vietnam War in the 1970s, as well as to the writings of Judith Herman, who extended the reach of trauma studies to women, minorities, and other traditionally marginalized groups. In his interviews with Vietnam soldiers, Lifton found instances not only of what later would be diagnosed and labeled as PTSD but also evidence that susceptibility to combat-related stress and psychological dysfunction was connected to childhood and previous life history, early survival experiences, and a constellation of guilt-inducing and emotionally numbing responses. Herman has combined these findings with her concern for the mistreatment of women and children and her contention that an implicit male bias has meant that PTSD has been defined too narrowly and without recognition that the condition was originally seen as a female disorder.[20]

The powerful effect of the Vietnam War on a generation of writers—plus the recognition of the effect of PTSD and its formal labeling as a medically diagnosable condition in veterans of the Vietnam War—has made the Vietnam experience a particular focus of the study of trauma and has produced evidence that war experience combined with earlier psychological wounds can contribute to psychological breakdown. In his study, *A Trauma Artist*, Heberle points out that Tim O'Brien's literature stresses his experience in combat only as part of a combination of early life psychological wounds and painful life experiences that led to his post-Vietnam breakdown. "Nam lived on inside me and I just called it by another name—I called it life," O'Brien wrote. "Nam, divorce, your father's death—such things live on even though you think you're over them. They come bubbling out." Heberle describes how O'Brien's personal emotional issues, particularly with his father, an alcoholic who was periodically institutionalized and someone that O'Brien felt he could never please during his growing up years, left him "with a hole in my heart," as he put it, and became part of what Heberle calls a "traumatic triad" in

O'Brien's life. This included his combat experience, his childhood and other adult traumas, and his writings (described by Heberle as "fictionalized testimony" or what O'Brien calls dealing with the "Vietnam in me") that have served as therapy and vehicles of recovery. O'Brien's two summers spent as a reporting intern with the *Washington Post* have been credited with giving him the discipline to do his best writing and putting him in the tradition of Hemingway and others who have used journalistic training to help tell of their war experiences.[21]

Unlike O'Brien, many of the journalist-literary figures studied here engaged the journalistic penchant for avoiding self-examination and analysis. Most were not confessional writers or highly introspective thinkers; instead they were most interested in things outside of themselves and engaged in what journalists commonly do: chronicle the lives of regular people that they saw and met, describe the world of their senses, encounter life through the direct experience of it, construct real (or semireal) characters on a foundation of truth as they perceived it, and position themselves as observers of and commentators about the world rather than as people who saw themselves as deeply personally affected by it. From the earliest days of the novel, when the sometimes introspective Johnson declared his preference for the psychologically complex novels of Samuel Richardson over those of the fluent story-spinner Defoe, Defoe has set the tone for a journalistically influenced form of writing that often reveals very little about the writer (and often focuses on characters who have minimal psychological insight into themselves). Even today, we know very little about the inner life of Defoe based on the voluminous amounts of journalism and fiction that he wrote during a prolific literary career.[22]

However, one can find exceptions to this rule. There are examples throughout literary history of a journalist-literary figure revealing in regular periodical work a good deal about inner emotional struggles and the life events that may have contributed to them. Boswell's "Hypochondriack" column in the *London Magazine* from 1777 to 1783, where he discussed the effects of depression and anxiety on him, is one notable example. However, Boswell was derided in his time for his openness about his inner life (even though his deepest secrets—as revealed in his accounts of his whoring and his bouts of venereal disease, his fear of insanity, and his anguish for the state of his soul and his prospects for the afterlife—were only made public with the discovery of his private journals in the early part of the twentieth century). Other highly personal and confessional forms of public writing by journalist-literary figures—such as Johnson's discussions of his painful social anxieties in his

Rambler newspaper contributions, Thomas De Quincey's *Confessions of an English Opium Eater*, and William Hazlitt's *Liber Amoris*, a thinly fictionalized but recognizable account of his courting of the coquettish daughter of his landlady who spurned the aging suitor's overtures—were notable for their unexpected candor.[23]

Typically, one gains the deepest insights into the impact of trauma in the book-length memoirs and autobiographical writings of the handful of journalist-literary figures who chose to chronicle painful periods in their lives. Richard Wright's autobiography, *Black Boy*, detailed in highly personal ways the abuse he suffered from his religiously fanatical family and the humiliations of growing up poor and black in the Jim Crow South. James Agee's memoir, *A Death in the Family*, where he chronicled the impact of his father's death on his six-year-old self, gave a moving glimpse into the tensions and repressions of his family circumstances and the effects of a traumatic event on a youthful psyche. Theodore Dreiser's stories about his professional traumas in his memoir, *A Book about Myself*, in which he described what it was like to be dismissed from Pulitzer's *New York World* and his tribulations in other newspaper jobs, are remarkable for their directness and insight about journalism's capacity to create disillusionment in an idealistic youth. In contrast, the examples of remarkable journalistic circumspection include Henry Adams writing nothing about the suicide of his wife in his autobiography, *The Education of Henry Adams;* Edith Nesbit using children's fable writing to counterbalance her early life losses (a father and a consumptive sister) and a philandering husband who pushed her to help raise his offspring with one of his lovers; and Hemingway telling biographer Charles Fenton to "cease and desist" in his probing of Hemingway's youth. "If I had written about Oak Park you would have a point in studying it," Hemingway remarked. "But I did not write about it."[24]

In fact, Hemingway's self-mythologizing built around a peripatetic life of emotional evasion provides an important example of why it can be valuable to rely on biographers and scholarly analysts to map the impact of trauma and stress on a journalistic and literary life. Hemingway stands out in the way that virtually his every psychological trait and early life experience seem to fit with what psychologists would identify as sources of traumatic stress. Hemingway biographers and scholars have found it irresistible to psychoanalyze Hemingway at every opportunity, particularly because his well-known personal philosophy of macho denial invites analysts to expose what Hemingway would not look at in himself. (To some degree, Hemingway was aware of this—and resented it. "I am opposed to writing about the private lives of living authors and psychoanalyzing them while they are alive," he said. "Criticism is getting all mixed up with a combination of the Junior F.B.I.-men, discards from Freud and Jung and a sort of Columnist peep-hole and missing laundry list school. Every young English professor sees gold in them dirty sheets now.") However, in evaluating the relationship of trauma and stress to literary achievement, it is important to note how many of the sources of trauma in Hemingway's life were turned to his advantage as a journalist and a novelist, even if his life strategies did not psychologically sustain him much past midcareer or keep him from suffering a terrible physical and emotional demise.[25]

Family mental health and family system's issues. Hemingway once said, "Happiness in intelligent people is the rarest thing I know"—and he learned this lesson from his home life growing up. He was raised by a physician father whose sporadic nervous collapses, "rest cures," and eventual suicide influenced Hemingway as much as did his father's convulsive rages, feverish enthusiasms, and subservience to Hemingway's controlling mother. Jamison used the Hemingway family—including the suicides of Hemingway's father, sister, and brother, and the psychological ailments of two of his sons—as a prime example of her contention that the inheritance of emotional instability has played a profound role in the life of many artists.[26]

Relationship with mother. John Dos Passos once said that Hemingway was the only man he ever met who truly hated his mother. A charismatic but domineering personality, she was the source of Hemingway's venom throughout his adult life (he regularly referred to her as "that bitch"). From a young age, his mother dressed Hemingway as a girl, gave him dolls, and treated him as if he was a "twin" of his older sister. Meanwhile, Hemingway's father, despite regularly yielding to his mother's wishes, took every opportunity to strengthen Hemingway's sense of masculinity by involving him in the outdoors and sporting life. With his mother as the "dark queen" of his inner world, as one biographer put it, Hemingway developed a deep insecurity about his personal sexual identity and showed a strong interest in androgyny and "manly" women throughout his life.[27]

Dealing with own issues of mental health. Although there is limited evidence of Hemingway's formal diagnosis, Jamison believes that he was bipolar and suffered from manic-depressive illness. Other biographers and analysts have applied a host of diagnoses to his mental condition, particularly in his failing years as he was checked in and out of the Mayo Clinic in the months before his suicide, including alcoholic psychosis, paranoia, psychological disassociation, chronic depression, morbid anxiety, and obsessive-compulsive syndrome. Hemingway acknowledged his vulnerability to profound mood swings (he described himself at times to friends as "terribly low," "damn near cuckoo," or "suffering from nervous fatigue" and often referred to his fascination with suicide).[28]

Risk taking. Hemingway's life on the edge of risk, in many ways, has come to define him. This included his youthful volunteering for the ambulance service in World War I (where he was gravely wounded but recovered after a long rehabilitation) to his front-line coverage as a journalist in the Spanish Civil War and World War II to his many outdoor adventures (big game hunting, sports fishing, and traveling the globe in search of high-risk adventures, where he survived two small plane crashes). Hemingway also took great risks in his personal life—including carrying on an affair with his first wife's best friend (thus leading to his divorce and second marriage) followed by a succession of affairs that became preludes to his divorces and third and fourth marriages, all of which involved some level of abuse (apparently mostly emotional) of his spouses.[29]

Experiences in war. Hemingway's traumatic wounding at age eighteen in World War I, when he suffered a severe shrapnel injury as a Red Cross ambulance driver while delivering candy to front-line troops in Italy, became the basis for much of his early fiction, including serving as the foundation for his fictional protagonist, Jake Barnes, in *The Sun Also Rises.* Jake's depression, apathy, and detachment fit with Hemingway's portrayal of both journalism and war service as places where young people learn to become tough on the outside no matter how much they may be suffering inwardly. Many a critic has psychoanalyzed Jake—and by extension, Hemingway—in the course of noting the psychic wounds left by Jake's (and Hemingway's) war experiences, their long hospital recoveries, and their difficulties reintegrating themselves into society. As was often the case with Hemingway, he seemed to have deeper intuitions into his psychic wounds than his personality reflected—and this was manifested in his literature, which can seem so much wiser than he appeared to be in his own life. "The world breaks everyone and afterward many are strong in the broken places," he wrote in foreshadowing his own fate. "But those that will not break it kills."[30]

Substance abuse. Hemingway became one of the most celebrated alcoholics in literary history as much for the way that he romanticized drinking as the miserable end that it helped to bring to his life. In following in the tradition of the laconic, glib, hard-drinking journalist—already raised to stereotypical levels in the lives and writings of such journalist-literary figure predecessors as Jack London, O. Henry, Stephen Crane, and Ring Lardner—and then elevating it to the level of literary symbolism (alcohol served as a truth serum for the characters in *The Sun Also Rises,* as well as an aphrodisiac, a lubricant for the action, and a symptom of their preference for anesthetizing their inner pain rather than dealing with it), Hemingway fixed the notion of companionable boozing as both a stoical and epicurean way of life within literary lore for the journalist who embraces the heroic, as well as the tragic, professional stance. Hemingway was proud of the prodigious amount of drinking his body could endure, and he viewed his ability to write and be productive despite the effects of alcohol as a sign of the robustness of his constitution (rather than as the signal of a death wish, as others have contended).[31]

Grandiosity. Hemingway lived his life on a mythic scale, and many of his troubles stemmed from his desire to sustain the legend of virility and adventure seeking that he had created for himself. The Hemingway myth has become synonymous with the image of the celebrity writer profiting from a trademark lifestyle, and a number of other journalist-literary figures both before and after him projected a public image and celebrity status that rivaled or eclipsed the impact of their literary works. Dorothy Parker, for example, who also suffered from issues of grandiosity, emotional recklessness, and substance abuse, was a great admirer of Hemingway and was impressed with Hemingway's notion of the bravado life carried on by the literary hero on his or her terms only.[32]

Rootlessness. Hemingway's restless movements after he attained literary success and financial independence also signaled his discomfort with life lived on ordinary terms—leaving home as an eighteen-year-old to take a cub reporting job in Kansas City, volunteering to be shipped to the Italian front in World War I, living the ex-patriot writer's life in Toronto and Paris, and participating in or covering as a journalist most of the major wars in his lifetime, before settling in such exotic spots as Sun Valley, Idaho; Key West, Florida; and Havana, Cuba. Hemingway's love of travel and the outdoor sporting life helped him to sustain a heightened sense of experience and to fend off his regular bouts of depression and melancholy.[33]

Job troubles. Hemingway's conflicted relationship with a *Toronto Star* editor Henry Hindmarsh was more traumatic than Hemingway ever fully admitted and explained a good deal about Hemingway's philosophizing throughout his life about the limitations of a newspaper journalist's career. Following a number of years as the *Star*'s European correspondent, Hemingway returned to Toronto in 1923 where he found himself working for Hindmarsh (a "sadistic" editor, as one Hemingway biographer described him). Determined to teach a cocky upstart some humility, Hindmarsh sent Hemingway around Toronto writing un-bylined stories about concerts and one-alarm fires. Hemingway's loathing of his editor became journalistic lore in the *Star* newsroom where

Hemingway reportedly plotted a novel in which he planned to make Hindmarsh the villain (which he never wrote) and contributed after he left the newspaper to a union campaign to organize the *Star* newsroom ("to beat Hindmarsh," as Hemingway put it in a note).[34]

Stimulation of art. Hemingway not only looked to his art for needed stimulation and the opportunity for enhanced experience, but he also found fiction writing to be a place where aberrational emotions could be validated and where thoughts and feelings not fully acceptable in regular society could be expressed. The pleasure Hemingway took in adding "imaginative details" to the semirealistic characterizations in his novels has been commented on extensively (many of his acquaintances paid a high price for having Hemingway as a friend, quipped one analyst). Hemingway rooted his literary philosophy in the lesson that he took from his early home life: that a writer needed to reach deep within in order to avoid expressing himself or herself in ways that were programmed into a person by family and society.[35]

Religion. Hemingway—who grew up in a religious home, read the Bible carefully, and filled his novels with allusions to religious themes—became, in the end, a symbol of the burned-out, hedonistic existentialist-artist who had decided to live by a carpe diem philosophy and looked to elevated human experience for his only spiritual sustenance. However, Hemingway's longing for spiritual connection and the lost consolation of religion is an important feature of his fiction, and his characters often comment on the emptiness they experience in trying vainly to get in touch with religious feeling. Throughout his writings, Hemingway tried to counter this by imputing spiritual meaning to real-life activities, and particularly so the "manly" activities of bull-fighting, big game hunting, and sport fishing.[36]

The connection that scholars have made between Hemingway's life experiences and his literature serves as an example of how trauma can be studied at the intersection of art, journalism, and biography. The well-known "war-wound theory" of Philip Young has been a dominant paradigm in the way critics have interpreted Hemingway's novels and short stories in the context of his injury and rehabilitation as a front-line ambulance attendant in World War I. In this interpretation (which Hemingway himself subscribed to, at least to some degree), his protagonists Frederic Henry in *A Farewell to Arms* and Jake Barnes can be seen as autobiographical figures in the sense that they reflected Hemingway's own disillusionment and emotional disconnection after his World War I experiences. Some have gone so far as to interpret his two fictional war veterans—as well as Hemingway himself—as suffering from a form of PTSD and of weaving those effects into his literary themes.

In particular, Jake Barnes, who as a journalist and the novel's narrator uses journalistic shorthand to establish the stylistic pace and to allude to, but only obliquely delve into painful emotions, is the embodiment of Hemingway's strategy of asking the reader to read between the lines to glean the novel's message. Both in his "hard-boiled" persona (as Jake describes himself) and in his cryptic comments and ironical asides, Jake's attempt to maintain a "neutral" journalistic front in his response to life allowed Hemingway ample opportunities to signal to the reader, as his well-known "iceberg" theory of writing has it, that only one-eighth of the novel's meaning is above the surface and the rest lies below.[37]

One can take this analysis even further in examining the impact of trauma on the journalism industry's fashioning of a writing style in a general sense. Modern journalism's "neutral" style developed, at least in part, as a way to provide journalists and their audience a means to distance themselves from the emotional impact of trauma as it was used as a repetitive formula in the conveyance of news about warfare, natural disasters, crime, and other traumatic occurrences. Hemingway's use of this style to both point to the feelings attached to trauma and to provide a surface cover for their evasion fits well with journalism's time-honored schemes for allowing reporters and readers to separate themselves psychologically from the full force of traumatic experience. Hemingway's blending of the traits of the traumatized personality into the archetypal journalistic protagonist (as in Jake's case) may have been done for character development reasons alone—but it also is a comment on the way that graphic news content and the gathering of information about trauma have required a hardening of the journalistic persona.

As is the case with Hemingway, the patterns that can be found in the life experiences and psychological symptoms of the journalist-literary figures studied here are organized around the research categories identified by investigators as connected to traumatic emotions and psychological instability. With some of the categories (e.g., depression and growing up with a depressed and emotionally troubled parent, familial links involving alcohol and mental health, work life as a factor in mental health), there are so many research findings that I have cited them only with search terms that can be accessed on the Web of Science and have listed the number of studies.[38] It should be noted that this explosion of knowledge about the relationship of trauma, stress, and emotional illness was not available to journalist-literary figures who lived before contemporary theories of psychology and family systems, the rise of the modern research university, and government subsidies of the psychological sciences.

It is important to point out that these categories do not simply provide a method to lament the difficult inner and outer life experiences of the journalist-literary figures in this study. In many cases, the pain and difficulties they suffered helped to produce something positive out of the negatives: great art. The apparent complexity of the influence of traumatic experience on the writing process needs to be kept in mind throughout this analysis. Inner pain often has been turned into higher literary accomplishment, and the learning and wisdom that can grow out of suffering can play a profound role in the creative process, and particularly so for writers who have been drawn to journalism as a profession and then transcended it with their move into the fields of fiction and literary writing.

The four chapters in this book examine the sources and the consequences of traumatic experience in the lives of these writers, as well as the ways that their experiences in journalism may have contributed to their psychological stress and played a role in their mental health history. Chapter 1 discusses their life stories in the context of childhood history, mental health symptoms, and categories of traumatic experience that today are recognized as "triggers" of psychic conflict. The pressures of the journalists' job and the traumatic experiences of women, minorities, and journalist-literary figures from historically marginalized groups—as well as those who have investigated social problems and/or used journalistic literature to advance social reform causes—are the subject of chapter 2. Chapter 3 examines the traumatic history of journalist-literary figures as military correspondents and observers of and participants in war, including the part they have played in developing the "code" of courageous conduct that has come to shape the "heroic" ideal of the journalist operating under dangerous conditions. The high prevalence of alcoholism, substance abuse, and general mental health difficulties among journalistic writers is detailed in chapter 4, as are the connections that can be made between addiction and compulsive behaviors and the experiences in journalism that may have helped to foster them.

Even though I suggest that one should be wary of overinterpreting the psychological condition of literary figures of the past, I have proceeded under the belief that the establishment of a historical foundation for examining the impact of trauma on the journalistic personality can be a valuable step in developing a fuller understanding of the role of psychic pain among writers who have experienced a journalistic work life. Although focused on journalists who have become important literary figures, it is hoped that this study will offer meaningful insights into the nexus of emotional and behavioral issues that surround the impact of traumatic experience in human life and in comprehending how these issues may have played out in journalistic and literary history. The chapters that follow trace the life patterns and emotional characteristics that can be found in many of the journalist-literary figures who experienced early life emotional abuses, losses of loved ones, mental health problems, traumatic employment circumstances, and other painful life events and will hopefully provide a helpful framework for establishing an expanded understanding of how trauma may have worked and be working within a profession with its traditions of machoism, stoicism, and the unexamined life.

1

Stories of Harm, Stories of Hazard

*Childhood Stress and Professional Trauma
in the Careers of Journalist-Literary Figures*

"No man knows he is young while he is young."
—G. K. Chesterton

Many people would call it a nervous breakdown when Sherwood Anderson, a thirty-six-year-old owner of a mail order paint company and editor of a series of business publications, walked out of his office in Elyria, Ohio, one day in 1912. He was later found wandering the streets of Cleveland, haggard, disoriented, and muttering confusedly of his grievances against the world. Anderson, however, came to see the incident as a matter of artistic escape—as the moment when he turned his back on the life of a Rotarian and business journalist to set off to fulfill his dreams of becoming a great artist and writer.[1]

The fact that Anderson—raised by an economically harried harness maker and house painter father in small town Ohio and filled with emotional turmoil rooted in unresolved childhood psychological conflicts—fulfilled his ambitions to become a celebrated novelist and short-story writer is perhaps less notable than it might seem. He is only one of a procession of journalistic writers who have overcome childhood hardships, early life family distress, and stressful experiences in journalism to succeed as novelists and literary journalists. The external and internal turbulence that helped to shape their literary vision can be seen in Anderson's capacity to turn the negatives of his "mid-life crisis" into an artistic virtue. In Anderson's case, his break from his small-town businessman's and editor's existence toward a Gauguin-like reach for the artistic life rose to legendary proportions, at least among Anderson scholars and in his own cultivation of his triumphal life story. However, in interpreting the "pervasive psychological motifs" found in a letter mailed to his wife by Anderson during his disoriented wanderings, Irving Howe, one of Anderson's biographers, interprets Anderson's inner issues (violent aggression against his role as an adult male, a regression to early levels of childhood, a resentment at too sharp withdrawal of maternal attentions, and a general confusion as to sex role and paranoia at imagined feminine assaults) as representing something more profound than anything in Anderson's autobiographical writings ever revealed.[2]

At the time of his crisis, Anderson had been dabbling in business journalism, and he was motivated to exit his small-town life, in part, by his frustration at having to express himself within the cant and the boosterism of the business world. As much as it made Anderson feel ashamed after his rise to literary success, his provincial business and journalistic experience proved instrumental in helping him to probe and transmit the mentality of small-town Americans in his early writings, as did his earlier work in the advertising industry, which helped to shape his view of the psychology of the American consumer and citizen. In fact, Anderson's manifestation of psychoanalytical themes—both in his personal life and in his literary works—puts him at the forefront of the many modern writers who have shifted the territory of artistic exploration into the Freudian recesses of their characters' psyches and made the examination of abnormal mindsets, traumatic experiences, and dysfunctional behaviors a feature of their literature. Anderson was an advertising executive in the days when Freudian concepts were becoming widely accepted throughout society, and he had come to recognize that people's repressed fantasies, sexual longings, and complicated inner lives could be exploited to sell them products no matter where they lived. In his own case, he came to think of himself as "before" and "after" personalities—the before person a Chicago advertising copywriter who became a small-town business owner and editor; the after personality a seeker of artistic freedom who divorced his first wife, moved from one big city to another, and searched out the company of journalists, artists, and bohemian types, often without having a residence more permanent than a hotel room.[3]

Anderson's masterpiece, *Winesburg, Ohio*, is widely recognized for its portrayal of small-town people as anything but the stock and shallow characters of much bucolic fiction. The rustics, urban exiles, and village characters in the novel are far from being narrow, conforming, or self-satisfied, on the one hand, or wholesome people to be sentimentalized and treated nostalgically. Instead, Anderson's small-town "grotesques," as he called them, are a parade of eccentrics and the emotionally undone who harbor shadowy grievances and strange but lost dreams and who express their loneliness in bizarre but poignant ways. In the novel, Anderson explored the despair among his small-town characters through his fictional town reporter, George Willard, who moves among them listening to their stories. Anderson's strange, incoherent, often tortured characters reflect intense inner turmoil, guilt, regret, fear, confusion—namely, many of the emotions that Anderson himself experienced when his "badly splintered personality" led to his breakdown and the beginning of his artistic odyssey. His searching out of "lonely and deformed souls" both in his art and in his companions left him feeling a profound sense of sympathy for the stricken, the helpless, and the unloved in any human setting and made him the model for the contemporary novelist who recognized the power of life's traumatizing events to forge life's destiny.[4]

In *Winesburg, Ohio*, Anderson's "grotesques" become so, as he put it, because they confront the "truths" of their traumatized lives in sharp and distressing moments of emotional insight or in revealing confrontations with others. These painful epiphanies and keenly felt revelations were conveyed in a series of character sketches that can be interpreted as fitting the pattern for what psychological researchers would identify as sources of traumatic emotion: death of a parent ("The Thinker") about a depressed boy with a deceased father and a dependent mother who feels cut off from the life of the town and cannot access his feelings except as they may affect his mother's; growing up with a mentally ill parent ("Mother") about a psychologically troubled woman who becomes fixated on her confused son's future and her hopes that he will break away from the circumstances of her own constricting life and unhappy marriage; abandonment ("Adventure") about a woman whose life and emotions become frozen in time while she waits vainly for the return of a lover who took her virginity; sexual abuse ("Hands") about a former teacher who grows increasingly neurotic and obsessive after having been accused of inappropriately touching his students; wounding of a narcissistic parent ("Godliness, Part Two") about an emotionally disturbed and violently unhappy woman who was unwanted in her childhood and the effect on her son when he goes to live with his grandfather who had rejected her. Typically, Anderson ended each vignette with a powerful revelation, as happens with Alice Hindman in "Adventure" after she is possessed with the desire to run naked through the streets before crawling back mortified to her bedroom ("turning her face to the wall, [she] began trying to force herself to face bravely the fact that many people must live and die alone, even in Winesburg").[5]

In his Freudian-inspired accounts of the stunted lives of Winesburg's citizens, Anderson chose to present journalism as a dubious device for the exploration of truth and his central character as a catalyzing figure in the confessions of the town folk and their strange and perplexing behavior (such as the spinster Kate Swift in "The Teacher," who bursts into the *Winesburg Eagle*'s office one evening and lets Willard take her in his arms, before pounding his face with her fists and fleeing). Anderson's sensitivity to the impact of trauma working in the lives of average people—combined with his belief in the power of the American Dream to combat it—was reflected in the ways that he used Willard's role as the town reporter to comment on the disingenuous nature of American public discourse. Willard's "discoveries" about Winesburg's citizens, confounding as they are to him, could never be printed in a small-town newspaper, and there is no evidence in the novel that they ever are. The unreported secrets that are revealed to Willard demonstrated Anderson's recognition of fiction as a superior device for expressing the symbolically rich and emotionally layered psychological material that Freudian-oriented character development requires. However, Anderson's sympathy for Willard's ambitions for himself—and his contrasting the young reporter to the defeated figures he encounters throughout the novel—reflected Anderson's own release of buried emotions when he made his artistic break. Anderson's romantic faith in life's possibilities and his lifelong search for the ideal lifestyle can be seen in his upbeat editorials and other writings in the small-town newspapers that he purchased in 1927 and edited near his Virginia retirement home—and which brought his own life odyssey full circle in its return to its provincial and journalistic roots. Unlike in his early business journalism, where he was forced to traffic in hackneyed slogans and boosterish bromides, Anderson wrote his most impressive journalism after he had published his most highly regarded novels, when the harsh conditions of the Depression led him to take on the journalist's mantle in the nonfictional *Puzzled America* with its exposés about joblessness and economic deprivation. At the same time, Anderson's declining fiction-writing talent and his persistence in producing poorly received novels were apparently what brought him back to the small-town life that his character, Willard, forsakes when he leaves behind the traumatized citizens of Winesburg and heads off for the big city. Willard's pretense of energetically looking for news items in a town of disfigured souls is reminiscent of the entrepreneurial young Anderson hustling odd jobs around town while coming to grips with his hard-drinking father's failings as a breadwinner and the emotional tensions of his family life. The many ironies involved in Anderson's writing career—first experiencing the falseness of promotional journalism, then using fiction and its portrayal of journalism's truth-telling limitations to explore the hidden stories of traumatic experience to be found in a small town, and finally finding refuge in country journalism as a means of escaping the traumas of critical rejection—illustrated the complex but powerful union that the intermingling of fictional techniques with the lessons of journalism can have in addressing the effects of traumatic experience as they play out in the hidden recesses of the American psyche.[6]

Since the rise of the modern commercial periodical in the late seventeenth and early eighteenth centuries, journalism has held out great hope for bright, talented young people with aspirations to become literary figures. Generations of writing hopefuls like Anderson—often without family connections and little formal education but with a powerful ambition to rise above their circumstances—have made up a notable cadre of literary figures whose experiences in journalism have helped to shape their literary vision and the literary canon in the United States and the British Isles. In a remarkable number of cases, these journalist-literary figures endured in their early lives stressful events and in their journalism jobs traumatic experiences but managed to use positions in print shops or as neophyte journalists to educate themselves about writing and literature, to bootstrap themselves onto better jobs, and then to move into fiction writing when they found themselves hemmed in by the formulaic writing practices at the news organizations where they worked. The frustrations encountered by this group, who often had a strong need to express their sense of humor, irony, or anger at what they felt were journalism's inauthentic portrayals of the world, were based on their recognition that the so-called objective or neutral methods for treating events on the news page often disguised a whole system of self-serving news judgments, self-dealing business practices, and toadying to the settled ways of the establishment. Novel writing, on the other hand, offered to free them from the commercial, social, and legal restraints of conventional journalism, even if they had to fictionalize their stories (sometimes only slightly). The circumstances of the journalist on the typical commercial publication—along with the higher status that artistic literature has come to occupy with critics and scholars—helps to explain the ironical situation in which so many well-known writers, schooled in the methods of so-called factual journalism, gravitated toward fiction writing in order to express their "honest" vision of life. This was particularly the case when a writer wanted to explore the impact of trauma on human beings beyond the stock conventions of newspaper crime-and-violence reporting or to probe the traumatic foundations of his or her own emotional struggles outside of a journalistic culture that had come to be dominated by callous and case-hardened thinking, emotional denial, and cynical views of human nature.

What could novel writing do that journalism did not in terms of conveying the emotional impact of traumatic experience?

- The use of imaginative storytelling forms as a means to woo audience attention was recognized early on by the pioneering writing
  figure Daniel Defoe, who is studied as one of the first great modern
  periodical editors and as a founder of the genre of the novel in English prose. Defoe's production in 1722 of a volume of nonnarrative
  journalism, *Due Preparations for the Plague*, and his semifictional
  novel of the same year, *A Journal of the Plague Year*, was based on
  the research that Defoe did in municipal archives as a means to warn
  the public of a possible reoccurrence of the plague that hit London
  in 1665. Although both works use municipal records and statistics as
  their foundation (such as figures about the number of burials in the
  city each day, orders of quarantine for affected homes, trade restrictions on ships coming into harbor, infection rates in various regions
  of the city), *A Journal of the Plague Year* was constructed around
  the chronicle of a fictionalized survivor of the plague who presents
  in vivid fashion its impact on regular people as Defoe imagined it,
  whereas *Due Preparations for the Plague* is a largely didactic treatise
  with little narrative appeal. In showing the protagonist of *A Journal of
  the Plague Year* wandering London and recounting scenes of suffering
  and death, Defoe dramatized the plague's horrors so that no reader
  could miss the personal implications in his warnings. Perhaps not
  unexpectedly, the novel elicited a stronger public response than did
  the journalistic account (even though Defoe was accused with both of
  fear-mongering for spreading his warnings about the plague, which
  was dying out on the European continent and never materialized
  again in England). Although he was writing in a period before the
  genres of journalism and the novel were defined in the modern sense,
  the opportunistic and entrepreneurial Defoe saw the benefits of using
  his imagination to embellish a tale for dramatic purposes (although
  he continued to maintain in disingenuous fashion that his novels
  were "just histor[ies] of fact," as he described *Robinson Crusoe* in the
  book's preface). Interestingly, as journalism, *Due Preparations for the
  Plague* was a major advancement in the use of investigative reporting techniques to illustrate the factual underpinnings of an important
  story, whereas *A Journal of the Plague Year* is a crude and embryonic
  example of a novel, with its disjointed narrative; its desultory use of

dramatic techniques borrowed from stagecraft, journal writing, and early biographical forms; and its lack of serious character development. But the narrative form that most informed the novel—the use of brief but powerful vignettes of human drama and suffering—was drawn from the journalistic techniques developed by Defoe (whose innovations in the London *Review* included the leading article, the foreign news analysis, and the gossip column) and other editors of the time, most notably Joseph Addison and Richard Steele in their *Tatler* and *Spectator* newspapers, whose witty and stylish short narratives and satirical personality sketches can be seen as forerunners of the modern short story.[7]

- The use of novel writing to camouflage the traumatized feelings of the author by shifting them to a fictional character became a key feature of early fiction—and particularly so as journalism industrialized in the nineteenth century and commercialized written expression became circumscribed by the economic imperatives of market-driven media operations. After he entered journalism in 1831, Charles Dickens found it frustrating to have his literary impulses constrained in his first reporting job for the *Mirror of Parliament*, where he was forced to conform to the stenographic practices of nineteenth-century political writing. Dickens's success in moving into serialized novel writing allowed him to probe themes that pricked his social conscience, and he came to believe that the novel's capacity for dramatizing human suffering and pulling at readers' heartstrings made it a more powerful instrument for social reform than the journalism of his day. The use of the thinly veiled autobiographical character was advanced in his novel *David Copperfield*, where Dickens used his own youthful travails to imply that the emotional residue of traumatic circumstances can be universal despite differences in the specific experience of individuals. For example, he portrayed David Copperfield as suffering the death of his father before his birth and the beatings and neglect of a cruel stepfather and his sister, whereas Dickens's own major early life trauma involved his father's incarceration in a debtors' prison; David's abandonment experiences included being sent away to school, whereas Dickens felt abandoned when his parents pulled him out of school; David went to work in the counting house of his stepfather's wine-bottling business, whereas Dickens was forced to find employment in a shoe blacking factory. Dickens used David's experiences training and working as a newspaper reporter covering

Parliament to comment on "the facts of dry subjects" encompassed by Victorian political reporting ("I am . . . joined with eleven others in reporting the debates in Parliament for a Morning Newspaper. Night after night, I record predictions that never come to pass, professions that are never fulfilled, explanations that are only meant to mystify. I wallow in words").[8]

- Even more than semiautobiographical characterization, authorial feelings could be injected into fictional characters in ways that could be presented as reflecting only indirectly on the real emotions of the author, as well as creating in the scenario of a novel some distance between genuine and fictionalized inner pain. Ernest Hemingway— with his manly public image—was, in a sense, also the many characters in his novels, such as Jake Barnes in *The Sun Also Rises*, who could express the inner pain that Hemingway evaded exploring in his real life; whereas Hemingway presented himself as a man of action and courage, Jake could cry at night over his thwarted love for Lady Brett Ashley and lament, "It is awfully easy to be hard-boiled about everything in daytime, but at night it is another thing." The depressed and alcoholic Ring Lardner—who in his own life was professionally stoical and reticent to the point of emotional paralysis—could explore through the characters in his short stories the evasions and dissembling of the secret drinker ("The Love Nest"), male complacency and insensitivity leading to a broken marriage ("Ex Parte"), and physical and emotional late-life traumas not unlike his own ("Insomnia"), as well as other themes of despair and emotional desperation that underlay his ostensibly satirical cameos of the voluble and shallow American personality type. Damon Runyon and Raymond Chandler, who both grew up with heavy alcohol use in the home and periods of single parenting, projected onto their gangland characters, in Runyon's case, and his detective protagonist, Philip Marlowe, in Chandler's case, the tough guy exteriors that they tried to emulate in their own journalistic and literary professional lives but which failed as exercises of life imitating art. Both authors found that their effort to maintain the tough talking, emotionally detached personas of their protagonists fell apart under the weight of alcoholism, depression, institutionalization, and a suicide attempt (in Chandler's late life) and the all-night lifestyle of Runyon, by which he ignored his family during long stretches of work, was prone to moody outbursts followed by depressive silences, and sat stone-facedly in bars and speakeasies until the early hours of the morning listening to the colloquy of gangsters, chorus girls, bookies, and various street-life characters.[9]

- Feature writing became extensive in journalism in the nineteenth and twentieth centuries, but, as practiced in the commercial press, did not typically allow for a full portrayal of the human psyche in the way a story touched up with imaginative details could. Novel writing, on the other hand, evolved within a different literary and legal tradition, and particularly so as serious fiction writing attracted a sophisticated audience able to handle themes of sexuality and moral deviance and was given added protections by the courts, which came to deem imaginative prose expression as outside the realms of many privacy and libel restrictions. For example, the death of a promiscuous party girl who dropped off a yacht into the harbor could be grist for extensive coverage in the New York City tabloid press—as was the case with the ill-fated young woman who served as the real-life model for Gloria Wandrous in John O'Hara's novel, *BUtterfield 8*. Although exposed by the New York City newspapers as an unstable alcoholic, a mistress to wealthy men, and a victim of sexual abuse, O'Hara's fictionalization of the life of the victim went much deeper in dramatizing the impact that early life sexual exploitation by a family friend—and the mishandling of the situation by parents—can have on the adult psyche. As a former journalist at a number of New York City dailies during the late 1920s, O'Hara's familiarity with the techniques of tabloid journalism (in the novel he used a journalist as a minor character in helping to unearth the details of Wandrous's life history) led him to create a revealing portrait of a victim of traumatic abuse that went far beyond what the conventions of commercial journalism would allow in discussing the background of an identified personality. The mixing of the real-life details with O'Hara's imaginative expansion into the realms of what journalists would call speculation, subjective interpretation, and amateur psychological analysis nonetheless enabled him to place the reader in a position to empathize with and more clearly understand the emotional connections in the life patterns of a person who could easily be written off (as the tabloid newspapers did) as a tramp, a strumpet, or a gold-digger.[10]
- In this sense, fiction writing has allowed journalists to veer outside the restrictive writing formulas of commercial journalism by using the same subject matter but expanding on it in ways that have allowed them to express themselves more intimately and feelingly

than within the confines of "objective" reporting. Martha Gellhorn's war journalism has received growing attention from scholars who believe that her powerful and vivid reporting was superior to that of her husband, Hemingway, who was covering many of the same events of World War II as she was. However, it was in her fiction about her war reporting experiences—where she often polished and recycled phrases from her journalism into her novels—that Gellhorn most directly tackled the moral issues that troubled her about the way journalists covered combat and the victims of war. Most notably in *A Stricken Field*, Gellhorn's fictional alter ego, the correspondent Mary Douglas, steps outside the detached role of the correspondent and involves herself in issues relating to the plight of refugees from Hitler's annexation of the Sudetenland region of Czechoslovakia in 1938. In trying to help the refugees, Douglas confronts the issue that Gellhorn said she herself faced ("Why don't you *do* something about it?") by speaking to a British refugee official in behalf of the refugees (Gellhorn acknowledged that she did something similar during a visit as a reporter for *Collier's* magazine to the Czech prime minister) and then smuggling out of the country an account of the treatment of the Sudetens (Gellhorn again did something similar to this; she delivered a report on the displaced Sudetens to the League of Nations High Commissioner for Refugees). Interestingly, Gellhorn's philosophy as a journalist was to have the reporter be there in the text as little as possible—but she added, "I was always cutting and deleting from my articles, to eliminate as much as possible the sound of me screaming." Phrases that have been used to capture her reporting philosophy— "The unflinching gaze"; "Close your eyes to nothing"—only served a limited role in satisfying Gellhorn's need to act as the "eyes for (people's) conscience," as she put it. In the end, it was her fascination with the struggles of the woman reporter covering war—Kate McLoughlin has listed ten of Gellhorn's fictional works that have women journalists as characters—and the freedom she found in fiction writing that allowed her to explore in a richer fashion the themes of conscience that she often had stripped out of her journalism.[11]

- Given the novel's traditionally greater latitude to discuss issues that are outside the dimensions of commercial journalism, themes could leak out in the fiction of journalist-literary figures that had no place in their more conventional journalistic writing. Scholars' fascination with the life story of Djuna Barnes—and the degree to which her father may have sexually abused her as a girl—has led to allusions that they have teased out of the subtext of her experimental fiction. Her first novel, *Ryder*, about the male head of a family who believes in free love and exploits the women of the household, and her verse drama, *Antiphon*, about a woman who is taken advantage of sexually by her father with her mother's collusion, have been read as evidence that Barnes was the victim of incest (or at least her father's facilitation of the loss of her virginity by an older acquaintance). Barnes's cult status as a participant journalist turned avant-garde fiction writer has been enhanced by the rise of the recovered memory movement and the growing belief in some quarters that certain traumatic "truths" may exist in the emotions that cannot be accessed in the straight-forward act of human recollection. Barnes's ways of alluding to the traumatic events of her early life also have been tied by scholars to her role as a flamboyant stunt reporter in New York City (she once joined with a group of women activists in order to write about what it was like to be force fed in jail), her renown as an interviewer of celebrities where she often elicited "shocking" confessions, and her fascination with people who performed potentially harmful or highly revealing acts for public display (such as a dentist eager to demon-strate his "painless" techniques in public). Barnes's work as a reporter for the *Brooklyn Eagle*, *New York Press*, *New York World*, and *New York Morning Telegraph* in the early decades of the twentieth cen-tury fit into the sensationalistic practices of the time (the story of the dentist, for example, was headlined, "Twingeless Twitchell and His Tantalizing Tweezers"), but she also showed her eagerness to expand the boundaries of journalism (such as including a fictional character in one newspaper account) that she pushed to even greater extremes in producing the nonlinear, imagist, and surreal atmosphere of her novels ("I have a narrative," says the doctor protagonist of her novel *Nightwood*, "but you will be hard put to find it").[12]

- In recent years, writers allied with the field of journalism have made inroads into the traditional domain of novelists and their claim that imaginative writing is the superior venue for conveying the "higher" and deeper truths of the human condition. The rise of the so-called new journalism movement of the 1960s and 1970s has let journalists reclaim some of the territory that restrictive reporting practices had allowed to be ceded to imaginative writers. The work that launched this movement—Truman Capote's "nonfiction novel," *In Cold Blood*—

has been praised for its blending of narrative fictional techniques with journalistic reporting methodology, and Capote's celebrity has grown with the release of movies and biographies that explore the parallels between Capote's own deprived childhood and that of his killer-protagonist, Perry Smith. Capote's comments about seeing himself in Smith (when Smith blamed his unhappy background for his actions, Capote reportedly said, "I had one of the worst childhoods in the world, and I'm a pretty decent, law-abiding citizen") has led scholars and critics to probe issues ranging from Capote's ostensible attraction to the diminutive and delicate-appearing Smith to their sharing of abandonment issues with mothers who did not stick around for them and fathers who came and went in their lives. The biographical overlay of Capote's life to the interpretation of his passages about Smith ("I was always thinking about Dad, hoping he would come take me away. . . . Only Dad wouldn't help me. . . . Told me to be good and hugged me and went away," said Smith in echoing comments of Capote about his own largely absent father) has added an intriguing element to the debate among writers as to whether journalism can present a picture that is as profound in the portrayal of the human psyche as is conventionally credited to fiction. That Capote has been accused of fictionalizing his account in a few places—as well as engaging in practices that would be forbidden to a conventional journalist (such as speculating about what went on in the mind of the murdered family members during their last day of life)—has not lessened the impact of Capote's accomplishment in expanding what is meant by the genre of journalism (and the reporting of crime and traumatic events in particular) in the minds of contemporary critics and the writers who have imitated his practices.[13]

For many of the journalist-literary figures discussed here, there is a strong connection between their journalism career and their traumatic life story that often came into display with the development of a fiction writing career. (See table 1 in the appendix.) Of the 150 journalist-literary figures that are the focus of this study, more than two-thirds experienced one or more of what I have deemed traumatic experiences in a journalism job. Those traumas included firings or loss of columns, coverage of crime, violence, or war, the suppression of journalistic projects that had great emotional importance to them, family or marriage crises with partners or spouses who were journalists, mental health collapses while employed in journalism, the death under trying circumstances of a cherished publication that they were editing or publishing, jailing or detention, and workplace humiliations, such as being pushed into sexually compromising circumstances. (See table 2 in the appendix.) A number of the writers in this study are better known as novelists or fiction writers than they were as journalists—but all had important experiences in the field of journalism that helped to shape the contours of their writing career.

As figures who became established in journalism jobs, many of the journalist-literary figures in this study found themselves attracted to the intensity and stimulation of journalism's professional culture, with its focus on the criminal world, tabloid topics, and the aberrational in life, in order to provide ballast against their own emotional turmoil. James Boswell's belief that his inner life had no meaning unless he chronicled it drew him inexorably to periodical and journal writing, including his publishing for many years a column ("The Hypochondriack") in which he discussed the challenges of living with depression and anxiety. Similar scenarios played out in the professional lives of Samuel Taylor Coleridge (who became a laughingstock when he was baited into making problematic contributions to *Blackwood*'s magazine whose editors knew of Coleridge's hunger to be a popular periodical writer despite being ill-fitted for the role), John Ruskin (whose mental illness became ever more apparent in the erratic and painfully personal revelations he wrote in his periodical, *Fors Clavigera*), and Hutchins Hapgood (who lived a tumultuous personal life in Greenwich Village, in part to deal with his ever-present and overwhelming sense of anxiety). As the romantic poet, newspaper reporter, and opium addict Coleridge put it, the appeal of journalism tends "to narrow the Understanding and . . . acidulate the Heart . . . Life were so flat a thing without Enthusiasm—that if for a moment it leaves, I have a sort of stomach-sensation attached to all my Thoughts, like those which succeed to the pleasurable operation of a dose of opium." (Or as Hunter S. Thompson put it in modern "gonzo" language: "I have spent half my life trying to get away from journalism, but I am still mired in it—a low trade and a habit worse than heroin.")[14]

For others who dealt with precarious mental health and carried the weight of troubled childhoods, journalism could overstimulate their already overwrought nervous systems and have both manic and depressive effects on their lives. The stresses of the job, the grim and unsavory circumstances that made up their reporting world, the blows to the ego in a profession where firings and workplace mistreatment were common—for these reasons and others, the fragile dispositions of a number of journalist-literary figures came unraveled on the job. For a number of these figures, their experiences in journalism played an ever more decisive role in embedding them in the traumatic circumstances that came to consume their lives, and they were encouraged by the culture of the profession to engage in activities that damaged their physical and emotional health. Two of the prominent practices identified with the journalistic workplace—high-stress reporting and drinking as a way to deal with the pressures of the job—brought low a significant portion of the writers in this study. This situation could be compounded when early life trauma was added to the mix. With the caveat that cause-and-effect relationships should not be presumed here nor should one generalize beyond the group studied, it is instructive to note that more than three-quarters of the figures in this study who lost parents as a young person, suffered early life abandonment issues, or grew up with an alcoholic or psychologically ill parent also demonstrated emotional health problems in later life and/or engaged in heavy drinking or drug taking. Although already internally troubled in varying degrees when they entered the profession, combat reporting also left a number to deal with the lingering symptoms of trauma, as it did those who were traumatized as military combatants or medical support staff and were later drawn to journalism and fiction writing, at least in part, as a way to "write out" their traumatic experiences.[15]

As with so many elements involving the complexity of human psychology, it should not be forgotten that human dysfunction—whether involving depression and anxiety, drinking and drug taking, or other forms of compensatory behavior for inner suffering—has played an important role in the production of great art. Some studies show that depression may be an unpleasant but adaptive response to affliction in ways that contain positive elements—as a sign that "we don't suffer in vain," as Jonah Lehrer has put it. Depression as a condition that can produce positive side effects has been a source of study and speculation since the time of Darwin (who plunged into a deep depression at the death of his ten-year-old daughter from fever; some believe that his depression was a clarifying force that propelled him to pull together his research and publish *On the Origin of Species* eight years later in 1859). Depression's capacity to create intense focus has been connected to literary production by researchers who have found a striking correlation between artistic activity and mental health disorders. However, those who talk of the "virtues" of mental suffering have been countered by other researchers who argue that there are many depressive conditions—deep and chronic depression, paralyzing self-hatred, hopeless and circular rumination—that should not be minimized, nor should this kind of emotional pain be seen as anything but a psychiatric disorder and potentially traumatizing in itself.[16]

Historical Limitations of Our Understanding of Trauma's Role in the Lives of Early Journalist-Literary Figures

The conceptual underpinnings of modern psychological and family systems research—that the pain of early life traumas can live deep within the body and be retriggered by stresses and traumatic situations later in life—have become a widely held position with many post-Freudian literary scholars and biographers who have been influenced by psychological theory and research. However, it is important to recognize the way that writers have dealt with trauma and emotional difficulties in an historical context. In some cases, it can appear that a journalist-literary figure took parental loss and other childhood traumas in stride—and particularly so in periods when life spans were shorter, medicine was less advanced, and the deaths of children and young people were regular occurrences. The writers of these eras were raised when people were not encouraged to "process" their emotions, and there is generally less documentation of their actual feelings for biographers to explore. Both the beginning and the end of Jonathan Swift's life are shrouded in mystery, for example, with scholars debating the credence of his story that he was stolen as an infant by a nursemaid and taken away to be raised by her (although most acknowledge that he was separated from his mother for many years before reuniting with her when he was twenty) and the accounts of his "going mad" at the end of his life (there is speculation that he suffered from some form of senile dementia). We know so little about Defoe personally—despite a prolific output of journalism and novels during his more than twenty years as a prominent editor of London periodicals and a vanguard fiction-writing figure, Defoe was remarkably closemouthed in writing about his own personal affairs—that scholars can only guess the details of his growing-up years and what were the health problems that he hinted at as an elderly scribbler during the late-life period when he wrote his most famous novels.

One reason that fiction writing proved to be a profitable place to analyze traumatic issues was the role it could play in camouflaging direct and identifiable allusions to journalist-literary figures' own inner struggles and the events that may have caused them. In the early years of journalism, when censorship by the authorities was common practice and modern free speech and press protections were not yet in place, the journalist-turned-novelist Swift honed the use of parody, code words, hidden digs, satirical parables, and allusions with disguised and multiple meanings while serving as the anonymous editor of the cleverly partisan Tory newspaper, the *Examiner* of London, from 1710 to 1711. Critics have pointed to the way that Swift imported these techniques into *Gulliver's Travels* and other fictional works that he wrote, at least in part, to retaliate against his political foes after the fall from power of his Parliamentary allies. In Defoe's and Swift's time, when writing in the public arena could involve a dangerous cat-and-mouse game with the authorities, there could be severe repercussions if editorial anonymity was stripped away, as happened when Swift was revealed to be the editor of the *Examiner* by his rival, Richard Steele. With its masked aspersions, its cynical fascination with the dark side of human nature, and its protagonist who is symbolically cast loose into a bizarre world that he cannot understand, *Gulliver's Travels* has been interpreted by critics in the context of Swift's psychological and abandonment issues, including the death of his father while he was in his mother's womb, his fascination with scatology, his strange relationships with women throughout his life, and the frantic bouts of exercise that he used to create the mood bursts necessary to dispel his episodes of depression. An Anglican clergyman and a lifelong bachelor, Swift's life, as well as his art, was colored with a cast of loneliness, isolation, resentment, cynicism, and a deep bitterness to the point of paranoia that the world was arrayed against him. These feelings were compounded by his loss of church preferment that resulted from his political entanglements, and he spent his last years in Ireland in a lesser church post writing spiteful, allegorical tales about his enemies and nursing grievances against humankind until he grew impossible and was deemed to have lost his mind.[17]

A few years later, Swift was Samuel Johnson's inspiration in demonstrating the topsy-turvy manner in which the use of fictional techniques by journalists could be the safest way to avoid the potentially traumatizing repercussions of frank expression in eighteenth-century England. After Parliament barred publications from carrying its debates in 1738, Johnson's *Gentleman's Magazine*'s ruse for handling the situation was to print what it said were the proceedings of the Lilliputian Senate brought back by the grandson of Gulliver. Even though he was virtually never in the House of Commons gallery, Johnson spent two-and-a-half years spinning "out of his own head" the magazine's accounts of debates from notes provided by assistants. For many years thereafter, the magazine's speeches—printed with the "coy" device, as one biographer put it, of using fictitious but easily recognizable names—were almost universally admired as authentic, including eloquent ones thought to have been delivered by William Pitt and Robert Walpole, until Johnson confessed to friends that much of the language in the speeches was really his.[18]

As was the case with Swift, the journalist-literary figures of the eighteenth and nineteenth centuries had limited cultural and social resources for handling emotional stress and psychological afflictions, and often their writings were their only outlet for dealing with trauma and loss. However, because the customs of their day allowed few opportunities to discuss trauma in a personal sense, they often projected their interior issues onto their literary characters and tried to profit from the public appetite for tales of trauma while revealing little about themselves and staying just within the boundaries of socially acceptable expression. Defoe's literary sleights of hand meant that he sold his accounts of profligacy, criminality, and human deviance as something that served a moral and instructional purpose. In *Moll Flanders*, he framed Moll's story—involving incest, criminal exploitation, and other libertine adventures—as the lessons of morality and contrition (or lack thereof). As he did in the preface to *Robinson Crusoe*, Defoe insisted that he was simply the editor of Moll's true-life chronicle whose job it was to make the material fit for respectable readers ("In a word, the whole relation is carefully garbled of all the levity and looseness that was in it, so it is all applied, and with the utmost care, to virtuous and religious uses," Defoe wrote). In her search for money and security in men, as well as in turning to thievery and deception, which gets her locked up in Newgate prison for a time, Moll presents readers with a picaresque tale of a bawdy adventuress who moves through tragic events and traumatic experiences with a cheeky attitude and light-hearted pluck. However, Defoe—who in his journalism advocated for the betterment of women's conditions—understood the dire situation for widows and women of his time who were left without means, and there is a serious undertone to his portrayal of Moll's tribulations. This is even more the case in his most psychologically complex novel, *Roxana*, where he described Roxana's desperation after she slips from a prosperous marriage into a life of promiscuity, affairs, and opportunistic relations with men. The events that follow her husband's desertion turn Roxana into a tormented figure who, as some critics have noted, experiences similar financial worries and emotional health issues that may have faced Defoe himself. ("There was a dart struck into my liver, there was a secret hell within. . . . I grew sad, heavy, pensive, and melancholy; slept little, and [ate] little; dreamed continually of the most frightful and terrible things imaginable; nothing but apparitions of devils and monsters, falling into gulfs, and off from steep and high precipices,"

Roxana says.) Her self-loathing and determination to see herself as a whore no matter how many men hope to make her an honest woman have been interpreted as Defoe's allegorical way of reflecting the traumatic events (his imprisonments, his business failures, and his editorial machinations that led to the severing of his political connections) that preceded his exile into a fiction-writing profession where he traded in tales of the traumatic effects of social marginalization, ostracism, and shame.[19]

Nearly a century later, the romantic essayist Charles Lamb demonstrated a different approach to how a journalist-literary figure used writing to maintain balance in a trauma-wracked life. Lamb never dwelt directly with his personal difficulties in the self-effacing humor of his periodical writings—the stammer that kept him from pursuing a university education, his confinement in an asylum during a period of "madness," as he put it, after a failed love affair, and his life helping to care for an invalid mother, a senile father, and a manic-depressive sister. The extent of his sister, Mary's, emotional illness became fully apparent one evening in 1796 when she killed their mother with a carving knife during dinner preparations. Lamb's burdens—his lifetime role in caring for Mary, who was in and out of mental institutions, his recurring bouts of depression often linked to her institutionalization—were barely alluded to in his popular "Elia" column in the London Magazine. Only close family friends understood how Lamb's journalism, his drinking (and his struggles to keep it in line), and his half-hearted efforts at writing poetry helped to distract him from his traumatic life tasks. Yet, Lamb's inner life was often one of misery, as he expressed in his private correspondence after one of Mary's breakdowns: "I am completely shipwreck'd.—My head is quite bad . . . I almost wish that Mary were dead."[20]

Across the Atlantic, the romantic movement's connection to journalism was personified in the newspaper editor-poet Walt Whitman, whose optimistic temperament and faith in journalism and poetry as tools for democratic nation-building made him—like Defoe—a groundbreaker in the expansion of journalistic practices into higher literary achievement. Whitman maintained a relatively healthy-minded approach to life, given that he came from a family with a father who experienced periods of heavy drinking, a mother who was nervous and a hypochondriac, a sister who was neurotic and possibly psychotic, a brother who was retarded and epileptic, another brother who became an alcoholic, and a third who died in an insane asylum. Throughout his life, Whitman carried a heavy burden of family worry and responsibility—but this was little reflected in his idealistic journalism and his mystical and passionately populist poetry (which often contained transposed elements of his

journalism put to free verse). Given the circumspect lives of people and the
repressive social patterns in Victorian times, we do not have a clear record
of the role of traumatizing experiences in his life—most notably, an instance
in which biographers have found evidence that he was forced to give up a
school teacher's post because of what town residents felt was an inappropriate
relationship with a student. Whitman's tendency only to "allude" to themes of
sexuality in his poetry while keeping the exact nature of his private life private
has meant that, whereas most scholars view him as a gay or bisexual person
advocating for a more open and sensual approach to human relationships,
the record is filled with enough ambiguities that one cannot know for sure
the nature of his sexual orientation or whether and to what extent he suffered
from keeping much concealed about himself.[21]

As the "dean" of nineteenth-century American letters, William Dean Howells's bouts of morbid anxiety and his obsession with hydrophobia as a youth
(the disease was a fixation of his publisher father who once editorialized in
his town newspaper that every suspected dog should be destroyed to avoid
the "terrible effects of madness") were the hidden story of Howells's life of
respectability and decorum. In veiled and seemingly contradictory ways,
his secret suffering provided the psychic energy that propelled the realist
literary movement and Howells's promotion of truth-telling as a method for
liberating American literature from its polite and disingenuous conventions
of expression (as well as presumably relieving the pressures of growing up in
a home environment of repression and hidden parental psychological suffering). Howells's own fragile disposition limited his sense of what he could
undertake in life—including newspaper reporting, which in his memoirs,
he indicated that he wished he had explored more so that he could have
encountered other "phases of life." Howells, who gave up a position at the
Cincinnati Gazette after a brief tenure of dealing with sordid wife beatings,
assaults, and attempted suicides, described how his psychic condition deteriorated to the point where he could not even read the headlines in the
newspapers. Although Howells came to blame his psychological struggles on
overwork, biographer Edwin Cady says that Howells's fear of hydrophobia
was symptomatic of "profound psychic turbulence" rooted in family tensions,
high levels of anxiety, and cultural alienation. Scholars have speculated about
the time the "bottom dropped out" (a phrase that Howells used to a friend)
during his composition of *The Rise of Silas Lapham*. In fact, Howells—despite advocating an uncompromising honesty toward life in his realist literary philosophy—was highly guarded in discussing how the residue of his
youthful hypochondria, depression, and panic attacks (he once described

how even the splash of water would lead to his dreaded fears of hydrophobia) played out in his adult life and writing career.[22]

Another of the so-called realists, Bret Harte manifested his literary reticence by doing what journalists have long done in simply not writing about the parts of life that are personally upsetting or that they believe their audience would find too unsettling. As a journeyman reporter-printer at the Humboldt County *Northern Californian*, Harte wrote only once about a traumatic employment event in 1860 that cost him his job and taught him a lesson about how much "reality" his readers would tolerate. In filling in while his editor was out of town, Harte learned about the massacre of sixty natives by axe-wielding town residents during a tribal celebration on the outskirts of Uniontown (called Arcata today). Harte chose to investigate the circumstances, and then to report on his findings, even after locals had taken away the mutilated bodies and organized a conspiracy of silence. "Old Women wrinkled and decrepit lay weltering in blood, their brains dashed out and dabbled with their long grey hair," Harte wrote in an editorial. "Infants scarce a span long, with their faces cloven with hatchets and their bodies ghastly with wounds." When the paper's editor returned, he and Harte agreed that it would be impossible for him to stay on—thus helping to steer Harte toward a magazine editing and short story writing career that would take off within a few months of his return to San Francisco. It is difficult to know how much the incident affected Harte, who was known for his emotionally distant demeanor and for putting little of his own personality into his writings beyond his role as impersonal storyteller. But whether the reasons were practical or psychological, the market savvy Harte presumably understood that there was a limited audience among the readers of his sentimental stories about the California Gold Rush years for accounts of the real "dark side" of frontier life. However, as Gary Scharnhorst has noted, Harte's portrayals of Native Americans and people of mixed white and Native American heritage, which he had written about somewhat derisively in his early journalism, were treated sympathetically and less stereotypically in his later fiction.[23]

The fact that the nineteenth-century writers we call the "realists" so consistently let cultural inhibitions override their truth-telling philosophy is a sign of how ingrained has been the response even of avowedly candid writers in trying to avoid traumatic subjects and to limit their picture of reality to what was considered acceptable within the public attitudes of their day. The necessity of living with repressed and unexamined emotions was particularly the condition for women journalists, such as George Eliot (a.k.a. Mary Ann Evans). Eliot probably would not have adopted a male pseudonym if she had not been forced to work, first as a journalist, and then as a novel writer, under circumstances in which professional women often operated anonymously and accepted difficult and sometimes humiliating work conditions as the price of involvement in the Victorian publishing world. Eliot faced the typical options for a nineteenth-century woman whose life path did not promise marriage and a man to provide her with social status and financial security. Following her mother's death, Eliot found herself in the role of surrogate wife for her aging father on the Warwickshire farm that he had managed—a dull, heavy burden that contributed to her tendency toward low moods and depression. She was able to escape this life, but at a high cost—John Chapman, the editor of the prominent *Westminster Review*, who discovered Eliot writing for the *Coventry Journal*, brought her to London, made her his mistress, and moved her into his home with his wife and governess, another mistress. After establishing Eliot as the de facto but anonymous editor of the *Review*, Chapman told her he could not love her because of her homeliness; at the same time, he performed the public role of editor, such as in the magazine's dealings with high profile male writers, while Eliot was forced to keep in the background. Eliot finally exited these employment circumstances and Chapman's home through her relationship with fellow journalist-literary figure, Henry Lewes. He encouraged her to launch her fiction writing career as a way of dealing with the isolation and social stigma that she experienced after the two decided to spurn Victorian convention by living together outside of marriage. Still, Eliot stayed exquisitely sensitive to the painful slights of life, which critics have seen as the basis of the finely textured prose of her novels with its hypervigilance to human feelings.[24]

Religion as the Early Framework for Understanding Trauma and Traumatized Emotions

In the eighteenth and nineteenth centuries, religion was often the context in which people understood and wrestled with their anxieties, their depressions, and the meaning that they imputed to traumatic experience. Religion has served as both a source of personal anguish and of spiritual questing, and journalist-literary figures, who have tended to be idealists, skeptics, seekers of both higher meaning and empirical truths, and even mystics sometimes all rolled into one, have had a propensity to intensely involve themselves in the religious debates of their time. Because religion has been a place to explore the meaning of suffering, many found their childhood wounds and the emotional turmoil of their adult lives tangled up in their experiences of and views about religion.

Defoe presented Robinson Crusoe's introspection as a function of his religious reflections—his trying to divine God's will in the disastrous events of his early life, his recognition of his sinful actions, and the religious epiphany that led him to dedicate himself to God while living in isolation on his island. Defoe's dissenting Protestant views were behind his championing of a number of stylistic techniques that have come to be identified with modern journalism and the popular novel—that writing should be simple and colloquial and accessible to average people, that abstract words and complex meanings should be avoided, that life should be about trying to discern the role of Providence and God's plan (a form of the "news" and an interpretation of natural events in Defoe's time), that character improvement and personal transformation could explain much about the journey of the individual. In *A Journal of the Plague Year*, Defoe portrayed his protagonist as deciding to stay in London rather than flee the plague because he feels that God has told him to do so (as a good Calvinist, he also wants to keep an eye on his business). This fictional device allowed Defoe to dramatize in eye witness fashion scenes of great trauma (a mother who grows hysterical in seeing the marks of the plague on her sleeping daughter, a grief-stricken father who cannot break himself away from the caskets of his family members as they are dumped into a mass grave pit, tavern revelers who blaspheme God and the notion of the plague as the work of God before they are struck down by the disease) that were constructed on the assumption that audiences would be drawn to up-close accounts of the suffering and explanations of why it had occurred. Defoe built a number of his novels around the fact that Calvinists often were blind to their own faults, such as in the case of the heroine in *Moll Flanders*, who is oblivious to her own spiritual and moral dishonesty. As a secularized Puritan, Defoe tried to have it both ways in the creation of Moll's character; he could moralize while also drawing the reader in with the titillating and traumatic elements of her story. At the same time, Defoe had enormous sympathy for the real struggles reflected in the lives of his fictional characters (including destroyed marriages, rapes and desperate descents into prostitution, shipwrecks, and escapes from the plague). Perhaps this was because Defoe, as a Protestant who refused to take communion in the Anglican Church and an outsider who was forced to suffer social ostracism and imprisonments, understood traumatic isolation (critics have noted, for example, the parallels between Defoe's own beleaguered life and Robinson Crusoe's lonely existence on a deserted island). Although religion could still

be a cruel business, the emergence of modern liberalism and expanded notions of religious tolerance were beginning to have an influence in Defoe's
time. Despite his run-ins with the authorities—Defoe was jailed for his in-
debtedness and for his writings against the established state religion—the
trauma of the experiences did not alter his generally optimistic outlook and
his generous and humane impulses. This can be seen in the imaginative sympathy he showed in his fiction for criminals and reprobates and other ren-
egade figures (almost certainly reinforced by his own time spent in prison),
as well as his tracts advocating for wealth redistribution and government
programs to help the disadvantaged.[25]

In a more personally revealing fashion, the mental health issues of Boswell
and Johnson also played out with religion as the backdrop. As writers of biography, and in Boswell's case, detailed journals about his association with Johnson, the two left an intimate record of their psychological ailments and how
they were connected to their writing activities. Johnson's debilitating bouts of
depression—which kept him bedridden and required that he be ministered
to by friends and loved ones—often took the form of trepidations about his
salvation and worries that certain Christian concepts might not be real. The
age of reason was fraught with fear for those who found it painful to experience religious consolation ebbing away and their doubts about, or loss of faith
in, the notions of an afterlife, of Jesus as a figure of salvation and redemption,
and of the many promises made by church teachings caused great stress, and
in some cases, what might be viewed as trauma. In discussing the passing of
his mother, as he did with Boswell in *The Life of Samuel Johnson*, the Anglican
Johnson indicated that he did not know how he could carry on without the
promise of being reunited with loved ones in the afterlife. Boswell's emotional
struggles also took on a religious cast in his mind (their shared experience of
morbid anxiety and religious questioning was a major reason that Johnson and
Boswell bonded), and he often wondered whether he was damning himself
by his profligate ways. Boswell's guilt over his incessant whoring, his bouts of
venereal disease, and his compulsive gambling and drinking was a response
to the melancholy that he described in his "Hypochondriack" column—but
which we only have learned the full details of because of the discovery of his
personal journals (published as *Boswell's London Journal*) in the twentieth
century. The tensions created by the inroads of secular, Enlightenment thought
can be seen in the exchange in *The Life* where Boswell and Johnson discuss
their acquaintance, the philosopher David Hume, and his alleged atheism and
nonbelief in the afterlife, as he lay on his deathbed (which led to Johnson's
anxious acknowledgment—while insisting that Hume could not really be such

a sanguine disbeliever in the face of his personal extinction—that many of the same doubts had passed through Johnson's own mind).[26]

The tensions during the Victorian age between a writer's public persona and the sufferings of his or her private self manifested themselves in a cultural environment where the hold of religion was weakening and the concept of human motivation as a function of subconscious psychological drives was rising up to challenge Christian explanations. Modernist views about Christian teachings and the coming of what is today called the "culture wars" created divisions, including within the families where a number of journalist-literary figures grew up. Eliot, who was greatly interested in Christianity (she translated David Friedrich Strauss's *Life of Jesus Critically Examined* from the German) but emerged a skeptic and a freethinker on religious matters, became alienated from her father and brother for refusing to go to church as a young woman. Eliot was deeply affected by the Darwinian challenge to Christian cosmological explanations and the "higher criticism" of the Bible that grew out of the work of Strauss and his questioning of the "facts" of Jesus's life as presented in the Bible. But even as she came to the conclusion that the church's portrait of Jesus was constructed out of evangelical myth, Eliot found Strauss's efforts to strip away all that was "miraculous and highly improbable" from the Gospels to be oppressive and joyless. She even complained at one point that she was "Strauss sick" (she performed much of her translation work in a melancholy mood, with a statue of Jesus before her on her desk). However, Eliot remained tough-minded in her refusal to embrace a theology that made no rational sense to her, and—stoical in her willingness to endure emotional pain for her disbelief—she never turned to spiritualism or other explorations of the occult as did other Victorian agnostics.[27]

With his bitter heterodoxy and his contemptuous views of Christian piety, Mark Twain played one of the most high profile roles among journalist-literary figures in challenging the notion of religion as a balm against traumatic experience. Twain's early family tragedies—his father's death that led to his family's economic struggles and his dropping out of school to work in print shops—were overshadowed by the late life losses of his beloved wife, Olivia, and two of his three daughters that contributed to his growing embitterment at a God who could inflict such pain on people. Twain, who in his youth briefly toyed with the idea of going into the clergy (he lacked "the necessary stock in trade, i.e. religion," he once wrote his brother), poured out numerous literary works with religion as a major theme—the most famous being *The Adventures of Huckleberry Finn*, with its ironical critique of Christian values (Huck saying that he was not going to "try for" heaven if the pious Miss Watson is there; Huck's celebrated exclamation—"All right, then, I'll *go* to Hell"—when he decides to embrace the "wickedness" that he was "brung up to" and snatch the runaway Jim back out of slavery) and *Letters from the Earth*, which Twain's surviving daughter kept from being published for many years after his death because of its perceived infidelity. As he grew more depressed in his later years, Twain's notions of God grew increasingly cynical and resentful, and he often implied that it was only the foolish and the naïve who would see God as anything but a cruel monster responsible for the "blood-drenched history" of conquest in the Hebrew scriptures. "These people's God has shown them by a million acts that he respects none of the Bible's statutes," Twain wrote. "He breaks every one of them himself." Unlike many aging people, Twain's experiences of loss and physical decline never humbled him or led him to seek spiritual solace in a power larger than himself; instead, his personality became crustier, his bitterness grew to colossal levels, and his ego expanded in proportion to his disenchantment with life. In his relentless attention to the "bad" things that happen to human beings, Twain became Job-like in his complaints. However, one senses that, like Job, Twain's bitterness might not have run so deep if his expectations of life had not been so high—and certainly if his view of himself as a favored one (if not by God, then at least by his audience) was not so great.[28]

The connection between journalist-literary figures' experiences in journalism and the collapse of their religious beliefs was made most explicitly by Theodore Dreiser, who recounted how the irreverent views of his journalistic colleagues in the 1890s—"hard, gallant adventurers" who were largely "confused by the general American passive acceptance of the Sermon on the Mount and the Beatitudes as governing principles"—helped to undermine the faith he had absorbed from his pious German Catholic father and his Mennonite mother. Dreiser recounted how he had his religious moorings uprooted by reading Herbert Spencer, Julian Huxley, and other writers influenced by Darwin. Spencer "nearly killed me, took every shred of belief away from me. . . . Until I read Huxley, I had some lingering filaments of Catholicism trailing about me, faith in the existence of Christ, the soundness of his moral and sociologic deductions, the brotherhood of man. . . . Now in its place was the definite conviction that spiritually one got nowhere, that there was no hereafter, that one lived and had his being because one had to, and that it was of no importance," Dreiser wrote in *A Book about Myself*. Yet, as bleak as were his conclusions about the emotional cost of the loss of religious faith, his discovery of life without the restraints of religion lifted a weight from his moral conscience. In his memoirs, Dreiser connected his loss of religious belief to his embrace of a "pagan" view of sex and a philosophy of personal gratification that many critics were aghast at finding reflected in the amorality of his literary heroes and heroines (particularly his heroines) who did not experience the "traumas" of sexual guilt or fear of punishment for their transgressions in the way of traditional Victorian female protagonists.[29]

The bitterness that Twain displayed against Christian teachings had seeped broadly into the culture by the mid–twentieth century, and the divisions that today we associate with the culture wars can be seen reflected in longtime *New Yorker* writer Peter De Vries' *The Blood of the Lamb*, his semifictional account of his ten-year-old daughter dying of leukemia. De Vries' main character, Don Wanderhope, loses his faith in a benevolent God and is tortured by what he comes to feel are religion's unsatisfactory explanations for suffering in the world. In a story written with "heart-breaking verisimilitude," as one critic put it, Wanderhope enters a church and throws a cake left in a church pew at a statue of Jesus shortly after his daughter has died. At an earlier point in the novel, a father, whose daughter is being treated for leukemia at the same hospital as Wanderhope's daughter, says to him, "What baffles me is the comfort people find in the idea that somebody dealt this mess. Blind and meaningless chance seems to me so much more congenial—or at least less horrible. Prove to me that there is a God and I will really begin to despair." As with Twain and a number of other journalist-literary figures, De Vries, who was raised in a strict Dutch Calvinist community, found the structure of the novel a useful place to intertwine themes of trauma with religious questioning and to put his resentments against God into the mouths of a variety of characters. Those included Wanderhope's impious older brother, their depressed and doubting father, and other more reverent family members, who debate in witty, sardonic, Twain-like fashion the imponderables of theology and the religious meaning to be found in traumatic human events. (Or as the youthful Wanderhope says at one point, as he ponders his older brother dying of pneumonia and God's responsibility for it: "*Why doesn't He pick on somebody his size?*")[30]

In contrast to the bitter impiety of Twain and De Vries, religion has had a positive impact on a handful of journalist-literary figures, most notably Graham Greene, G. K. Chesterton, and Evelyn Waugh who became midlife Catholic converts, in helping to ease the effects of traumatized emotions. Chesterton was perhaps the most outspoken of this group in defending Christian orthodoxy in his writings—and perhaps the one whose religious conversion had the most to do with his mental suffering. With his early struggles with depression and his youthful fascination with suicide and fear of insanity,

Chesterton felt much "healed" by his conversion to Catholicism. This became the basis for a lifetime of writing that had enormous appeal to intellectuals who also were believers but felt embattled by the growing secularism and hostility toward traditional religion that they found within the twentieth-century intelligentsia. Another Catholic convert, Dorothy Day, experienced such gratitude at the birth of her daughter and joy at her conversion ("It was because through a whole love, both physical and spiritual [that] I came to know God") that she went from freethinking skeptic to Christian believer. Day's transformation into an important Catholic journalist and founder of *The Catholic World* was even more dramatic given the opposition of her father, a whisky-drinking, race track enthusiast and journalist, who disapproved of both her taking up journalism and her involvement in religion. Day's traumas connected to religion—including the guilt and confusion she suffered after undergoing a preconversion abortion while living with a group of bohemian activists in New York City (the father, who left her, suggested the abortion and later wrote her a letter telling her that he hoped she would "get comfortably married to a rich man")—exemplified the manner in which religion has been both a panacea and a source of pain in human dealings with trauma.[31]

Trauma and the Romantic Movement

An increasingly less conventional attachment to traditional religious values also was at the heart of romanticism, which grew up as a powerful force in literary as well as journalistic circles in the late eighteenth and early to mid–nineteenth centuries. Beginning with Coleridge, the romantic movement was a response to the dissatisfaction in intellectual circles with both Christian doctrine and Enlightenment rationalism, and it swept up a number of the major journalist-literary figures of the era, including Lamb, Edgar Allen Poe, Whitman, Ruskin, Thomas De Quincey, Leigh Hunt, and Margaret Fuller. The embrace of passion and emotional experience was a defining issue with the romantics—but the romantic endorsement of suffering as a life stance can sometimes make it difficult to ascertain when emotional wounds were genuinely debilitating. Given the romantic fascination with the spontaneous side of human nature, the romantics' dislike of formalized religion also was a feature of their mindset, but it often was softened by their embrace of "spirituality" and their pantheistic views of nature. Coleridge, like Poe and De Quincey, discovered the trauma of substance addiction (he began taking opium as a pain-relieving medicine, laudanum, and—without fully understanding its addictive properties—became dependent on it), and he helped to establish the romantic image of the suffering artist using whatever means available to deal with emotional pain and sacrificing all for the sake of art. However, with his prolific philosophical writings and his one-time interest in the ministry, Coleridge also is considered something of a theologian today, and he was deeply influenced by both the Christianity of his pious, minister father whom he greatly admired and his own spiritual experimentation, which included dabbling in a form of utopian communalism with fellow poet Robert Southey. In fact, while Coleridge might have had reasons to consider his religious upbringing abusive—he was abashed when he was sent away to a strict, religious school as a young boy—he always expressed appreciation for the clergyman who ran it and seemed to suffer the most from being forced to live apart from his family.[32]

The romantic movement's influence on the developments in nineteenth-century philosophy expanded awareness in journalistic circles of the notion of the subconscious mind in operation and the importance of childhood experience ("That youth and I are house mates still," Coleridge wrote) before the appearance of Freud. But a naivety about the force of subterranean emotional influences in directing human behavior still inhibited many Victorian authors, including many of the journalist-literary figures of the period, from exploring the deeper psychological implications of their literary themes or personal stories. Although fully a romantic in temperament, Dickens conformed to the posture of rectitude and repression that characterized his age and largely kept his emotional issues hidden from public display. With his own youthful traumas reflected in a variety of his literary characters (abandoned young people, helpless young women, children in poverty exploited by adults, victims of abusive families and harsh educational settings), Dickens preferred melodrama and sentimental stereotypes in the expression of his romantic impulses. However, despite experiencing bouts of depression, manic periods of work, and nervous disorders, he never fully explored the roots of the truly psychologically unhinged personality in his fiction nor did he present the unbalanced psyches of his villains outside the good-versus-evil stereotypes used in the popular press of the period or connect adult criminal compulsions to histories of childhood trauma. The tension between romantic idealism and the exploration of deeper feelings of youthful trauma also came into play for other romantically influenced but divided figures of this period, such as Twain and Harte, who satirized romantic posturing in their journalism and humor writing while creating sentimental depictions of childhood and frontier life in their own fiction. Twain, in particular, never escaped his own romantic questing, nor did he settle on a vision of youth that could quite rid itself of the recognition of how much traumatic experience could influence even a rough-and-ready boy. ("It was kind of lazy and jolly, laying off comfortable all day, smoking and fishing, and no books or study. . . . But by and by pap got too handy with his hick'ry, and I couldn't stand it," said the iconic victim of child abuse, Huckleberry Finn, of life on the river with his drunken "Pap," "I was all over welts.")[33]

The literature of Poe, whose short life found him walking a narrow line between suicidal impulses and self-destructive behaviors, was interwoven at every turn with traumatic experiences, romantic expression, and the practices of the sensational press of his time. With a drunkard father who abandoned the family when Poe was an infant and a mother who died just before his third birthday, Poe felt victimized by his early life experiences. He brought this resentment into his journalism career, where he identified with the landed gentry connections in his family background and would complain about the hackwork that he felt was beneath his literary talents and standards. Poe's emotional turbulence and his attraction to sensational story formulas (he was already suicidal and alcoholic when he argued with his first editor at the *Southern Literary Messenger* that what his publication needed were more stories of the bizarre and the grotesque) led to the intermingling of his hopes for founding a popular literary magazine (a goal that obsessed him, but which he never attained) with the many external devices (alcohol, periodical job hopping, critical attacks on famous authors) that he employed to try to numb and divert his inner pain. In his way, Poe found the environment of journalism a congenial, if frustrating, one in its tolerance (even though usually only temporary) of his unreliable work habits, its encouragement of him to put to paper his fantastical tales for an audience that loved Gothic and sensationalistic formulas, and its willingness to give second and third chances for a sick but brilliant talent.[34]

Poe's recognition of the attraction of popular crime formulas combined with the unique patterns of his obsessed and fevered imagination to produce his groundbreaking detective stories and tales of the macabre and the mentally unstrung. Poe identified with popular fictional authors of the "voyeur style" of George Lippard and G. W. M. Reynolds, who came out of the sensationalistic press and blended the "peril" accounts of the Penny Press newspapers with fictional writing formulas; although, Poe fancied that he did it in a more adroit literary fashion and in a way that served the "scientific" ends of forensics and official police investigations. Perhaps his most famous story, "The Tell-Tale Heart" (which has served as the model for countless television and movie scenarios ever since), was inspired by the 1830 trial of Joseph and Francis Knapp for the murder of Captain Joseph White, the notorious "Salem Murder," as well as another highly publicized homicide involving a rich banker. "The Mystery of Marie Roget" was Poe's attempt to apply his own investigative insights to the real crime of a murdered New York City cigar girl. Pseudoscience and romantic notions of the power of criminal impulse had a big impact on Poe, and he mixed themes of phrenology, animal magnetism, and occultism into what he liked to pretend were case studies to aid criminal probes. Both in his stories and his public persona, Poe recognized the advantages of self-dramatization, and his overpowering compulsions meant that he understood intimately how to put trauma to professional use, as well as how to balance his own inner turmoil with his mastery of the multiple ways (the updating of trauma-related archetypes rooted in Gothic and folk tale formulas, the creation of fictional works that remixed these formulas into haunting literary narratives, and the development of a public reputation based on manifesting the same symptoms as many of his literary characters) in which he saw that trauma could be marketed in a mass society. Poe's inability to keep the traumas of his inner life from mastering him in the end cemented his legend and made him one of the earliest of the prominent journalist-literary figures—like Agee, Capote, Brendan Behan, Dylan Thomas, and others who would come after him—to trademark a tragic public style that put on display the compulsive behaviors that were killing him at the same time.[35]

The romantic tradition of confessional writing became a key factor in the development of the image of the suffering journalist-literary figure trying to drown the effects of broken hearts, life disappointments, and other romantic longings in alcohol and drug use. De Quincey and Lamb, friends and public confessors of their opium and alcohol addictions, respectively, asked their readers to understand and forgive them their problems with substance abuse. Lamb and De Quincey used the tradition of the guilt-ridden confession of immoral or weak-willed conduct in parallel with the developing tradition of Wesleyan and Christian evangelical condemnations of sinful conduct and the antidote of conversion and reformation. Critics have read into Lamb's drunkard's confession connections to his traumatic experience in witnessing his mother's murder by his sister, as they have De Quincey's references to the "incidents of my early life" that he said made up the "substratum" of his dreams as much as his opium use. De Quincey's portrayal of what Susan M. Levin calls the gap between the "coherent unity we start recognizing in a mirror at an early age and the neurotic, uncontrollable bundle we feel ourselves to be" is at the heart of romanticism's entanglement with the traumatic issues of the inner life. De Quincey acknowledged that his confession, first published in *London Magazine* in 1823, was as much an embarrassment to him as a solace (he said that he was reluctant to make himself into another Jean Jacques Rousseau who had undertaken "acts of gratuitous self-humiliation" by making a "spectacle" of himself and "obtruding on our notice his moral ulcers and scars"). De Quincey tried to elevate his revelations by writing in the language of the utilitarians of his time and to imply that his approach was scientific and an examination of the good of opium weighed against the bad, as well as the underlying causes of what might make a person turn to drug use. In this, one can find in De Quincey incipient insights into romanticism's connections to the field of psychology that Freud would advance by arguing that only the light of reason could subdue the irrational self that was capable of causing much pain in a person living the unexamined life.[36]

The politically outspoken and independently wealthy Ruskin had the resources to underwrite his newsletter, *Fors Clavigera*, which he said was aimed at the working people of England (even though he was never willing to drop the cost so that any working person might have been able to afford it). Few except his friends and acquaintances read the publication—which was filled with "incoherent confessionalism and Carlylean misanthropy," as one critic has put it. Described as an "unpopular anti-periodical," Ruskin used *Fors* to insult a wide range of people he considered his readers, and his comments were both intrusive and highly personal in nature. His confessions became increasingly awkward as Ruskin, who suffered from periods of mania and paranoid schizophrenic behavior, engaged in "utter self-revelation," as he put it (one passage in *Fors* described the morning that Ruskin mistook his bathrobe for his greatcoat and "walked through the full market-place, and half-way down the principal street, in that costume, proceeding in perfect tranquility until the repeated glances of unusual admiration bestowed on me by the passengers led me to the investigation of the possible cause"; in another he told his readers of "the state of morbid inflammation of brain which gave rise to false visions" and the "transitional moment of the first hallucination, entirely healthy, and in the full sense of the word 'sane'" that enabled him "to discern more clearly, and say more vividly, what for long years it had been in my heart to say"). Ruskin's most outrageous quotes spread through the literary grapevine and led to the termination of a number of relationships (including with much of the Victorian press). His paternalism led the humor magazine *Punch* to mimic Ruskin writing to his working class readers this way: "What right have you to put yourself on a level with me? . . . Read my books. If you say you can't afford them, I beg to remind you that by abstaining for five years from bread, beer, spirits, and tobacco, you will be quite able to afford a volume of *Fors Clavigera*."[37]

J. M. Barrie's life tells a story of how repression, romantic impulses, and warped life experience could intertwine with traumatic emotions to create one of the great children's mythical stories and yet leave scholars and biographers wondering what really was up with Barrie's peculiar behaviors. Barrie's creation of the Peter Pan play and books at the same time he maintained an intense relationship with the Llewelyn Davieses, a London family with five young boys, has led to scholarly speculation as to Barrie's underlying motives and his sexual nature. The Llewelyn Davies boys are commonly viewed as the model for the "Lost Boys" of the Peter Pan story, and the summer that Barrie spent with the family (he invited them to his family cottage after meeting the mother and boys in London's Kensington Gardens in 1897) telling stories about pirates and adventures to the boys and photographing them (often in provocative poses) as the inspiration for the play. Peter Davies (who many have seen as the namesake for Peter Pan, although Barrie insisted that Peter was a composite of the five boys) later commented, "contemporaries thought the whole business pretty odd." As the boys grew older, they came to resent the way that they had become objects of obsession of Barrie and how the press chronicled everything that happened to them in the context of the Peter Pan story. Barrie's strangeness was apparent early on in his journalism for the *Nottingham Journal* in which he mixed cynicism, sentimentalism, and a fixation on "pretty boys," which was the title of one of his columns. "Pretty boys are pretty in all circumstances, and this one would look as exquisitely delightful on the floor as when genteelly standing, in his nice little velvet suit with his sweet back to the fireplace. . . . When you leave the house, the pretty boy trips politely to the door and . . . holds up his pretty mouth for a pretty kiss," he wrote. "If you wish to continue on visiting terms with his mother you do everything he wishes." (Biographer Andrew Birkin says that Barrie's humor did not particularly amuse the newspaper's provincial readers, and his employment was short-lived.) The repressions of Victorian life and the sentimentalizing of childhood in Barrie's time have left scholars to speculate about the Freudian motifs involved with his fascination with children and childhood—his claims that he was never really happy around adults, his childless, probably unconsummated marriage with an actress who eventually left him for a younger man, and the cruelty and even sadism that some saw behind his willingness, despite his own personal reserve and shyness, to reveal the most intimately neurotic truths about himself and his family in print ("My God! . . . I would write an article, I think, on my mother's coffin," he said). The most dramatic speculation has centered upon the suicide in 1960 of Peter Davies (who once told an interviewer who was questioning him about being the namesake for Peter Pan, "Please forget that. I'm grown up now, you know"). Despite their suspicions, today's psychologically oriented commentators will never fully know how the traumas of Barrie's own dysfunctional upbringing may have manifested themselves in traumas visited on other children—and to what degree he may have acted on his emotional peculiarities (and what those peculiarities really were).[38]

Richard Harding Davis, as the most publicly "romantic" American journalist-literary figure, at least in the self-caricature sense, embodied the fusion of the journalist-literary figure with the public image of the intrepid war correspondent that became a popular manifestation of romanticism as the United States entered into the colonial sweepstakes in the late nineteenth and early twentieth centuries. Davis's neuroses—his dependence on and attachment to his mother, the journalist-novelist Rebecca Harding Davis, his celibate relationship with his first wife, and his depressive episodes—underlay the foundation of the public Davis, who was both admired and ridiculed for his dandyism and his Sir Galahad–like posturing. Biographer Gerald Langford maintains that Davis's histrionics and self-dramatization were camouflage for his basic insecurity, and his globe-trotting and his attraction to the thrill of combat were "therapy" to deal with his depression and moods of self-doubt. His mother's affection—which Langford says was "crippling" to her son—was a Freudian counterpoint to Davis's derring-do image in the public mind, and his dutiful efforts to disguise the gap between his real feelings and his presentation of an ideal self caused him considerable tension throughout his life (his mother, in reflecting the model of family system's theory, suffered herself from severe depression during and after her pregnancy with Richard, which psychologists would say increased the chances of her son suffering from depression, too). Davis's life of repression and denial—overlain with his battles against his "nerve storms," as he called them—made him the perfect figure to portray warfare in the romantic and heroic, if not always forthright, terms that suited a young nation pursuing its "manifest destiny" by expanding America's armed presence around the world. Davis's personal immaturity (he had few serious dealings with women until he was thirty-five and was willing to marry a woman who was interested in a "platonic" marital relationship) was mirrored in a national press that—in taking Davis's lead—often glossed over the ugly realities of war in favor of portraying America's battlefield exploits always in a noble light. The death of his mother—who, in classic Alice Miller fashion, had indoctrinated Davis to subordinate his feelings to her needs (she wrote him letters that read: "I can't do anything but think how you look and how hungry I am for the sight of you and the touch of your dear arms around me . . . I want you always to know . . . how happy you have made me in my old age")—led first to a major emotional collapse but then to a sense of personal freedom that allowed him to end his first marriage and wed Bessie McCoy, an actress whom he loved deeply and who brought him domestic happiness late in his life. Davis's "coming of age" can be seen as a parallel to the United States' entry into World War I—which Davis covered in his last overseas assignment—and the end of an era of glorified American views of war that came with the colossal loss of life, the poison gas attacks, and the years of stalemated trench warfare on the French-German front.[39]

Trauma and the Age of Freud and Psychology

The merging of modern psychology with the sensationalism of the big city newspapers and the use of Freudian patterns to provide interpretive frameworks for stories about crime and deviance soon became so widespread that writers could not escape their reach. By the early decades of the twentieth century, many journalist-literary figures were so immersed in Freudian ideas and concepts that they could hardly perform their work without having someone psychoanalyzing it. Not only were Anderson's "grotesques" presented in forms that invited Freudian interpretation, but other psychologically motivated characters who operated out of subconscious drives and distorted emotional impulses became commonplace features in the novels of Barnes, O'Hara, Erskine Caldwell, Richard Wright, Virginia Woolf, E. M. Forster, and others who recognized the role of emotional trauma that could be traced to family trauma. A greater awareness of psychological theory and the operations of the subconscious was not only seen in the fictional characters and the plots of their writings but also in the way that post-Freudian critics and biographers came to relate their journalism and fiction to their traumatic and early life experiences. In their writings, Edmund Wilson, George Orwell, H. G. Wells, H. L. Mencken, Rebecca West, John Dos Passos, E. B. White, Katherine Anne Porter, and Mary McCarthy wrote with insight into the psychological roots of human motivation, and they often demonstrated more than the usual popular understanding of Freudian theory. At the same time, only a few journalist-literary figures—including Agee, White, Dorothy Parker, Heywood Broun, Dorothy Thompson, and V. S. Pritchett—tried psychoanalysis in controlled settings as a way to get at the source of their own emotional issues. For the most part, the Freudian-oriented journalist-literary figures tended to write about psychological themes when they wanted to explore them, and their interest in the field was less about involving themselves in personal therapy than it was in using art tempered by psychological insight to expand the range of their literary investigations. (This attitude was captured semihumorously by the humorist, James Thurber, who once said, "I do not have a psychiatrist and I do not want one, for the simple reason that if he listened to me long enough, he might become disturbed.")[40]

With his well-known taste for booze, prostitutes, and opium smoking, Greene is a good example of a journalist-literary figure who trafficked in trauma as a way to build his literary and his journalistic reputation. Greene was known for traveling the world to find the lush and forbidding settings for novels, such as *The Heart of the Matter* (Sierra Leone), *Travels with My Aunt* (Paraguay), *The Quiet American* (Vietnam), *A Burnt-Out Case* (the old Belgian Congo), *The Comedians* (Haiti), *The Honorary Consul* (Argentina), *Our Man in Havana* (Cuba), and *The Captain and the Enemy* (Panama), in which his protagonists often participated in the dissipated expatriate lifestyle that so attracted Greene himself. Greene would work for news organizations and/or sell freelance articles as a way to help cover his expenses and give him access to people and scenes that became the grist of his fiction. His problematic role as a journalist (that included allegations that he sometimes also spied for the British Secret Service) added to the pleasure he gained in vexing the world by changing his political colorations and engaging in subterfuges that have left scholars and biographers debating whether he was really a leftist sympathizer and a Catholic convert or just a self-promoting trickster. Greene's controversial activities as a journalist were legion. He once confessed to having communist affiliations as a way to embarrass his then employer, the pro-American Luce publications; at the same time, his journalism for Luce about the French military campaign in Vietnam in the early 1950s was too sympathetic to the communist forces and never used by his editors at *Time*. Greene often would pen parallel journalistic and fictional books—such as he did from his visit to Mexico in 1938 with his nonfictional travel book, *Lawless Roads*, and *The Power and the Glory*, the story of a tormented, alcoholic Mexican priest that was based on the persecution of the Catholic clergy that Greene documented in his nonfiction, or *Getting to Know the General*, a journalistic celebration of his late-life friendship with the Panamanian leader, Omar Torrijos, and the fictional *The Captain and the Enemy*, set amid the treachery and intrigue surrounding the politics of Panama's dictatorship. The part of Greene that so enjoyed displaying the dark side of his personality found the line between truth and imagination an irresistible one both in his fiction writing and in the way he told his life story, and scholars and biographers still debate how much to connect the suicide of his police commissioner protagonist in *The Heart of the Matter* with Greene's thoughts of suicide as a schoolboy or whether to believe his claims that he played Russian roulette, as dramatized in his short story, "The Revolver in the Corner Cupboard."[41]

Those who have questioned Greene's sincerity tend to see him as a person who looked at everything—whether it was religious agonizing, psychological suffering, the pain of human relationships, or the struggles of life lived in dangerous and exotic circumstances—as a source of material for his writing and not a reflection of real angst. However, his literary characters—whether the whisky priest in *The Power and the Glory* or the cynical, opium-using journalist, Thomas Fowler, in *The Quiet American*—present compelling fictional accounts of the themes that Greene hoped his readers would associate with his own life. His conversion to Catholicism, for example, which he said gave him insight into his numerous fictional characters who use religious motifs as the framework for exploring their emotional torment, their longing for spiritual connection, and their experience of evil within themselves, was viewed with skepticism by some, including his friend and fellow convert, Evelyn Waugh. (On one occasion, for example, Greene was telling the cynical Waugh about the plot of *The Quiet American*, and Greene said it would be a relief not to write about God for a change. "Oh?" Waugh replied. "I wouldn't drop God, if I were you. Not at this stage anyway. It would be like P. G. Wodehouse dropping Jeeves halfway through the Wooster series.") Biographer Michael Shelden said there is evidence that Greene embraced the role of the believer because it offered him opportunities to break rules from the inside while posing as a friend of the church and to add biographical intrigue to his literary probing of the mysteries of the human psyche. "I had to find a religion . . . to measure my evil against," Greene once said. How much comments such as this were a tactic on Greene's part—and how much it was a genuine reflection of his own troubled life—is a matter that, in the end, is as open to interpretation with Greene as it is with Major Scobie in *The Heart of the Matter*, whose wife says to a priest after her husband's suicide, "The Church knows all the rules. But it doesn't know what goes on in a single human heart."[42]

Willa Cather is a fascinating study in how a personality—private, self-protective, highly reticent in her expression of personal emotions—has become a fixation for post-Freudian scholars who have speculated about the internal traumas that she must have endured in concealing her alleged lesbianism and in dealing with harsh criticism as her political and literary views grew more conservative. Cather was so little forthcoming about her private life that scholars do not know for sure what was the nature or the cause of a nervous breakdown that she appeared to have suffered in 1922 when she returned to Red Cloud, Nebraska, and joined her hometown Episcopal church. Cather, who lived the last forty years of her life with a woman friend, Edith Lewis, in their Greenwich Village apartment, was so determined to deflect examination of her private life that she instructed Lewis to burn much of Cather's private correspondence after her death. However, this has not stopped a flood of scholarship about the nature of Cather's sexual orientation, and in particular, her relationship with a youthful friend, Isabelle McClung, as well as the challenges she faced as a woman who used journalism as a ladder to literary and fiction-writing success. Scholars have interpreted a number of Cather's novels and short stories in the context of her advocacy of the independent women's professional life, as well as tried to tease out of her texts and her life history hints that she was homosexual. Cather strongly identified with the male world—dressing like a man as a college student, expressing her preference for male authors, writing with a male persona as narrator, as she did in *My Antonia* (which she said she better understood how to do after serving as a ghostwriter for S. S. McClure's autobiography while she worked at *McClure's* magazine). When she became the *Pittsburgh Leader's* telegraph editor in 1895—even though her age, sex, and inexperience were working against her—she came to be considered "one of the fellows" and was respected for her ability to handle herself unselfconsciously in a bastion of male editors. Cather viewed with great skepticism the romantic passion that she saw as filling up too much women's literature, and she coined a number of phrases for why she spurned marriage in a society where a woman usually had to sacrifice her professional ambitions for husband and family. ("He travels the swiftest who rides alone," she was fond of saying, as well as "married nightingales seldom sing.") As a rule, Cather said, "if I see the announcement of a new book by a woman, I—well, I take one by a man instead," adding, "I have not much faith in women in fiction. They have a sort of sex consciousness that is abominable."[43]

However, Cather's ambivalent views about what in her time was called "the woman question" have not kept contemporary scholars from finding in her texts and the biographical record that she tried to conceal enough evidence to put her into the camp of gay literary figures. The correspondence between Cather and McClung has been the subject of particular attention—as have Cather's letters (the ones that were not burned) that are kept at Duke University and which scholars have access to (per Cather's instructions) only if they agree not to quote from them. It has become widely accepted among Cather scholars that she experienced trauma when McClung decided to marry in 1916. However, the foundation of this interpretation is largely speculative and demonstrates how prone some contemporary critics are to state inference as fact when they look for repressed or concealed trauma in the lives of historical figures. Biographer James Woodress argues that Cather critics commonly do not acknowledge that in her day, unmarried women often became live-in companions, and it was quite customary for these arrangements to be platonic. He said it is impossible to know if Cather's ties to women resulted from inherent tendencies or from the fact that her principle aim was to retain an inviolability of self, and that relationships with women avoided involvement with men and the issues of marriage and children. Cather's creation of Alexandra Bergstrom in *O Pioneers!*—with her determination to build a prosperous farm on the Nebraska frontier without the aid of a man and her concern about her brother's tragic attachment to a high-spirited neighboring farmer's wife—exemplifies Cather's great suspicion of passion in life and her view that women can have highly fulfilling lives without marriage (or sexual relations, for that matter).[44]

As is the case with Cather (who had a problematic relationship with an imperious, genteel, and depressive mother who tended to dominate her children and husband), Alice Miller's theories can be applied to Barrie, Hemingway, George Kaufman and other products of middle-class families who were forced to deal with the narcissistic needs of a troubled parent as a matter of childhood survival. Miller says that mothers of disturbed patients often were insecure and depressed, and that what they failed to find in their own parents they attempted to find in their children; a child, in turn, has an amazing ability to perceive and respond intuitively and subconsciously to the need of the parent who is using his or her children to help manage psychic stress. The list of Kaufman's psychological and psychosomatic manifestations of his traumatic relationship with his ill mother was extensive, and he was aware of their source in his childhood travails ("Some scars don't show on the skin," he said). Although Kaufman dealt with his phobias largely by laughing at such things in his stage comedies, his friends knew, as Parker once put it, that he "was a mess." Born shortly after the death of his older brother from intestinal illness at age two, Kaufman became the fixation of his mother's obsession with her children's health. In her determination that Kaufman not suffer the fate of his brother, she excluded milk and water from the tap from the family table, would not let him play games or strenuous sports, and forbade close contact with anyone who might have a disease. Kaufman came to have an overwhelming fear of being touched, a hypochondriac's dread of contracting illness (a friend once found him with more than thirty bottles of medicine on his night table, virtually all unneeded), and a loathing of shows of emotion (his mother was prone to throwing jealous fits and emotional tantrums that drove his father out of the house). Throughout his life, it took acts of courage for Kaufman to take an elevator to a high floor or to cross a heavily trafficked thoroughfare or even to fall asleep (because he feared dying in his sleep). As a collaborator with other well-known journalists-dramatists (Lardner, Parker, Alexander Woollcott, Ben Hecht, Charles MacArthur, Edna Ferber, John P. Marquand, and Marc Connelly), Kaufman was often derided as a gag-smith who brought a newspaper columnist's humor to the stage—and he largely adopted this self-deprecating view of his success. With his self-image struggles, Kaufman was mortified in his first journalism job, as a columnist for the *Washington Times*, when he was dismissed after the newspaper's owner, Frank Munsey, identified him as Jewish. Eventually, Kaufman developed a self-protective strategy in such matters (he once left an Algonquin Roundtable gathering when Woollcott jokingly referred to him as a "Christ-killer," saying, "This is the last time that I am going to sit here and listen to my religion being slurred").[45]

In using identifiable people in his satirical writings, Thurber paid a price (the resentment of his mother, his estrangement from an older brother) for venting in an open literary forum his grievances against his dysfunctional family system. Thurber's boyhood loss of an eye in a William Tell–bow-and-arrow incident with an older brother had filled him with grief, remorse, and bitterness, and it carried into his attitudes as a journalist and humor writer. (Thurber's underlying philosophy of humor is perhaps best captured in his statement, "The laughter of man is more terrible than his tears, and takes many forms—hollow, heartless, mirthless, maniacal.") Thurber's blind eye was not removed right away by a local doctor, which eventually led to his other eye going bad, and Thurber blamed his mother, a Christian Science dabbler, for not taking him to an eye specialist. Although he dealt with his resentment by writing hard-edged, humorous stories built on exaggerated misdeeds of his eccentric family members, Thurber was quiet, shy, a true Walter Mitty personality (his famous short story hero) as a boy, in contrast to his mother, a powerful figure who (along with his first wife) became the prototype for the domineering "Thurber women" of book and cartoon fame. His portrayal of the "giddy madness" of his family in *My Life and Hard Times*—which one biographer called "cheap psychoanalysis" and an "exorcising" of the demons of growing up in Columbus, Ohio—led his mother to say, "People will think we are trash." Although he eventually had a daughter with his first wife, Thurber resisted having children for a long time and once pledged, "never to bring any children into this old vale to inherit the Thurber nervousness."[46]

Other Psychological Themes: Parental and Family Loss

As with all individual human beings, the journalist-literary figures studied here handled stressful early life emotional events differently depending on their temperaments and the age in which they lived. A number who lost parents, beloved siblings, or had abandonment experiences in their youth seemed less scarred emotionally than in later eras when life span expectations were greater and exposure to death at an early age less common. Yet, for some, the experiences were devastating and permanently life-shaping. The shock of his older sister Elizabeth's death in 1792 when De Quincey was six, coming on the heels of the death of a younger sister, left him feeling a "terrible separation" and "colored his dreams" throughout his life. Nellie Bly, also six at the time, was distraught when she lost her father in 1870, and biographers have connected the trauma to her lifetime of severe headaches, fearful depressions, and frantic pursuit of professional success. The poet-journalist John Masefield, who experienced a pattern of severe depression and institutionalizations, struggled emotionally after his mother's death when he was a boy, as was the case with Poe, Woolf, Porter, and Parker, as well as with Agee and Gail Godwin (with the loss of their fathers that they turned into powerful novels of family dysfunction and tragedy, *A Death in the Family* and *Father Melancholy's Daughter*). The death of Woolf's mother in 1895, when Woolf was thirteen, precipitated the first of a series of nervous breakdowns and emotional collapses that preceded her suicide in 1941. Woolf had a grandfather, mother, sister, brother, and niece who all suffered from recurrent depression; in addition, her father and another brother were manic-depressive. Woolf was repeatedly treated and admitted to hospitals for psychotic episodes and depressions (she once described them as the "violent moods of her soul"). Despite her sufferings, Woolf accepted the role of emotional illness in the production of art and believed in the importance of melancholia and even madness in the exercise of her imaginative powers.[47]

In the loss of their brothers, Robert Benchley and Jack Kerouac experienced devastations similar to De Quincey's. Kerouac's older brother died from rheumatic fever when Kerouac was four (he was reprimanded by his father—after gleefully running to tell him the "special" news of Gerard's passing—which led to an enduring sense of guilt over the event). Benchley's older brother was his mother's favorite, and, when news came in 1898 that he had been killed in battle in the Spanish-American War, she reportedly screamed uncontrollably, "Why couldn't it have been Robert?" This so disturbed friends and relatives that it was agreed that the eight-year-old Robert—who was present for this outburst and whose anguish surrounding his brother's death was a source of pain throughout his life—should be taken to his aunt's house until his mother was back in her right mind.[48]

A number of journalist-literary figures chose—despite the availability of counseling and psychoanalysis—not to deal with the pain of early traumas outside of their art, but they and/or their biographers have connected their early life troubles to distressed personal and professional lives. The tragic circumstances surrounding Porter's mother—she lost her third child to influenza while she was pregnant with her fourth, Katherine; her mother then died just two months shy of Katherine's second birthday—caused Porter much lingering emotional anguish. Porter—whose father, an impoverished Texas farmer, brought in his widow's mother to help raise the children—suffered all her life from melancholy and depression. Somewhat similarly to Porter, who wondered in her own writings how much her psychological struggles had their origins in her early childhood traumas, Angela Carter's melancholic characters have been connected by critics to her experience of losing a mother (as the depressive Carter did in childhood). Joel Chandler Harris also found in writing and journalism an escape from an oppressive family situation—his unmarried mother, who bore and raised Harris with no father around, eked out a living in their small Georgia town by working as a seamstress and living off of the support of town benefactors—by going to work at age thirteen on the nearby plantation of the printer, Joseph Addison Turner, in 1862. When the shy, stuttering, and lonely Harris was not learning the printer devil's trade, he would hang around the slave quarters, where he heard the stories that he turned into his popular Uncle Remus tales after he became the editorial page editor of the *Atlanta Constitution*.[49]

Perhaps, given the stiff-upper-lip traditions of the journalism business, it is not surprising to find that the pain of childhood trauma has not always been made explicit or fully explored in the journalism, memoirs, or the fiction of a number of journalist-literary figures. Psychological suffering and emotional distress in a pre-Freudian age frequently were expected to be held inside, and particularly so in eras when custom demanded a high degree of social restraint and psychological repression. In later periods, the professional image of the reporter as a tough-minded cynic could make it difficult for journalists to deal openly with emotional pain in their writing or their professional lives, and they were attracted to writing modes that encouraged them to keep their true emotions hidden. For example, O. Henry's difficulties growing up with an alcoholic father, the trauma he experienced during his imprisonment for embezzlement while a bank officer, and his own alcoholism stand at a great distance from the sentimental characterizations and clever plot constructions of his short stories. In fact, some of the most emotionally damaged in youth or within their marriages emerged to write children's stories (Nesbit, Barrie, Harris, Lamb), light drama (Parker, Kaufman), humor and satire (Twain, Benchley, Thurber, Wodehouse, Evelyn Waugh, James Russell Lowell), and romance literature (Margaret Mitchell), which touched on the authors' traumatic experiences only by inference and what can be gleaned from textual interpretation. Much the same can be said for the popular tale writers Runyon and Harte, whose urban underworld (in Runyon's case) and western frontier characters (in Harte's) tended toward caricature and local color typecasts and did not directly connect with the authors' own experiences of parental loss, fractured family lives, and stressful adult careers that contributed to their emotional problems.[50]

In a number of cases—including with those who had suffered some of the most shocking events surrounding a parental death—a journalist-literary figure produced his or her own chronicles, some in the form of fiction, some nonfictional, or something in between. The death of Wiesel's mother and younger sister in the Nazi campaign to exterminate Jews (he lost his father, too, who died just before the Allied liberation in 1945 in the same camp where Wiesel was imprisoned) was something that he could not write or talk about for many years. Wiesel initially found conventional journalism (he was a journalist for Paris *L'arche*, Tel Aviv's *Yedioth Ahronoth*, and the *Jewish Daily Forward* beginning in 1949) a refuge for avoiding his feelings and the processing of his camp experiences. But a French novelist whom he was interviewing finally persuaded him to let loose of his memories, and then the books poured forth. Although *Night*, his account of a teenage boy afflicted with guilt for having survived the camps, is semiautobiographical, Wiesel used the techniques he had practiced in journalism to establish some distance between himself and his protagonist, Eliezer. Wiesel's taut, compressed prose set the tone for later writers describing terrible events by letting "the story tell itself," as biographer Ted L. Estess put it. However, even nearly fifty years later, in his preface to a new translation, Wiesel was adding painful refining details, including of the account of his father's "plaintive, harrowing" voice calling his nearby son's name while being beaten by German SS officers. "My father no longer felt the club's blows; I did," Wiesel wrote.

"And yet I did not react. I let the SS beat my father, I left him alone in the clutches of death . . . I shall never forgive myself. Nor shall I ever forgive the world for having pushed me against the wall . . . for having awakened in me the basest, most primitive instincts." With his guilt, his wounded religious sensibilities, and his lament that it was God that had broken the covenant with humans ("As for me, I had ceased to pray. I concurred with Job! I was not denying [H]is existence, but I doubted His absolute justice"), Wiesel has suggested that one can never fully penetrate into the meaning of evil and horrifically traumatic events. "I'm still not sure it was . . . the right move," he said of his decision to write about his experiences. "That is, whether to choose language or silence."[51]

When the six-year-old McCarthy and her three orphaned younger brothers were left in Minneapolis with relatives after the death of their parents in the 1918 flu epidemic (first with her father's parents, then with an austere great aunt and her husband), she found herself in a situation that she later described as a disaster for herself and her brothers. Also recuperating from the flu, McCarthy was at first told nothing of her parents' death by her grandparents; after she and her siblings were handed over to her great aunt and uncle, their treatment—which included beatings and severe punishments—left her starved emotionally as she detailed in her memoir, *Memories of a Catholic Girlhood*. McCarthy suffered from debilitating episodes of depression and anxiety throughout her life, combined with an attraction to men with their own personal problems (including the alcoholic critic, Wilson, whose tempestuous marriage to McCarthy became a legendary literary union before its breakup in 1946). She was one of a number of women journalist-literary figures who were drawn to older writers and fellow journalist-literary figures (West to Wells, Gellhorn to Hemingway, Parker to MacArthur, and Dorothy Thompson to Sinclair Lewis, which one biographer called "two bruised souls" joining together) that ended in self-recriminations on the part of the women as they later analyzed the unhealthy elements in their own emotional history (as well as the workaholic environment of journalism and the insularity and incestuous nature of the writing world that commonly brings together equally driven and emotionally wounded writer couples) that contributed to the failure of their relationships and marriages.[52]

James Agee lived for years with a deep anxiety about his own self-worth that manifested itself in a primitive, uncontrollable fear, which he illuminated in his semifictional memoir, *A Death in the Family*, about his father's perishing in an automobile accident when Agee, like Bly and McCarthy, was six years old and forced to deal with parental loss. Joy always had the face of anguish for Agee, said biographer Geneviève Moreau, every happiness seemed transitory and fragile, and sadness marked the most perfect times in his life. This "duality" of experience left him with an acute sense of solitude and an obsession with death that he linked with the feeling of deprivation that settled over him when he was told about his father's fatal accident. When Agee reached the age of his father at his death (thirty-six), he realized that he needed to come to grips with his sufferings as a child if he hoped to overcome the self-destructive urges that had begun to master him. He found a Jungian therapist who told him that he needed "to work this out in analysis or write it out." Agee did both—he entered an on-again, off-again regimen of personal therapy for three years, and he began the novel that would become *A Death in the Family*.[53]

Agee and McCarthy handled the trauma of parental loss differently in their two memoirs—and yet in ways that had similarities. Both books raised philosophical questions about the relationship of memoir to the genre of nonfiction, with McCarthy acknowledging that there were places where she simply was not sure whether she was remembering something or was making it up; Agee never addressed that issue directly in his manuscript, but the liberties he took with journalistic methodology, despite his obsession with accuracy in the creation of the manuscript, were extensive in places. "Indeed, I really had a wicked uncle who used to beat me," McCarthy wrote. Even though it was in "everyone's interest, decidedly, that we should forget the past," McCarthy said that she considered herself clever for figuring out the fate of her parents when no one would tell her. ("I believe I thought they were dead, but their fate did not greatly concern me; my heart had grown numb.") She compared her grandmother's comments about McCarthy's loss ("She doesn't feel it at all," her grandmother allegedly would tell those who inquired) to what someone might say about a "spayed cat." "We orphan children were not responsible for being orphans, but were treated as if we were and as if being orphans were a crime we had committed," McCarthy wrote. (But in recognizing memory's role in sometimes distorting the facts, she also commented that in her bitterness she might have been unfair to her grandmother.)[54]

Agee, in contrast, took more fictional liberties in crafting *A Death in the Family* so that the reader is repeatedly faced with poignant scenes of the trauma as his six-year-old self experienced it and what he imagined his younger sister, Catherine, experienced. He described Catherine as remembering her father's whiskers and the way he ate breakfast and his waving when he went to work ("Ever any more," Agee recounted his sister as thinking. "He won't come home again ever any more. Won't come home again ever. . . . But why's he not here?"). Rufus, Agee's narrative counterpart, is described as telling himself, "He's dead. He died last night while I was asleep and now it was already morning. He has already been dead since way last night and I didn't even know until I woke up. . . . I am awake but he is still dead and he will stay right on being dead all afternoon and all night and all tomorrow . . . and he can't come back home again ever any more."[55]

Interestingly, McCarthy used the same central symbol (a tin butterfly) as did Agee (who described a butterfly landing on his father's casket as he was being interred) to allude in literary terms to the spiritual (in Agee's case) and the ironic (in McCarthy's) elements of the meaning that they imputed to their parental losses. McCarthy connected the tin butterfly to the children's rescue from their harsh circumstances by their maternal grandfather, who took action after hearing the children's story of how McCarthy was punished severely for not producing a lost butterfly toy of her brother's (and which, it turned out, had actually been hidden by her caretaker uncle). Consistent with Agee's more religious orientation, his use of the butterfly image was mystical and symbolic; one of his uncles described to Rufus how a butterfly rested on his father's coffin as it was being lowered into the earth. His uncle told the boy it meant that "it was good for his father and that lying there in the dark-ness did not matter so much. He (Rufus) did not know what this good thing was, but because his uncle felt that it was good, and felt so strongly about it, it must be even more of a good thing than he himself could comprehend."[56]

Even more so than Agee and McCarthy, other journalist-literary figures have recognized that the extraordinary nature of their youthful traumas made it virtually impossible that the effects would not be felt in their adult emotional lives. Conrad Aiken's father—who was suicidal, paranoid, and manic-depressive—shot his mother at the family home after a late evening fight in which he had accused her of unfaithfulness. When the eleven-year-old Aiken heard the shots, he ran into his parents' room to find a .45-caliber revolver and the bodies of his parents. Before notifying police, he closed the doors to the bedroom where his two younger brothers and sister were in their cribs sleeping. Later, backed by an educated Freudian perspective, Aiken ascribed the "horrified and lack-lustre restlessness which prevents me from loving one person or place for more than a season" to his father's crime. Kurt Vonnegut Jr.'s mother suffered from depression and killed herself with an overdose of pills while Vonnegut was home on leave soon after he had enlisted in the U.S. military following the Japanese bombing of Pearl Harbor. This proved particularly painful for Vonnegut, because his mother had told him that he—and her worries about his well-being in the military—was the source of her unhappiness. Critics have noted the impact of his mother's suicide as a reference point in the way Vonnegut portrayed the mental health of his fictional characters, and Vonnegut alluded to his own fragile mental condition in a number of his personal writings and conversations.[57]

Others of the journalist-literary figures who lost a parent in their youth did not make it the explicit focus of their writing or necessarily connect it to their own emotional troubles—but their biographers have. Parker's life story, for example, was built around a narrative of herself as an unloved and abandoned young girl that she transposed as an adult into a wry but fundamentally self-pitying authorial voice. Even though she screamed terribly as a five-year-old at the news that her mother was dead, Parker later would write, in what became her trademark off-hand style, that her mother "promptly went and died on me." After her father's remarriage, Parker came to hate her stepmother, until she suddenly died, too, leaving Parker once again motherless at the age of nine. Taking on early the acerbic persona that she would perfect as a put-down journalist and writer of clever verse and short stories about the pathos of single and professional womanhood, Parker became famous for her sardonic digs that circulated through the press—but which were largely a cover for a life filled with episodes of depression, suicide attempts, alcoholism, and disastrous affairs. In effect, Parker marketed herself as the literary equivalent of "damaged goods," and her flip view of men (largely worthless) and her pursuit of the literary version of the 1920s flapper lifestyle have made her a prominent proponent of the viewpoint (also advanced by her idol, Hemingway) that a traumatic past, a romantic inner life, and a tough outer exterior could serve the aspiring writer quite well.[58]

Although temperamental differences have played a large role in this, other family traumas of the journalist-literary figures in this study have triggered intense emotional reactions—the loss of their children experienced by Twain, Howells, De Vries, Rudyard Kipling, and Fanny Fern; the early death or suicide of a spouse by Fern, Poe, Orwell, Mencken, Henry Fielding, Henry Adams, and Lillie Devereux Blake. But the twin traumas experienced by Joan Didion—and her candor in writing about her grief at the sudden death of her fellow literary-journalist husband, John Gregory Dunne, while they were engaged in the bedside monitoring of their fatally ill daughter, Quintana Roo—is remarkable as a contemporary document in its analysis of the role of loss and bereavement in life. In *The Year of Magical Thinking*, Didion managed to merge deep feeling with her characteristic clinical detachment in recounting her response to Dunne's fatal heart attack while she was preparing dinner in their apartment after returning from a hospital visit to their daughter. In places, Didion revealed herself as the clear-eyed observer that she has become known for in her richly atmospheric journalistic accounts of the fractured social and political events of the 1960s and 1970s and in her novels about broken people wandering an empty American cultural landscape. (At one point, a social worker handling her husband's death described her as "a pretty cool customer"; when her doctor asked her how she was doing, she responded, "I just can't see the upside in this.") Yet, throughout the book, Didion showed herself to be the meticulous observer of the ambient in life by her careful probing of the medical details and commonplace experiences that are connected to the death of a loved one, followed by penetrating expressions of powerful personal feeling ("Grief is different. Grief has no distance. Grief comes in waves, paroxysms, sudden apprehensions that weaken the knees and blind the eyes and obliterate the dailiness of life"). Didion's willingness to turn her discerning writer's eye and her carefully crafted journalistic prose onto the subject of her own grief is magnified in impact when one realizes that her daughter, who is still alive at the end of the last chapter, died shortly after the book's publication. With the blending of the confessional tradition with her postmodern consciousness, Didion forswore the tendency in her younger years to dismiss as "whining" and "self-pity" the expressions of those who found it difficult to handle the loss of a longtime spouse ("time is the school in which we learn," Didion wrote) and acknowledged that "we might expect if the death is sudden to feel shock. We do not expect this shock to be obliterative, dislocating to both body and mind. . . . We do not expect to be literally crazy, cool customers who believe that their husband is about to return and need his shoes."[59]

Other Psychological Themes: Abandonment, Marginalization, and Abuse

The experience of abandonment shows up time and again in the life story of many journalist-literary figures—and it was a major source of both their personal insecurities and what drove them to literary and journalistic achievement. Thackeray's father, who served in the British civil service in India, died three years after Thackeray's birth and left the young boy in a strange, ambiguous world of family secrets and betrayal fitting for a Victorian novel. Before her marriage to his father, Thackeray's mother had been in love with a young military man. Her parents thwarted the marriage, first by telling Thackeray's mother that her lover was dead and then telling the soldier that she did not want to see him again. Soon after Thackeray's birth in 1811, with the family settled in India, his father came home one evening with the same young soldier, Henry Carmichael-Smith, who had been in love with Thackeray's mother. After his father understood the situation, the marriage was never the same again. When his father died of fever a few years later, Thackeray's mother arranged to marry Carmichael-Smith but not until the five-year-old Thackeray was dispatched to England to boarding school where he did not see his mother again for three years. "Twang goes the trunk, down come the steps. . . . I smart the cruel smart again; and, boy or man, have never been able to bear the sight of people parting from their children," Thackeray later wrote. The underlying sadness of Thackeray's life—despite the gentleness and good humor of his fiction and his satirical journalism—was reflected in his inept and unrequited efforts to find female companionship (while supporting his insane wife for years in private care), his endless rounds of socializing where he ate and drank himself into corpulence, and his lethargy and his indifference to his health as it deteriorated, even as his literary successes made him the toast of the London social world.[60]

As the illegitimate child of a vagabond astrologer and a spiritualist who had run away from her well-to-do-home in Ohio, London as a small boy always had the feeling of terrible calamity about to befall him. His mother had made two sensational suicide attempts in the weeks after his father—in learning that she was pregnant—had abandoned the relationship. Eight months after London's birth, she married a man that London was led for many years to believe was his real father. Often melancholy, angry, or preoccupied with her séances and spiritualist practice, London's mother was a perplexing figure to him, as was his stepfather, who spent much of his time dealing with the family's financial difficulties. By age ten, London was largely on his own, having dropped out of school, working odd jobs around the Oakland waterfront, and drinking and fighting. He converted to socialism soon after he was jailed for vagrancy in Buffalo, New York, while hoboing across the country—a degrading experience that he said taught him about the depths of the down-and-out life in America and why the country needed to be radically politically reformed. "Jack was most a socialist when he was depressed and the nightmares rode him," said biographer Andrew Sinclair, and he needed a system that protected the unlucky and unfortunate. When London felt good, he believed that survival of the self and the race determined all human behavior, and he would preach a form of Aryan superiority and a Nietzschean superman philosophy that would vex his socialist colleagues. When London learned in his early twenties of the scandal of his birth in the files of San Francisco newspapers, he was violently disturbed (he wrote to his real father but received only evasive answers), and this exacerbated the manic-depressive tendencies that he demonstrated throughout his life.[61]

Dos Passos was born the illegitimate son of a prominent corporation lawyer who kept his mistress and his son living in hotels until his wife died. That did not happen until Dos Passos was fourteen, and it was only then that his father married his mother and let young John take the last name of his "guardian" (a ruse that had been kept up during the years when Dos Passos and his mother lived abroad and would meet his father at certain designated rendezvous sites). There was much emotional strain involved in the lies and deception required in such circumstances, and Dos Passos was intensely aware from the time he was a boy of his mother's suffering. Dos Passos never manifested overt psychological difficulties from this experience, but for much of his life he (like Lamb and Harris) stuttered whenever he grew nervous or agitated. Perhaps because of the duplicity involved in his growing-up years—and because he largely worked as a freelancer and never as a staff member of a journalistic publication—Dos Passos did not embrace fiction writing with the enthusiasm of some of his fellow journalist-literary figures, and he felt that his journalistic activities were both honorable and important. His distaste for deception was unabated throughout his literary life—including during the period that he gravitated from a leftist political outlook to a right wing one—and many of his literary works, including his fictional ones, have a strongly journalistic flavor and are filled with the insights that he never feared to express, even as he came to realize the cost in old literary friendships for a writer who deviated from the largely liberal outlook of the writing community.[62]

Although she eventually straightened out her life by finding work in journalism and establishing a national reputation as a poet, Maya Angelou's early life story—as she has told it in her autobiographical writings—was filled with the traumas that have not been uncommon for young women growing up in the poor black underclass. Angelou's divorced parents sent her at age three from St. Louis to Stamps, Arkansas, where for the next ten years her maternal grandmother reared her. At age eight, during a visit to St. Louis to see her mother, Angelou was raped by her mother's boyfriend ("a breaking and entering when even the senses are torn apart"), suffered the painful aftermath ("I wasn't sick, but the pit of my stomach was on fire. . . . My belly and behind were as heavy as cold iron, but it seemed my head had gone away and pure air had replaced it"), testified at the trial (where she screamed at the harsh questioning by the defense lawyer, "Ole mean, dirty thing, you. Dirty old thing"), and then was thrashed by family members for her sullenness ("when I refused to be the child they knew and accepted me to be, I was called impudent [and] . . . was punished for being so uppity"). Although her rape was avenged (her mother's boyfriend was murdered after he was let out of jail—presumably by one of Angelou's uncles), she wrote in her memoirs, "There isn't one day since I was raped that I haven't thought of it. . . . I have gotten beyond hate and fear, but there is something beyond that." Her mother became a professional gambler and moved her children to San Francisco after Angelou's graduation from eighth grade. While residing in the city's urban underground for much of her teenage years, Angelou started using drugs, lived homeless for a time, and at age sixteen gave birth to a son. When she graduated into prostitution, she got this advice from her mother: "If you want to be a whore, it's your life. Be a damn good one." After marrying a white ex-sailor (and causing her mother to explode that she was receiving a "hell of a wedding gift—the contempt of his people and the distrust of yours"), Angelou found herself divorced three years later. Her involvement with a South African freedom fighter, Vusumzi Make, brought her to Africa and journalism jobs in Egypt and Ghana before her reputation as a poet allowed her to consign her past life of drugs and sordidness to the world of her four-volume memoirs.[63]

Capote's biographer, Gerald Clarke, has noted that psychologists say that a child's greatest fear is that a parent, particularly a mother, will abandon him or her. Capote understood from an early age that his mother never wanted him (she was dissuaded from an abortion only by the scheming tactics of his father). A gadabout character who traveled to other cities to work and had many affairs, she and Capote's father, a peripatetic promoter and sometimes con artist, broke up permanently and left Capote at age six in Monroeville, Alabama, to be raised by three eccentric spinster relatives and their odd brother. Capote's mother would appear occasionally from some distant place where she was working; when she left, Capote would be desolate. His father would promise to take him places but seldom showed up. "Imagine a dog, watching and waiting and hoping to be taken away," Capote said. "That is the picture of me then." This experience left Capote with "an intense fear of being abandoned. . . . I remember practically all of my childhood as being lived in a state of constant tension and fear." When he became an adult, this feeling grew into a powerful, unrelenting sense of anxiety—which, as with Poe, Capote tried to mask with alcohol and, in Capote's case, prescription and recreational drugs. Capote's professional traumas also began early—he was fired as a *New Yorker* copyboy in 1944 when he was accused of passing himself off as a writer for the magazine at a New England arts festival—but his life eventually came full circle (his firing freed him to pursue his fiction writing career, which did not go well; this brought him back to writing non-fiction for *The New Yorker*, which in turn led him to the story that became the nonfiction novel that made his reputation). The traumas at both ends of his life (he complained repeatedly that the writing of *In Cold Blood* was killing him) were connected by the anxiety (his character, Holly Golightly, in *Breakfast at Tiffany's*, described it as "the mean reds") that neither drugs, nor alcohol, nor the fame he gained from his pioneering blending of journalism and fiction writing in *In Cold Blood* could assuage.[64]

Unlike Capote, most of the gay journalist-literary figures that preceded him lived closeted existences—often at great emotional cost to themselves. In this respect, Capote also was a pioneer in publicly acknowledging his sexual identity—but it did not come without heavy blows to his psyche. As an adolescent, Capote recognized that he was gay, and he never tried to hide it. However, this led to a series of painful encounters that only reinforced his sense of abandonment after he moved to Long Island as a teenager to live with his mother and stepfather but was soon sent to a military school to get him to behave in a more "masculine" fashion. Once when he learned that his mother was taking him to her doctor to get male hormone shots, he made her stop the car so he could get out; after she slapped him, he threatened to break her nose if she ever tried to make him feel ashamed of being a homosexual again. Later she told a group of her friends in his presence, "Well, my boy's a fairy," and once in a drunken rage, yelled at him, "You're a pansy! You're a fairy! You're going to wind up in jail. You're going to wind up on the streets." It was the fear of this kind of treatment that led the poet-journalist Hart Crane to conceal his homosexuality from his divorced parents throughout much of his adult life—including from his erratic and controlling mother who learned the truth of it (and who made his life miserable with hysterical fits and threats to tell his estranged father) only a few years before Crane's suicide.[65]

Trauma, in the context of many gay and bisexual British literary figures, was for many years defined in terms of the experience of Oscar Wilde, which hung like a specter over their secretive private lives. Critics, for example, have noted how much H. H. Munro was influenced by the witty paradoxes of Wilde in the construction of the short stories where Munro (as "Saki") whimsically probed the superficialities and hypocrisies of Edwardian society. However, Munro also was like most gay men of his time, who were forced by British law to keep private their sexual orientation or face the fate of Wilde, who was prosecuted and imprisoned for violating the nation's antisodomy statutes. Wilde—who edited a magazine, *Woman's World*, from 1887 to 1889—was a journalist as well as a fiction writer, as was Munro, who served as a columnist for the *Westminster Gazette* and foreign correspondent for the London *Morning Post* from 1896 to 1908. The fallout from Wilde's case spread through the community of gay men at the time (many decided to move abroad), and the fear it engendered in Munro and others was a reminder of the precarious nature of private existences always at peril of public exposure. Wilde's own traumatized reaction to his conviction in 1895 ("I sat amidst the ruins of my wonderful life, crushed by anguish, bewildered with terror, dazed through pain," he wrote) was followed by depression, fears for his sanity, and thoughts of suicide, and he died in 1900 soon after his release from prison while living in exile in Paris. That the bisexual Wilde, who believed that none of his male lovers would testify against him for fear of their own prosecution, turned out to be wrong left other public figures terrified that they also could be caught up in scandal. The most notable of those was the then prime minister, Lord Roseberry (Archibald Philip Primrose), whose apparent liaison with the older brother of Wilde's companion made Wilde and Lord Roseberry targets of the brothers' father, Lord Queensberry (John Shilto Douglas), who was determined to bring the seducers of his sons to justice. Although he was never prosecuted, Lord Roseberry suffered a nervous breakdown and removed himself from office for a time. "To lie night after night, staring wide awake, hopeless of sleep, tormented in nerves . . . like a disembodied spirit, to watch one's own corpse as it were . . . is an experience no sane man with a conscience would repeat," Lord Roseberry wrote.[66]

Other Psychological Themes: Family Breakup and/or Living with Psychologically Ill and/or Alcoholic Parents

Many of the journalist-literary figures in this study have exhibited powerful compulsions in response to their dysfunctional families—either by becoming like their impaired parent or parents or becoming vehement in their efforts to avoid their parents' syndromes. Although researchers do not know for sure if the cause is genetic inheritance or environmental circumstances or a combination of the two, studies have shown that there is a greater possibility of adult life dysfunction if a person has been raised by someone with addictive behavior or mental health issues. After the death of his mother at age three, O. Henry was left with a father, a doctor in North Carolina, who had a weakness for the bottle that O. Henry came to share. His grief-stricken father lost interest in medicine, as well as his children, and spent much of his time trying to invent a perpetual motion machine, leaving O. Henry—who would go on to become the classic drifting, alcoholic journalist—to be raised largely by his paternal grandmother and later with family friends in Texas. Evelyn Waugh's mother suffered postpartum depression after his birth; she stayed in bed for six weeks experiencing headaches and other emotional ailments. After her recovery, she became highly protective of him, and Waugh developed a strongly dependent relationship with her.

His father was distant and reserved (and depressed at times), and he favored Evelyn's older brother, Alec. Psychologists would not be surprised that Evelyn turned out to be a disinterested father himself, and that his son and fellow journalist-literary figure, Auberon, would carry his father's troubled disposition as a burden throughout his own life. McCarthy did not learn about her deceased father's serious drinking problems until she was in her late thirties. By then, her marriage to the critic Wilson, with his own drinking problems and his abusive behavior toward her, was over. (Wilson, in his divorce petition, referred to McCarthy's "acute hysterical condition" during her first pregnancy and called her "a psychiatric case"; McCarthy later wrote "the logic of having slept with Wilson compelled the sequence of marriage . . . I could not accept the fact that I had slept with this fat, puffing man for no reason, simply because I was drunk. . . . Marrying him, though against my inclinations, *made* it make sense.")[67]

A shared background of childhood struggle left Jimmy Breslin recognizing himself in the life of Runyon and contributed to Breslin's attraction to Runyon's image of the journalist as tough enough to overcome a dysfunctional upbringing. Breslin grew up with two alcoholic parents in working-class New York City, his father, a piano player, and his mother, a troubled personality who threw tantrums and showed little warmth to her children. Breslin's working-class roots and his blunt and salty prose helped him to become the prototype of the hard-living urban journalist. Breslin acknowledged that his lifestyle was based to a good degree on the profile of Runyon, whose colorful and romanticized stories about gangland figures and whose life devoted to saloons, race tracks, and nonstop work schedules made him Breslin's role model when he broke into the business. From the time his editor father sent the teenage Runyon to cover a hanging, his career also had become modeled on a stereotype of the vagabond journalistic life—in his case, the itinerant newsroom culture at the small-town Colorado newspaper that his father ran. When Runyon's mother died in 1891, his three sisters were sent to Kansas to be raised by relatives, but Runyon stayed in Pueblo with his father. Runyon's own life, where he battled alcohol and eventually went on the wagon, disappeared from his family for long stretches of work and play, and cultivated in bars and speakeasies the gamblers and gangland sources of his stories of the urban underworld, was not unlike that of his father, who spent much of his free time in saloons and would bring back women to their apartment while young Runyon slept in his own bed in the corner. (Like Runyon, Breslin also quit drinking at one point, but also famously said, "When you stop drinking, you have to deal with this marvelous personality that started you drinking in the first place.") In his sympathetic biography of Runyon, Breslin found much to identify with in Runyon's early life. ("I am going to tell you a story about a guy, Runyon . . . [because] I am about the only one who can do it because of the life I've lived," Breslin wrote in the preface.)[68]

Two who wrote extensively of their experiences growing up with an emotionally troubled and alcoholic writer parent were Susan Cheever, daughter of the novelist, John Cheever, and Auberon Waugh. Like many writers, John Cheever was more comfortable writing about the subtleties of setting and the texture of life than directly expressing emotions—and, as in many dysfunctional families, Susan Cheever grew up in an environment of emotional tension, spousal conflict, and family secrets (including, for many years, her father's alcoholism, prescription drug abuse, and bisexuality). As a *Newsweek* editor, Susan Cheever once interviewed her father and helped prepare an article about him for the magazine—all the while dealing with her own feelings of confusion about her father's emotional distance ("I didn't ask for help, and he didn't offer it," she says of her own novel-writing career. "When he did read my novels, he was polite but perfunctory"), his vague displeasure with his children ("Susie has completed a novel," her father wrote in his journal. "None of us, particularly me, are first rate but we do, I like to think, persevere"), and her sense that his disapproval meant that he "didn't love me, obviously; how could I love him?" As in many family systems where unhealthy syndromes were evident up and down the generational line (Susan Cheever, too, would struggle with alcohol, drugs, and other "acting out" behaviors in her personal life), her paternal grandfather had grown bitter and alcoholic after he had lost his factory and his investments in the Great Depression, and John Cheever felt himself to have grown up as an "orphaned spirit" (his mother, as John Cheever also liked to say, drank herself to death). "There is some connection between my need for drink and my need for love of some sort. . . . This may be a neurotic condition, some injury done in my childhood," he wrote. Not unexpectedly, Susan Cheever had similar things to say about her childhood wounds as she explored them in *Home before Dark*, her biographical memoir of her father's life, and in her own autobiographical writings.[69]

Like Susan Cheever, who quoted extensively from her father's journals (where she uncovered much of the evidence of his sexuality struggles and the extent of his drinking problems), Auberon Waugh found in his father's posthumously published private diaries painful confirmation of issues that he had wrestled with since childhood—his father's indifference toward his children ("My children were much in evidence and boring"), his particular disapproval of Auberon as a youth ("I have regretfully come to the conclusion that the boy Auberon is not yet a suitable companion for me"), and his lack of faith in what his children would become ("My children weary me. I can only see them as defective adults: feckless, destructive, frivolous, sensual, humourless"). In his own autobiography, Auberon detailed instances where their father chose to eat in front of Auberon and his siblings the fresh fruit that had been rationed to children by British authorities in World War II and where Evelyn made plans to evacuate his books from London under the threat of German bombing raids while summoning Auberon to the city (and writing in his diary, "It would seem from this that I prefer my books to my son . . . but the truth is that a child is easily replaced, while a book destroyed is utterly lost"). Yet, Auberon, who inherited many things from his father—his drollness, his conservatism, and his life as a novelist and prolific journalist—largely defended his father throughout his own autobiography. However, he also revealed some of the emotional pressures of being his father's son, including Evelyn Waugh's "unendurable" presence when he was melancholy and his "undisguised glee" (and his children's relief) when he was away from his family (the news of his father's death, Auberon recounted, "lifted a great brooding awareness not only from the house but from the whole of existence"). For many years after, he struggled to "break the habit of viewing every event with half an eye to the bulletin I would send to my father. . . . But the strain of living two lives, one on my own, and the other through his eyes, was greatly relieved by his sudden death," Auberon wrote. "Perhaps nobody is completely grown-up until both his parents are dead."[70]

How much their emotional symptoms were connected to triggered memories of youthful and other life traumas experienced by the journalist-literary figures studied here has been the subject of speculation by biographers, scholars, and critics. However, the way traumatic events, troubled psyches, and literary and journalistic expression were interwoven in their life stories has left a notable mark in the biographical, autobiographical, journalistic, and literary record. Determining the exact contribution of traumatic experience to journalist-literary figures' professional successes and failures, as well as to their mental health struggles, ultimately is an interpretative act. But it is hard to ignore the connections one can see between traumatic life experience, an attraction to the stimulation of journalistic work, and the emotional release found in their fiction, their literary writing, and the biographical accounts of their lives, even if it is not always possible to say for sure which was the cause and which the effect.

2

Trafficking in Trauma

Women's Rights, Civil Rights, and Sensationalism as a Spur to Social Justice

"We should be willing to go all the way. I mean that we should be willing to go live with them in their way and take it in the neck with them."

—Sherwood Anderson in urging his fellow writers to support a textile mill–workers strike during the Depression

Zora Neale Hurston was a unique mixture of traumatized personality, once-poor African American woman who had migrated from the South to the North, college-trained anthropologist, and fledgling journalist and fiction writer when she got off the train in central Florida in 1927 to study the folklore of the poor black community where she had grown up. Hurston's return to the small-town setting where she had experienced family abandonment and racial abuse played a profound role in her development as a folklorist and the author of *Their Eyes Were Watching God*, her 1937 novel about a middle-aged black woman who after two loveless marriages embarks on a journey with a reckless but romantic man who affirms her commitment to passion in life. Hurston's interest in voodoo and folk traditions, her mastery of dialect writing, and her determination to show the positive side of rural southern African American life already had been on display in her "Eatonville Anthology," which was published in *Messenger* magazine in 1926. The stories—a mix of fiction, biography, folklore, and the anecdotes about Eatonville, Florida, that she liked to tell at parties when she was a Barnard College student in New York City studying under the famed anthropologist, Franz Boas—foretold the atmospheric, dialect-rich prose that would make *Their Eyes Were Watching God* a "recovered" classic when Hurston's reputation was revived by writer Alice Walker and women critics in the early 1970s. Hurston's folklore forays to Jamaica, Haiti, the Bahamas—as well as her repeated visits to Eatonville and surrounding areas—demonstrated her fascination with black magic and folk healing as methods of survival and cultural identity for people living in marginalized circumstances. Her odyssey was even more remarkable when one considers the traumas she endured at both ends of it: a father who gave her up to relatives for raising and experiences as a teenage maid where she was dismissed for spurning the sexual advances of her white employer; after gaining notoriety as an anthropologist and novelist, she antagonized powerful members of the black writing establishment with her criticism of writers that she felt overstated the suffering in the lives of black people, such that she ended her days broke and forgotten, living on unemployment, and writing a column about voodoo and folk culture for a small Florida newspaper.[1]

In a middle-class variation of Hurston's odyssey, George Orwell decided to step out of his comfortable circumstances and purposefully experience trauma by joining the urban outcasts that lived by their wits on the streets and in menial jobs in London and Paris. Inspired by Jack London's chronicle of urban poverty, *People of the Abyss*, Orwell made secret expeditions to London's East End in 1929, where he spent his time in the company of tramps, beggars, and unemployed laborers. Orwell wanted to learn what it was like to live among the poorest of the poor, and (like London) he disguised himself in a shabby coat, rumpled cap, and faded scarf. These expeditions provided material for his first book, *Down and out in Paris and London*, published in 1933, where Orwell said he hoped to "get right down among the oppressed, to be one of them and on their side against their tyrants." This youthful expiation of middle-class guilt became commonplace, particularly among the journalist-literary figures who were radicalized by the suffering that came with the industrialization of the urban centers in the nineteenth century and the Great Depression of the 1930s. Orwell went so far as to endure three days without food in Paris after a thief stole all his money from his room (as he told it in *Down and out in Paris and London*, although he later conceded that the thief was really "a little trollop" that he had picked up in a café). Biographer Michael Shelden has noted the degree to which Orwell often turned his experiences into literary theater by pointing out that he had a favorite aunt in Paris who almost certainly would have been happy to feed him. In fact, critics have never been sure how much to view as fact or fancy in *Down and out*, given Orwell's penchant for self-dramatization and his acknowledgment that some of the stories in the book were not fully accurate.[2]

Journalist-literary figures' fascination with the worlds of poverty, transience, criminality, and the customs of the poor and the working poor is a consistent one since the days of Daniel Defoe—to such a degree that some even felt the need to serve an "apprenticeship" in the life of the down-and-out to earn their credentials to be real writers. In a tradition stretching back to Henry Mayhew's investigations that led to the publication of *London Labour and the London Poor* in 1851, Orwell, Hurston, London, Nellie Bly, Stephen Crane, Theodore Dreiser, Sherwood Anderson, Erskine Caldwell, Richard Wright, James Agee, Edmund Wilson, and John Steinbeck all made forays into the urban underground or scenes of rural poverty to chronicle the conditions of the underprivileged in society. By the coming of the industrial age, when technological developments were causing rifts in the social order and reform movements were rising up, a number of journalist-literary figures established themselves as frontline protesters against the political and economic factors that were causing human trauma. Some were dedicated social activists, such as Orwell, London, Dreiser, Anderson, Caldwell, Wright, and Wilson, who viewed their efforts largely in political and social reform terms; others, such as Hurston and Agee, became involved with the subjects of their investigations and held ambivalent feelings about middle-class reformers who condescended to the lesser privileged. In fact, throughout the nineteenth and twentieth centuries, sensationalistic tactics, exploitative literary practices, and the use of themes of poverty and human abuse were as often as not used with commercial and career-advancing purposes in mind as they were based in moral and reformist zeal. Still, the combination of journalistic, fictional, and literary writing proved to be a potent force for the advancement of social ideals—and particularly so in the hands of women who used periodical and novel writing to thrust issues of female oppression and traumatic gender experience into public discussion, minority writers who used narratives of racism and social injustice fueled by their own traumatic life stories, and other activist writers whose empathy for people's traumatic life circumstances made them willing to pay a personal and professional price for advocating for social change.

From its earliest days, journalism has given employment, opportunity, and exposure to a range of personalities who were drawn to the profession not only for its inherent excitement and stimulation but also to assail the foundations of custom, the entrenchment of prejudice and racism, and the social and economic inequities that have led to suffering in the population. In quite direct ways, the reform tradition, which rests alongside the modern commercial press's ethic of objectivity and detachment in presenting the news, has had a large impact on American and English literature via the politicized and radicalized journalist-literary figures. Many of these personalities openly pushed a literary and a political vision that was intended to transform the way the social order dealt with sexual roles, opportunities for women, and the treatment of minorities and the poor. In many cases, the journalism profession was eventually unable to hold them, and they burst the bonds of organizational life and shed the demands of deadlines, editorial control, and formula writing to pursue higher literary goals—although sometimes suffering "job trauma" in the process. Yet, it can be argued that many would never have been the social conscience groundbreakers that they were if it were not for their experiences in journalism. The tensions of working within a journalistic organization, the exposure journalism gave them to the underside of life and the unhappy aspects of the human condition, the mixture of irreverence and idealism that they absorbed from their fellow employees, and their abilities to manage their own traumatic backgrounds that often spurred them to want to address questions of social justice—all these elements provided a heady experience for those who were drawn to the journalist's and the novelist's craft as a way to make a difference in the world.

Charles Dickens, who was forced to drop out of school to work in a shoe blacking factory after his father was cast into debtor's prison, is viewed as the first prominent novelist to use reform themes as the basis for his fictional plots. Dickens threw himself into the causes of political justice, and his energy for "externalizing" his grievances against life and the social order in his fiction was monumental. "No words can express the secret agony of my soul," said Dickens of his youthful distress. "Even now, famous and caressed and happy, I often forget in my dreams that I have a dear wife and children; even that I am a man; and wander desolately back to that time in my life." *Oliver Twist*, the novel that established his reputation as a fictionist, is an example of the way Dickens merged his feelings about his own early life tribulations, the affinity it gave him for understanding the traumas experienced by the victims of the industrial age, and his support of reform movements that were trying to address these issues. Dickens employed melodrama in his fiction, in good part, because he recognized its marketability as a formula for confronting evil and for arousing reader empathy for the conditions of the economically and socially downtrodden. (Dickens, for example, once predicted that his story, "The Christmas Carol," would have a greater impact on the debate about poverty than any pamphlet.) With its accounts of the abuses of orphanhood and life among the urban underclass, *Oliver Twist* was intentionally cast in the context of the ongoing political debates about the poor laws during the mid–nineteenth century, and *The Times* of London once published

Dickens's scene of Oliver coming before the board of governors as if it were a social document rather than fiction. Critics have noted that, in appealing to the emotions and intuitive morality of his readers, Dickens worked within a structure that fit with popular crime narratives, including what has been called the "Newgate novel," in which there is a criminal element to the plot, a clear delineation of good and bad characters, circumstances revolving around mistreatment and victimization, and a restoration of moral order at the end. At one point, Dickens, who also did a good deal of investigative reporting into social and economic problems in his magazines, *Household Words* and *All the Year Round*, wrote to his friend, John Forster, "By Jove how radical I am getting! I wax stronger and stronger in the true principles everyday." Yet, Dickens was criticized (usually privately) by fellow writers, such as William Thackeray (who suggested that the "two penny newspaper" contained more about real life than Dickens's novels) and Harriet Martineau (who chastised Dickens for exhibiting human misery as an artistic study). In the end, Dickens became disillusioned at the possibilities for social change, and the idealism and melodramatic dramatization of poverty, child abuse, and abusive educational settings (*Oliver Twist, The Old Curiosity Shop, Nicholas Nickleby*) gave way to more inconclusive later novels where the monolithic nature of institutional injustice and corruption in the courts (*Bleak House*), the jails (*Little Dorrit*), and the factories (*Hard Times*) could not be fixed by simply removing "bad" people from the system. "I do reluctantly believe that the English people are habitually consenting parties to the miserable imbecility into which we have fallen, and never will help themselves out of it. . . . I have no present political faith or hope—not a grain," he wrote in one letter. [3]

George Eliot, too, grew immersed in issues of social justice—but in ways that have complicated her legacy with feminists and historians who view the Victorian era as a time when women and laborers were banding together to challenge entrenched historical practices of cultural and political oppression. Eliot herself was traumatized by her experiences in the work world of her day and in her encounters with the customs that made women highly dependent on their appearance, their ability to gain a husband, and their willingness to stick to the "woman's sphere" of domestic life. The travails that she endured as a freethinking but "fallen" woman in the eyes of Victorian society, while embracing a relationship that she viewed as a true spiritual marriage (Henry Lewes was separated from his wife, but she would not grant him a divorce, even though during their marriage his wife had born a number of children by Thornton Hunt, Lewes's coeditor of the *London Leader*) have become celebrated in the annals of artists living unconventionally and resisting the moral pressures of society. What her early journalism meant to the brilliant but cloistered Eliot, while caring for an ailing and widowed father in rural isolation, were contacts with members of the London intelligentsia that eventually provided her with an exit from a stifling existence. As a single and potentially unmarriageable Victorian woman, Eliot could look forward to a life of limited opportunities in a society where career options for women were few. Even advanced thinkers of the time, such as *Westminster Review* editor John Chapman thought himself to be, were not ready to accept a woman at the head of a distinguished publication. Yet, Eliot's behind-the-scenes work on the *Review* that Chapman edited became a calling card to a new kind of life. Her shrouded journalistic persona also prepared her for the act that has helped to define her literary reputation and has come to symbolize the dilemma of the talented woman trying to make her way in a man's world— Mary Ann Evans's jettisoning of her name for the pseudonym, George Eliot. Eliot became a symbol of Victorian women's emancipation when her novels were judged critical successes before critics and the rest of the public learned who George Eliot really was. ("They can't now unsay their admiration," said Lewes when the scheme was finally revealed.) Still, Eliot's pioneering role for women writers was diminished somewhat by the compromises she felt she needed to make (and the lies she felt forced to tell) to protect her literary identity from a world where she was shunned by even many of her old friends. Even more so, her mixed history of personally triumphing over the system of patriarchy that dictated a women's role in Victorian life but opposing the campaigns for voting enfranchisement and the expansion of political rights for women and workers has been a vexing matter for women's rights advocates and feminist scholars.[4]

Although largely remembered as the neurotic, one-book author of *Gone with the Wind*, Margaret Mitchell's drive for authorial success was catalyzed by her indignation at the way heroic women characters were treated by the patriarchal press of her time. While working as a features reporter for the *Atlanta Journal*, Mitchell produced a series on great women in Georgia's history, including an account of a woman who enlisted (in disguise) with her husband as a volunteer in the Confederate army; another who single-handedly captured a marauding group of British soldiers during the Revolutionary War; and a third, a Creek Indian woman, who married three white husbands but remained largely unacculturated. Soon after the first articles appeared, her editor presented Mitchell with a stack of protesting mail and cancelled the rest of the series. Mitchell went back to the role reserved for most southern women reporters in the 1920s, producing features with such titles as "Football Players Make the Best Husbands," "What Makes the Pretty Girl Pretty?," "Should Husbands Spank Their Wives?," and "Atlanta Boys Don't Want Rich Wives." Although seldom openly complaining, Mitchell chafed under the male hierarchy of southern journalism (including working for an editor at the *Journal* who said, "One thing that I liked about her was that she was always ready to take on any story—she never looked down on any story. And she wrote like a man"). Though highly sentimentalized, *Gone with the Wind* deals with the traumas of war and the traumas of womanhood in a way that appealed greatly to a popular audience, and her legendary character—Scarlett O'Hara—has shown that even a spoiled southern belle (Mitchell herself fit this category) could become a symbol of suffering but heroic womanhood in search of an independent path in life. Mitchell's satisfaction at making herself and Scarlett O'Hara into marquis figures was her revenge for the offenses she endured in an Old South newspaper culture (although the novel was a product of her stay-at-home life after she married a public relations executive who convinced her to quit her job at the *Journal*, and it incorporated some of the research that she did for a local history column that she wrote from home).[5]

Wright's use of journalism and novel writing to both escape and chronicle the abusive circumstances of his growing up years in the Jim Crow South can be seen in the memoir of his youth. In *Black Boy*, Wright talked of the many ways that experiences connected to journalism—a paper route as a young boy; his reading of African American newspapers brought to his hometown of Jackson, Mississippi, from the North; the printing of his short story by the local black newspaper; and his discovery of H. L. Mencken (a man he pictured as "fighting with words" and "a raging demon, slashing with his pen, consumed with hate, denouncing everything American"), Dreiser (whose *Sister Carrie* and *Jennie Gerhardt* "revived in me a vivid sense of my mother's suffering"), Sinclair Lewis (whose *Main Street* helped Wright to see his white boss at the time "as an American type" so that "I could feel the very limits of his narrow life"), and other journalist-literary figures—served for him as guideposts for what would be his eventual migration from the segregated South to an independent writer's life in the North. The writings of these journalist-literary figures became for him "like a drug, a dope. . . . It would have been impossible for me to have told anyone what I derived from these novels, for it was nothing less than a sense of life itself," he wrote in *Black Boy*. Wright—who endured traumatic family experiences as a young person, including a father who abandoned the family to a nomadic life of meager subsistence, a mother who once gave up Wright to a settlement house orphanage, and an uncle in

Arkansas who had been lynched by whites—ultimately found a home in journalism (he worked for communist publications in Chicago and New York City in the 1930s) and the Depression-era federal writer's program that nurtured his fiction career but left him with a lifelong belief that a black man could never fully be free of the pervasive pressures of racism no matter where he moved. Wright's temperamental incapacity to accept the subservient status of blacks led him to develop a traumatized worldview, where it became impossible for him to escape the internal turmoil that living as a second-class citizen created in him. "Tension would set in at the mere mention of whites and a vast complex of emotions, involving the whole of my personality, would be aroused," wrote Wright. "It was as though I was continuously reacting to the threat of some natural force whose hostile behavior could not be predicted."[6]

Journalism, Fiction, and Social Justice for Women

The controversies surrounding anonymous and pseudonymous publication of journalism and fiction played an important role in the movement of women into professional periodical circles and their use of journalistic and novel writing to probe social and political injustice. Beginning in the eighteenth century, but accelerating with the push throughout the nineteenth century by Victorian women for greater rights, the forum of the periodical and the pages of the novel became an arena where women contested the political and social restrictions of their lives and debated with the world—and among themselves—about how far their reach for cultural and political freedom should go. Commonly, journalism—and a journalism career that became a springboard to novel writing—drew women who had experienced traumatic domestic circumstances and failed marriages and were desperate for a way to have an independent career. This began in the eighteenth century with such figures as Delariviére Manley (the editor of the *Female Tatler*) and Eliza Haywood (the editor of the *Female Spectator*), who after the failure of early marriages braved the social stigma of taking up independent lives as Grub Street writers of salacious fiction and mild erotica and as editors who operated in the tradition of wit, gossip, and cultural parody of Joseph Addison's, Richard Steele's, and Jonathan Swift's periodicals of similar titles. Single women or those who saw the breakup of their marriages also came to populate the world of eighteenth- and nineteenth-century periodicals—including Charlotte Lennox (who was estranged from her husband while she cultivated a Grub Street editing and novel-writing career in which she satirized women's romance literature and sympathetically discussed women's difficulties in society), Mary

Wollstonecraft (the wife of the radical journalist and novelist William Godwin, whose unconventional personal life and whose advocacy for women's political equity, sexual freedom, and professional opportunity made her an important forerunner of modern feminism), and Martineau (who, as a single woman, endured regular rounds of criticism while working as a high-profile figure in the male domain of Victorian journalism and novel writing). This group of nineteenth-century women journalists and novelists also included Caroline Norton, Charlotte Tonna, Eliza Lynn Linton, and Margaret Oliphant, whose troubled and/or broken marriages (caused by desertion, bankruptcy, alcohol, and other ills suffered at the hands of their spouses) formed the basis of their views about the importance of women having opportunities to lead career lives free of the domination of men; Norton, Anna Maria Hall, Geraldine Jewsbury, and Emily Faithfull, whose advocacy of political reform and/or women's rights themes made notable contributions to the tradition of Victorian authorship as a tool in campaigns for social justice; and Oliphant, Linton, and Dinah Mulock Craik, who were more conservative figures in their views about women's political and social roles but nonetheless strong advocates for women's professionalism and the role of the independent woman writer. Some of the earliest novels that protested conditions in the factories and urban slums were written by women—most notably, Norton's 1836 *Voices from the Factories*, the Christian reformer Tonna's 1841 *Helen Fleetwood* and 1843 *The Wrongs of Woman* (closely resembling Wollstonecraft's feminist tract of similar title), and Rebecca Harding Davis's 1861 *Life in the Iron Mills*. Lydia Maria Child's 1824 novel about an independent heroine and her interracial marriage, *Hobomok*, was just the beginning of Child's career in agitating the readers of her day—in particular, with her determination to take up the cause of antislavery that cost her the editor's job at the magazine, the *Juvenile Miscellany*. Yet, despite their gains, women writers of fiction and journalism published until the mid–nineteenth century often faced censure if they resisted established forms of social or political authority or wrote without the veil of anonymity or pseudonymity. Martineau, for example, was considered radical by some simply because she published novels and articles under her own name (even though most of her journalism was written anonymously, including more than sixteen hundred articles she produced for the London *Daily News* between 1852 and 1866). Interestingly, Eliot emerged as a sharp critic of some of her fellow women writers in her 1856 essay, "Silly Novels by Lady Novelists" (published pseudonymously, ironically, under her George Eliot moniker in the *Westminster Review*) in which she complained about the evangelical women's reform novel that she saw as patronizing, sentimental, and excessively pious.

(Many novels of this period argued that, despite vast disparities in wealth and class among women, anyone could find gratification by adopting appropriate family values within a private domestic framework.)[7]

Yet, as Eliot knew from experience, Victorian women writers often were humiliated by the condescension of male reviewers, and at the same time— raised in environments of female repression, emotional concealment, and self-censorship—worrying that writing and public authorship might make them seem unwomanly. Martineau, as a single woman, was willing to follow the advice of her editor at the London *Morning Chronicle* who told her, "Keep to the text; write with strength; don't talk nonsense, and do your work like a man." (At another point, the irrepressible Martineau responded to an editor at the *Edinburgh Review* querying her about a potential assignment, "I'm your Man.") However, by the 1860s, Victorian women were making inroads into the masculine domination of the periodical world, and women's publications flourished. An interesting outcome of this development was the launching of criticism, often coming from women writers themselves, of female novelists who—denied participation in public life—overvalued love and romance and profited from promoting the domestic values that Eliot and others saw as holding back women. Like Eliot, Martineau and Oliphant criticized the overemphasis on love in women's novels. Margaret Fuller also joined in on this criticism, attacking "female scribblers" and calling them "the paltriest offspring of the human brain."[8]

American women of this period—including important women's rights figures—often came out of similar oppressive domestic backgrounds as their female British counterparts. Despite founding her own feminist newspaper, the *Forerunner*, in 1909, Charlotte Perkins Gilman showed how difficult it could be to carry childhood and marital trauma into professional life. Gilman's father abandoned his family when she was a young child, leaving her with great trepidations about marriage (she did not want to compromise her independence and repeat her parents' mistakes). After she wed in her early twenties, she promptly suffered a nervous breakdown that was compounded by postpartum depression after the birth of a daughter. From the start, she described her marriage as "mutual misery. Bed and cry." During a trial separation and "rest cure," she slipped into despondency and came near to "utter mental ruin," as she put it. At this point, Gilman and her husband agreed to divorce, which freed her for a life of independent journalism, feminist novel writing, and crusading against the cultural and social practices that held down women. "It seemed plain that if I went crazy it would do my husband no good, and be a deadly injury to my child," she said. Yet,

Gilman was criticized in the press of her time for her break with Victorian domesticity by giving up custody of her daughter in the divorce. (Ironically but perhaps not unexpectedly for the time, one of her severest critics was Ambrose Bierce, who virtually abandoned the raising of his children to his wife while he pursued his professional, social, and travel interests.)[9]

Similar difficulties faced Fanny Fern, whose brother, a New York City periodical editor, discouraged her from entering journalism and then told her she was a disgrace to the family when she did. A widow who had left her second marriage to an abusive husband, Fern was determined to forge on with her writing aimed at women like her who had suffered emotionally damaging marriages, traumatic divorces, and other indignities in dealings with men. In her long-running column for the New York Ledger, Fern wrote for an audience of powerless and demoralized women in witty and upbeat ways, even as she fended off the attacks of those who did not like her self-assertion and her belittling of social convention. Because of the grief she experienced during her hostile divorce and her struggles to make it as a single working woman, Fern always sympathized with unmarried and abused mothers, no matter what their economic class. She was persistently (and enthusiastically) provocative. She advised beaten women to leave their husbands, supported both women servants and professionals victimized by employers, and spoke out against sexual harassment and for equal pay for women. Despite the scandal of her divorce (her ex-husband slanderously accused her of treachery and infidelity in public notices) and her family's disapproval of her writing, Sarah Payson Parton chose to write pseudonymously (rather than anonymously) and ultimately changed her legal name to Fanny Fern.[10]

Although Fern's first novel, Ruth Hall, is fiction, it is highly autobiographical and a window into the trauma that Fern experienced before she became a breezy controversialist and saucy, lightning rod figure. In the novel, Fern told in poignant terms about the impact on Ruth and her husband in experiencing the death of a child, as Fern did when her oldest daughter died of brain fever at age seven. (In 1871, Fern wrote in the New York Ledger a response to a woman who had lost her child. "I know just how you go about, listening for the little appealing cry that you may nevermore hear; touching listlessly the little useless clothes that you fashioned, with your heart so full of love and hope. . . . [I] reach out my woman's hand, and clasp yours in sympathy, although we have never and may never meet in this world.") In a second instance in the novel, Ruth's husband, Harry, dies in circumstances similar to Fern's financially misdealing, first husband, Charles, who left her penniless after his death from typhoid fever. Fern's bitterness at the indifference

she faced from family members and friends as she lived in a Boston boarding house with her two daughters and tried to make a living as a seamstress
provided the energy behind *Ruth Hall* and her entry into journalistic work.
("Just go to work and hew out a path for yourself," she advised her readers.
"Get your head above water, and then snap your fingers in their pharisaical
faces! Never ask a favor until you are drawing your last breath; and never
forget one.") However, it was the family scorn that Fern had faced when—
after remarrying and then leaving a man who turned out to be tyrannical and
intensely jealous (her second novel, *Rose Clark*, follows the outline of this
episode in Fern's life)—that almost broke her. For Fern, the bitterest experience came when her editor brother, Nathaniel Parker Willis, wrote to her that
his reading of her writing samples meant that he saw no chance for her in
literature: "You overstrain the pathetic, and your humor runs into dreadful
vulgarity sometimes. I am sorry that any editor knows that a sister of mine
wrote some of these which you sent me." In *Ruth Hall*, Ruth's brother writes
such a letter; Ruth (saying to herself, "I *can* do it, I *feel* it, I *will* do it") decides
to persist in her writing aspirations anyway, as did Fern (who got even by
writing a satirical sketch about the social-climbing Willis for the *New York
Musical World and Times* in 1853 and deciding to base the portrait of Ruth's
cruelly indifferent brother on hers).[11]

Fern demonstrated the way that by the mid-1800s journalism and novel
writing were providing a platform that allowed spirited Victorian women
writers—who by philosophy and/or life circumstances found themselves
challenging traditional moral and domestic standards—to build a public
image and an audience following. Trauma became a theme of both their
journalistic and fiction writings, as well as the subtext of their own lives, and
their mixing of reform advocacy, sensationalistic and melodramatic literary
formulas, and socially defiant personal lives constituted a powerful draw in
the emerging mass media marketplace. Whereas the best-known Victorian
women novelists—Eliot, Jane Austen, the Bronte sisters—became famous
for their novels with women protagonists struggling against the social and
gender conventions of Victorian life, some of the more controversial, although less remembered, women journalist-literary figures of this period,
such as Norton, Faithfull, Mary Elizabeth Braddon, and Gertrude Atherton,
braved scandal and critical assault while writing for or editing periodicals
and producing novels that they filled with many of the same themes as their
personal lives. The vivacious Norton, for example, lived estranged from an
abusive husband who kept her from their children, publicly accused her
of adultery, and refused to grant her a divorce. Norton's journalism while

editing four periodicals and producing sentimental, Gothic fiction nonetheless was based on her strong social reform interests (fighting to gain more rights for women in divorce, writing some of the earliest examples of social justice fiction protesting industrialized factory conditions). Norton's own fatherless upbringing was reflected in her version of the Victorian woman novelists' archetypal plot—the young woman attracted to wild, passionate men—by having her heroine in *Old Sir Douglas* mend her ways by settling for a father-figure husband and a life of emotionally supportive tranquility. Braddon lived for fourteen years with a magazine publisher whose wife was in an insane asylum, producing five illegitimate children and surviving a nervous breakdown in 1868; *Belgravia*, the London Penny publication she founded and edited from 1866 to 1876, was rivaled in its raciness by her "sensation" novels (or what some critics scornfully called "kitchen literature") with their notorious heroines, illicit passions, and crime and mystery themes insinuated into the lives of her middle-class protagonists. Atherton, mercuric and confrontational, promoted her philosophy of literature as sweeping yet authentic in scope, and as a young widow left San Francisco for New York City in the late 1880s, determined to live out her belief that women could fashion independent, larger-than-life existences just as men could. In her journalism and her forty-three novels, Atherton wrote about women in quest of an identity beyond domesticity and procreation, and the "rotten spot" of her brain that she said was the source of her creativity produced a blending of realistic with romantic writing that Atherton associated with the windswept western landscapes that served as the symbolic backdrop of much of her fiction. The feminist and novelist Faithfull, who established the Victoria Press and *Victoria Magazine* as part of her printing establishment to promote employment opportunities for women in the mid-1800s, saw her reputation assailed when, in divorce proceedings, she was accused of sleeping with and trying to alienate the affections of the wife of a prominent admiral.[12]

A parallel development in the mixing of literary politics with trauma came with the emergence of a group of women leftist writers who found the combination of journalism and novel writing an effective forum for framing their personal, professional, and political grievances against the system. Like Gilman, Edith Nesbit, Katharine Glasier, Vera Brittain, and Rebecca West were self-proclaimed socialists; others (Dorothy Parker, Mary McCarthy, Meridel Le Sueur, Agnes Smedley) were communists during at least some period of their lives, and they wrote for and/or edited radical publications and fashioned controversial narrative fiction, often built on their leftist political perspectives. Trauma was a commonplace feature of their lives and political involvement: Le Sueur as a teenager witnessed the destruction by an antisocialist mob of the radical college where her mother taught; Smedley, who had chronicled the push by Mao's forces deep into China, was charged with espionage when she returned to the United States and died while flee-ing back to China; Parker struggled to keep alive a Hollywood screenwriting career when she was blacklisted during the Red Scare of the 1950s; Glasier suffered a nervous breakdown in 1921 after taking over as editor of the so-cialist *Labour Leader* while nursing her terminally ill husband and then was let go during staff in-fighting over how much the newspaper should support the Bolshevik cause. Ironically, the traumas experienced by two of the best known of this group, West and Nesbit, were brought about, at least in part, by the male socialists in their Fabian Socialist set, H. G. Wells (who, as West's lover, fathered a child by her in 1914 and then pretty much left her alone to raise it) and Herbert Bland (who, as Nesbit's chronically unfaithful husband, pressured her to help raise as their own his two children by a lover, who lived for a time in their household). West spent ten years as Wells's lover despite his ongoing marriage and his parade of other mistresses; when she bore their son, Anthony West, she was alone, having only seen Wells sporadically and receiving little financial support from him; when Anthony grew up, he viewed himself as unwanted and West as uncaring and more concerned with her professional interests (which caused West great hurt, as did Anthony's view that Wells was the more nurturing parent). That these women would end up being traumatized by the consequences of the "advanced" sexual attitudes within the socialist circles of their day did not diminish their important roles as journalist-novelists in pushing for women's and workers' political rights—but it did underscore the cost that could come in reconciling one's publicly progressive views with the realities of finding love and support in one's private life.[13]

As with Wells, others of the male journalistic-literary figures were guilty of perpetrating trauma on spouses and partners—even as one could sometimes see the sources of their behavior rooted in their own abused youth. Whether it was connected to philandering, substance abuse, or male-dominated cul-tural attitudes, the fame of a number of the men among the journalist-literary figures fostered a gargantuan sense of entitlement—and particularly with the women that they expected to support their artistic efforts, to nurture them in their insecurities, and to suffer their selfish ways. Some were considered sympathetic to women's ambitions—besides Wells, these included Dreiser, Hemingway, Erskine Caldwell, and Robert Benchley—but nonetheless were guilty of mistreating women in their lives. A number neglected their wives and families—including Dickens, who dispatched his wife (who had born ten children, often suffering postpartum depression afterward) into a "Victorian marriage" (she was moved into a separate house and put under the care of their oldest son) while Dickens engaged in a late-life affair with a young actress; Bret Harte, who would not allow his wife and family to visit him in Europe while he lived in an apparent ménage à trois with a woman and her husband; Benchley, who left his wife and family in the New York City suburbs for days on end while he drank and partied in the city and patronized whorehouses; Damon Runyon, who grew estranged from his children and whose newspaperwoman-turned-stay-at-home-wife became an alcoholic under the pressures of Runyon's affairs, patriarchal expectations, and all night lifestyle; and Caldwell, who would show up at the family home after extensive stretches of writing by himself in hotels and ask his wife to edit his manuscripts. Some were shockingly insensitive in their treatment of so-called loved ones. Greene—with a Catholic wife who would not grant him a divorce—would slip away to downtown London to visit brothels (including once spending the afternoon with a favorite prostitute after attending his mother-in-law's funeral in place of his pregnant wife). After his wife learned that Greene's goddaughter had become his lover, he came back from a trip with the young woman, told his wife that they planned to spend the night together, and insisted that she serve them dinner and make up the bed. Dreiser did similar things—once, while his friend, Mencken, was at dinner, he excused himself and headed off to a rendezvous with a mistress, leaving Mencken to chat with Dreiser's first wife until he returned; another time, he insisted that his live-in lover and the woman who would become his second wife cook breakfast after Dreiser had spent the night at their place with another mistress.[14]

There were a few women journalist-literary figures in this study (Norton, Atherton, Parker, and Lillie Devereux Blake) who gave as good as they got in the battle of the sexes. Parker was renowned for her parrying of male behavior with barbed retorts: "It serves me right for keeping all my eggs in one bastard"; "Snatch a lover and find a foe"; "Men don't like nobility in woman. . . . The men like to have the copyright on nobility—if there is going to be anything like that in a relationship." However, in her less armored moments, Parker (whose affair with Charles MacArthur ended in an abortion and suicide attempt) would complain about the no-win situation for women where their cultural conditioning and the latitude granted to men made it difficult to avoid being hurt. "He'll be cross if he sees I have been crying," she said during the collapse of one relationship. ". . . I wish I could make him cry

and tread the floor and feel his heart heavy and big and festering in him. . . .
I wish he could know, without my telling him. . . . They hate you whenever
you say anything you really think."[15]

Minority Writers and Journalism
as a Pathway to Protest Literature

Journalism that led into novel writing proved to be a valuable avenue to independence for members of marginalized communities who faced social and
political oppression. For those journalist-literary figures born into slavery or
who grew up black in the years of Jim Crow and de facto segregation in the
South and northern inner cities, their personal experiences of human cruelty
and family abandonment were compounded by harsh encounters with racism and economic deprivation. The escaped slave and abolitionist Frederick
Douglass, reared on a plantation in rural Maryland, had no memory of his
mother from the period before he was six (although apparently she lived
nearby, working in the fields). Although he was raised in the cabin of his
grandmother under relatively happy conditions, Douglass was delivered by
her to the home of the plantation overseer to serve as a household servant.
When the six-year-old boy found his grandmother had left him, he was disconsolate. "I was a SLAVE—born a slave—and though the fact was incom-
prehensible to me, it conveyed to my mind a sense of entire dependence on
the will of *somebody* I had never seen; and from some cause or other, I had
been made to fear this somebody above all else on earth," Douglass wrote.
Added biographer William McFeely of the boy who said that he "sobbed"
himself to sleep that night, "He never fully trusted anyone again." Douglass's
inner toughness was forged in his survival of the beatings associated with
his efforts to help other slaves learn to read and write and then his escape
from his owners in 1838. These experiences helped him to develop the fortitude to oppose his white allies after he became a leading African American
figure in the abolitionist movement. He did this when he ignored William
Lloyd Garrison's advice that he not start up a newspaper—but which he did
anyway (beginning with the *North Star, Frederick Douglass' Paper*, and other
publications, as well as writing a novel, *The Heroic Slave*)—because he felt
that it would help develop solidarity among black people and prove what an
African American person could accomplish. In reality, Douglass operated
in a world where he had every reason not to trust white people, including
his fellow abolitionists whose opposition to slavery did not necessarily alter
their views about the inferiority of black people. (For example, Edmund

Quincy, the assistant editor of Garrison's abolitionist newspaper, the *Liberator*, once complained in a letter to a friend of "unconscionable niggers" after Douglass asked for more money for his contributions than the publication wanted to pay.)[16]

In recent years, scholars have analyzed the manner in which postbellum African American journalist-literary figures negotiated the perils of segregation, racism, and bias in the periodical and book publishing industry; the psychological pressures of living as a minority in white culture; and the division of political thinking within the African American community. The variety of shrewd devices that they often employed to express their vision of black life without alienating the white (or, in some cases, the black) establishment was not only a feature of their literary strategy but says a great deal about how trauma was assimilated into their experiences and literary themes. Despite the difficulties of living as an African American between the Civil War and the adoption of the 1964 Civil Rights Act, W. E. B. Du Bois (who famously described the "double consciousness" that black Americans live with in looking at themselves through the eyes of others, "of measuring one's soul by the tape of a world that looks on in amused contempt and pity") possessed the temperament to forge ahead into controversy with his advocacy of Afrocentrism, Marxism, and black autonomy. In the *Crisis*, the publication of the National Association for the Advancement of Colored People, that he edited for nearly a quarter century, or the themes of his novel, *The Quest of the Silver Fleece*, which dramatized the economic conflicts that afflicted African Americans in the South during Reconstruction, Du Bois served as a critic of other black leaders—particularly Booker T. Washington—who wanted to cater to white expectations rather than to address grievances through protest and confrontation. A few African American journalist-literary figures, such as Victoria Earle Matthews, a prolific contributor to black and white newspapers in the late 1800s who penned historical fiction romances about independent-minded African American women in the South, managed to straddle the competing camps and emerge as a broadly influential advocate for African American women's rights. Others—including Pauline Hopkins, another important African American journalist and historical fiction novelist—were not so lucky. Also a critic of Washington, whose accommodationist rhetoric conflicted with her views of black pride and African American women's independence, Hopkins lost her influential position on *Colored American* magazine in 1904 when allies of Washington purchased the publication. In different ways, George Samuel Schuyler and Paul Laurence Dunbar paid a price for deviating from expected operational frameworks for African American journalists and novelists of the Jim Crow era: Dunbar when he wrote *Sport of the Gods*, which offered a biting social critique of the plight of black Americans that veered away from his local color fiction (or abandoning his "exquisite darky stories," as one white newspaper lamented); the one-time socialist Schuyler when he upset activist black writers and politicians (already troubled by *Black No More*, Schuyler's satire about a black doctor who turned blacks into whites for $50 and that ridiculed black and white stereotypes about each other) by challenging commonly held views in the African American community (as he did when he went to Mississippi for the *Pittsburgh Courier* and concluded that two-thirds of the accounts of lynchings and unjust prosecutions of blacks were not true) and by transforming into a Mencken-inspired conservative and an enthusiastic member of the John Birch Society.[17]

The contrast in strategies can be seen in the respective experiences of Ida Wells-Barnett and Charles Chesnutt in how they addressed hostility toward blacks in the segregated South. Wells saw herself as cut out of the same cloth as Douglass—she founded a newspaper, the *Memphis Free Press*, and wrote provocative editorials that protested injustice against blacks ("a Winchester rifle should have a place of honor in every black home, and it should be used for that protection which the law refuses to give," she wrote). She moved to New York City under threat of her life after a white mob burned down her newspaper office in 1892 in the wake of an economic boycott called for by the *Free Press* during a lynching controversy. After becoming editor of the *New York Age*, she became a tireless investigator of and campaigner against the lynchings of blacks by white southerners ("Not until the Negro rises up in his might and takes a hand in resenting such cold-blooded murders, if he has to burn up whole towns, will a halt be called in wholesale lynching," she wrote). Chesnutt—"a voluntary Negro," as one biographer described him (meaning that he was so light-skinned that he could pass as white but chose not to)—adopted a more indirect and less confrontational tactic in his 1901 novel, *The Marrow of Tradition*, about the race riots that took place in Wilmington, North Carolina, in 1898. Chesnutt's book—although fictionalizing the people and circumstances—challenged the accounts in the white press that portrayed white citizens as responding in spontaneous outrage to a black newspaper editorial suggesting that local white women were as eager to have clandestine relationships with black men as were local white men with black women. Chesnutt's privileging of oral history over "historical records" (including journalistic records) and his suggestion to readers through the novel's narrator that they should expand the sources from which they derived information about the riots was a strategy to deal with the delicate circumstances of black writers critical of the white (and the journalistic) establishment. Chesnutt's fictional approach—in which he infused his political and social points into his melodramatic plot revolving around a dramatization of the oppressive circumstances that blacks and people of mixed black and white heritage lived under in the Jim Crow South—can be seen as following in the tradition of earlier journalist-literary figures, such as Defoe, Swift, Fern, and Gilman, who found the devices of fiction a safer way to express unpopular truths. Even though Chesnutt, who like Dunbar, made his mark originally by writing largely inoffensive, southern dialect tales, demonstrated considerable circumspection throughout his career in dealing with white editors who were not particularly sympathetic to black aspirations, *The Marrow of Tradition* was not well received by critics, and this was considered to be a factor in Chesnutt's decision to give up writing for a time and to return to his court reporting business. As a person of mixed ethnicity, Chesnutt used literary themes that often focused on the absurdities of racial divisions in a country where so many people (including many who did not know it) had a blended racial heritage. But his experiences of living with the emotional residue of daily and continuous racial tension were no less traumatic than Wright's were. ("I am neither fish, flesh, nor fowl," Chesnutt once wrote. "Neither 'nigger,' white, nor 'buckrah.' Too 'stuckup' for the colored folks, and, of course, not recognized by the whites.")[18]

Wright also turned to novel writing in transforming his autobiographical insights in *Black Boy* into the ghetto world of Bigger Thomas, his protagonist in the 1940 novel *Native Son*, where Wright fictionalized the details of the real-life murder trial of Robert Nixon, a black Chicago youth who was accused of killing five women and raping others. Wright's own anger and his observations in *Black Boy* about his mother's suffering ("a symbol [of] all the poverty, the ignorance, the helplessness; the painful, baffling, hunger-ridden days and hours; the restless moving, the futile seeking, the uncertainty, the fear, the dread; the meaningless pain and endless suffering . . . [that] set the emotional tone of my life") informed his picture of Bigger's circumscribed existence in the slums of Chicago and colored his portrayal of Bigger's inner agitation ("A somberness of spirit that I was never to lose settled over me . . . that was to make me stand apart and look upon excessive joy with suspicion, that was to make me self-conscious, that was to make me keep forever on the move, as though to escape a nameless fate seeking to overtake me," Wright wrote in *Black Boy*). Wright's descriptions of Bigger's claustrophobia and resentment at waking up in his mother's ghetto apartment, his confused and frustrated reactions that manifested themselves in violent explosions of temper, and his mistrustful response to the condescension of the white communist characters in the novel who insist that Bigger take them to a restaurant in his neighborhood reflected Wright's raw sensitivity to the conditions of marginalization and alienation of blacks in American society (including among communists, with whom Wright ended his affiliation after he came to believe communism offered no place for African Americans). Although Wright needed the latitude of a fictional platform to explore the function of racial isolation in forming Bigger's psychic condition, the world of journalism played a background role throughout the genesis and narrative of the novel—from its inspiration in newspaper accounts of Nixon's trial (Wright read clippings spread out on his apartment floor as a way to impress the story into his imagination) to the role that Bigger's reading of fictional newspaper headlines and racist coverage of his crime played as the police noose tightened around him. In one of the most traumatic moments in *Native Son*, the jailed Bigger gets hold of another prisoner's newspaper that carries this account of Bigger's case: "slayer will undoubtedly pay supreme penalty for his crimes . . . there is no doubt of his guilt . . . what is doubtful is how many other crimes he has committed." As the shock sinks in, Wright described how Bigger was seized with "an organic wish to cease to be, to stop living" that grows into a powerful feeling of something just the opposite. "His face rested against the bars and he felt tears roll down his cheeks. His wet lips tasted salt. He sank to his knees and sobbed: 'I don't want to die. . . . I don't want to die. . . . '"—which was Bigger's last expression of painful feelings before he adopts the defiant stance that he takes to the electric chair.[19]

Hurston—who, like Wright, was a product of the Jim Crow South—was one of eight children, and she lost her mother when she was eleven. To appease his new second wife, her father sent Hurston from Eatonville to a boarding school in nearby Jacksonville, Florida, where she experienced racial hostility and feelings of isolation. At one point, her father stopped paying room and board and suggested the school adopt her. Eventually, Hurston returned home but was passed around to her stepmother's friends for rearing. When she refused sexual advances from a male employer as a fourteen-year-old maid in a white family and left its employment, she began to drift through a lifetime of menial jobs that (despite her intermittent successes as a journalist, anthropologist, and novel writer) was her lot until she died largely unrecognized while writing a column for a local newspaper, battling depression, and working as a maid in Fort Pierce, Florida. Hurston's early life trauma was compounded by the traumas she experienced as a writer-journalist—most notably, in her losing struggle with the proletarian/social realist black journalist-literary figures, Wright and Langston Hughes, who (in Wright's case) condemned Hurston's *Their Eyes Were Watching God* as portraying black southern life as "quaint" and doing for literature what minstrel shows did for theater. Wright's and Hughes's domination of black letters in the 1930s and beyond helped to ensure that Hurston's writings were generally forgotten and Hurston marginalized until she was rediscovered in the 1970s by Walker, who was moved by the power of Hurston's story of a black woman who found joy and independence in her quest for identity within black folk culture of the South. Hurston's neglect and renaissance put a twist into the more typical scenario of the left-activist writer squelched by the forces of the establishment—and Hurston's more conservative views (in developing her vision of racial pride and identity, she rejected what she called the "sobbing school of Negrohood" that portrayed black lives as deprived and lived largely as defensive reactions to white actions) and their unpopularity with fellow African American writers demonstrated that professional trauma could come from many sources, including from writers who themselves had been the victims of traumatic experience.[20]

The criticism that could come to an explorer of ethnic themes also has been visited on the multiracial journalist-literary figure, Sui Sin Far (the pen name of Edith Maude Eaton), who played an early role in bringing the conditions in Asian immigrant communities to public attention. However, her reform tendencies were couched in viewpoints that some critics today see as a reflection of cultural typecasting that was unhelpful to the Chinese community of her mother. As the product of a mixed marriage and a traditional middle-class upbringing in the house of her white father, Far's writings about Chinese immigrants made her as much a "voyeur" on the "exotic" Chinese in San Francisco's Chinatown, says Maria Ng, as an activist writer. Far's 1912 collection of short narratives, *Mrs. Spring Fragrance*, presented her protagonist as an idealized Chinese immigrant, who learns English, adapts to local customs, and drinks tea with neighbors. Although Far did not shy away from discussing the harsh side of immigrant life (such as in one story about a Chinese businessman shot by racist whites, and in another about an immigrant wife who kills her son rather than let him become "Americanized" by his acculturated father), Ng says the experiences of many Chinese immigrants—who worked long hours in sweatshop conditions and experienced racial discrimination if they worked outside of family businesses—were not adequately portrayed in Far's focus on middle-class life. Far's intentions were good (even though she did not speak Chinese, and thus had limited access to people's homes, she wanted to refute highly racist and inflammatory stereotypes of Chinese immigrants), and her stories of upwardly mobile life in a Chinese community were sensitively crafted. But it would be left to later, more politically oriented writers to satisfy contemporary critics who have not found in Far's work a radical enough critique of the circumstances of those of Chinese heritage living in America.[21]

Trauma, Naturalism, and Sensationalism

One cannot underestimate how much the industrialization of newspapers and periodicals throughout the nineteenth century—followed by the popularization of Freudian psychoanalytical theories at the turn of the twentieth century—accelerated the trend of fusing trauma into the formulas that news organizations used to appeal to audiences. The capitalizing on traumatic life events for moneymaking purposes by mass market publications encouraged savvy writers of journalism and fiction to produce stories that drew on the "sensational" realism of the natural world and provided heroes who triumphed over the brutal laws of Darwinian existence and heroines who flaunted social convention and pushed the boundaries of propriety by offering themes of feminine independence with risqué undertones. Both men and women writers capitalized on the public appetite for voyeuristic "exposes" that revealed social problems while selling newspapers and periodicals at the same time. Such was the case with W. T. Stead's "Maiden Tribute of Modern Babylon," which (in the tradition of Chartist reform writers such as G. W. M. Reynolds and Ernest Jones, who mixed scandal narratives with social justice advocacy as a way to appeal to working-class readers) dramatized the issue of child prostitution. However, Stead saw his July 1885 story in London's *Pall Mall Gazette* about childhood trauma morph into a real-life trauma for himself. Stead was convicted of kidnapping and served three months in prison when it was revealed that his "purchasing" of a thirteen-year-old girl was a "put up" job, and that he had arranged to have the girl placed in a bordello as a way to illustrate how easy it was to engage in white slavery. (Interestingly, Stead's notoriety did not mean that he was not a sincere follower of what was called the "social gospel" in his time; his book, *If Christ Came to Chicago*, was a powerful indictment of the failures of municipal government and industrialized society to follow the Bible's demands for just treatment of the disadvantaged.)[22]

A new growth in understanding of the multilevel complexity of the human psyche came with the arrival of the literary naturalists in the late nineteenth and early twentieth centuries—a number of whom suffered life traumas and emotional upheavals in their early years. They were the first generation of writers to draw on Darwinian principles and to pen important works as Freud was offering his theories of the power of repressed and hidden emotions over the human personality. Dreiser's own traumas—both family and professional ones in journalism—became the material of his two memoirs, *Newspaper Days* and *Dawn*, as well as his early fiction. His heroines, Carrie Meeber in *Sister Carrie* and Jennie in *Jennie Gerhardt*, were modeled on two of his wayward sisters and their hard-knock experiences (most notably his sister, Emma, who, as the inspiration for the creation of Carrie Meeber, had been the subject of tabloid headlines when she ran off with a married saloon manager who stole money to set themselves up in New York City), and the novels reflected his naturalist view of a world where people are buffeted about by internal and external forces largely beyond their control. Dreiser's abandonment of religious faith and his embrace of Darwinian explanations for the impersonal cruelties of life are well documented in his memoirs—as were the lessons he took from his work as a young, urban journalist that taught him to put a premium on opportunistic methods for survival over ethical concerns. At the *New York World* of Joseph Pulitzer, Dreiser described being sent to the city morgue to see if a drowned young woman was beautiful, as one of the newspaper's competitors described her. Once Dreiser established that she was not, his newspaper's interest in the story disappeared. Throughout his newspaper career, Dreiser connected his depressed feelings with the things that he was reporting on, and particularly so as he was reading and absorbing the evolutionary concepts of Darwin and other writers, such as Herbert Spencer, who were transforming Darwinian principles into a philosophy of "Social Darwinism," which maintained that human and social laws followed the "survival of the fittest" principles of nature. "Suicides seemed sadder since there was no care for them; failures the same. . . . Also before my eyes were always those regions of indescribable poverty and indescribable wealth . . . and when I read Spencer I could only sigh," Dreiser wrote. Dreiser blended the cynical feelings he came to have about newspapers' claim to a higher civic mission with the trauma of his reporting experiences in his short story "Nigger Jeff," where a reporter witnesses a lynching in its full brutality—but then is overwhelmed with excitement at the prospect of writing up the story. "With the cruel instinct of the budding artist that he already was, he was beginning to meditate on the character of the story it would make—the color, the pathos," wrote Dreiser.[23]

London turned his traumatic life experiences—witnessing the cruelties of hunting while on a sealing expeditions as a teenager, enduring a rugged Alaska winter in a cramped cabin during the Klondike gold rush, and learning to "survive with the fittest" while jailed for vagrancy during his travels as a tramp—into tales that he cranked out for popular publication. His experiences led him to develop a "might is right" philosophy that he saw manifested in Darwinian laws of survival in the natural world and the philosopher Friedrich Nietzsche's superman notions of a philosophical elite living on their own moral terms. London's shock at learning in his twenties that his stepfather was not his real father, but had been a fill-in for an itinerant astrologer who had abandoned his pregnant mother, was long-lasting, and he came to see his experiences of poverty and childhood neglect as evidence that he had survived only by proving himself to be one of the "fittest." London's mental deterioration, his descent into drug and alcohol addiction, and his sacrifice of the radical political values of his youth as he chased after the good life and preached a philosophy of Aryan superiority left him with a divided legacy— the wealth-seeking socialist, the populist radical who was a racist and an elitist, and the macho creator of swashbuckling heroes who developed a late-life fascination with Jungian psychology that he felt explained the traumatic events of his youth and gave him perspective on the compulsive internal patterns that came to control his life. That literary fame and psychological insight did not prove enough to ease his turbulence is a commentary on how powerfully trauma can affect the interior world of a personality who sought to understand its sources. London's death by a drug overdose at age forty can be seen as ushering in an era when public and private diagnoses of writers' mental health became commonplace but did not necessarily save them from a tragic end.[24]

London stands as an important figure at the intersection of journalism, literature, and trauma in the manner in which he borrowed from news stories and other journalistic accounts (to the point of being accused of plagiarism) for his adventure tales of the outdoors. His experience of living through an Alaskan winter in a ramshackle shack (where he suffered from boredom, short rations, and scurvy that cost him his four front teeth and that he used as the basis for his short story, "In a Far Country") became a model for his semifictional accounts of humans pressed to their limits by their experiences in nature. His story, "To Build a Fire," is one of his most vivid in this regard; it conveys the slowly developing horror of a solitary Alaskan traveler's realization that his fire-making implements have failed him and that he is going to freeze to death (which London illustrated in a harrowing scene of the traveler's panic and descent into a deep, deadly sleep). London's use of newspapers as sources for his stories became the subject of controversy when his short story

"The Love of Life," about a man in the agony of dying of starvation, was shown by the *New York World* in 1906 to have "deadly parallels" with a previously published account by another writer. London defended himself by saying, "I, in the course of making my living by turning journalism into literature, used material from various sources which had been collected and narrated by men who made their living by turning the facts of life into journalism."[25]

Frank Norris, one of the other naturalists London was accused of plagiarizing, was someone who did not suffer particularly from early life emotional scarring (he grew up in relatively benign and comfortable circumstances in a San Francisco merchant's family) and yet has been viewed as the most directly influenced among the naturalists by the coming of the psychological sciences. One can see in his novel *McTeague* (based on an account in the San Francisco newspapers of the stabbing death of a woman by her violent husband), the creation of an author with a strong sense of the notion of humans as influenced by internal drives that they can barely control or understand. However, he published the novel in 1899 before Freud had come to widespread public attention, and Norris's grasp of psychological motivation seems more intuitive than based on knowledge of psychoanalytical theory. Like the newspapers of the time, which often reveled in the cruel things people could do to each other, the motivation for the cold-blooded acts by the criminal dentist McTeague seems ultimately to be a mystery to Norris, and his naturalistic orientation (this is simply how things work in the harsh Darwinian natural world) can seem unsatisfying in the retrospective context of Freud's coming entry into public life. Yet, the convergence of these thought systems—Darwinian evolutionary theory, Social Darwinism and the "survival of the fittest" concepts of Spencer, naturalistic philosophy, and the psychoanalytical theories of Freud and Jung—would serve as a philosophical backdrop for the sensationalistic newspapers of the yellow press era, which did not need an intellectual justification for using trauma as grist for their audience-building but nonetheless came to see psychological journalism as a way to wring one more angle out of their stories of criminal motivation. The same can be said for the novelists who emerged from this journalistic workplace to mine the themes of "incredible realism" that sold so well to audiences whose taste for stories of the sadistic "superman" (Wolf Larsen in London's *The Sea Wolf*), the syphilitic and sexually unrestrained sensualist (Vandover in Norris's *Vandover and the Brute*), the human unconscious fused into the imagination of the beast (the dog, Buck, in London's *The Call of the Wild*), and the amoral and power-hungry industrialist

(Frank Cowperwood in Dreiser's *The Financier* and *The Titan*) had been well primed by their newspaper reading habits.[26]

Of the writers who carried the spirit of naturalism into the twentieth century, Caldwell was perhaps the most prominent in being accused of importing the practices of the sensationalist newspapers into his fiction. Caldwell had learned in his reporting career with the *Atlanta Journal* the value of employing direct expression and material with intense emotional impact, and he merged these with his recognition of the marketability of graphic and titillating themes in his portrayals of deprivation and depravity among the poor, rural, southern characters of his Depression-era novels. Caldwell profited from the market appeal of traumatic themes at every turn of his career—and particularly so as he addressed in his fiction the cruelties that he had witnessed as a journalist but could not discuss in the newspaper. His powerful fictional account of a southern lynching, *Trouble in July*, was inspired in part by his experience as a young reporter arriving at the scene where the body of a strung-up black man had not yet been cut down—but which his editors at the *Journal* were not interested in his writing about. In 1933, Caldwell investigated a series of lynchings in Bartow, Georgia, and wired stories to the *New Masses* magazine in New York. In his articles, Caldwell gave detailed accounts of the hangings and chastised the local press for ignoring them. Although he felt great sympathy for the impoverished circumstances of the rural southern whites that he had grown up among, he was highly ambivalent about their cultural values (he once lambasted southern whites for creating a "retarded and thwarted civilization"). As a social realist and a political radical, Caldwell often embellished material that he used in his journalism for his novels and vice versa—such as he did in the lascivious portrayals in *Tobacco Road* and *God's Little Acre* of poor white backwoods residents who engaged in wanton coupling at the same time they suffered from hunger and malnutrition. His 1934 series on rural southern poverty for the *New York Post*—which he wrote soon after the publication of *Tobacco Road* and *God's Little Acre*—garnered nationwide attention, including when he led a delegation of reporters to witness the conditions (big families and malnourished children crammed into tar-paper shacks, birth defects from incestuous unions, overworked black cotton mill hands who were paid only half as much as their white counterparts) after the local Georgia press questioned whether people really lived in such wretched circumstances. Caldwell's seemingly prurient fascination with rural southern customs—including the lustful practices of rural churchgoers that could be mixed in with their ecstatic spiritual states, which he dramatized in his novel about a corrupt preacher, *The Journeyman*—helped earn him a reputation as a sensationalist and exploiter of human trauma. But in his Freudian-inspired view of sex as the source of all human motivation and violence as a parallel impulse, Caldwell fit into the tradition dating back to the mid-1800s of tabloid editors, such as Reynolds and Stead, who demonstrated a reformer's interest in exposing social injustices at the same time they recognized the commercial benefits of dramatizing scenes of human suffering and licentiousness.[27]

Journalistic and Literary Forays into the Great Depression

With the advent of the Great Depression, a number of journalist-literary figures—besides Caldwell, this group included Dreiser, Anderson, Agee, Le Sueur, and Steinbeck—set aside their novel-writing activities to investigate as journalists the conditions of joblessness and economic misery that they believed were too dramatic to need fictionalization. Steinbeck's outrage at the conditions of the Oklahoma tenant farmers that he encountered in California's Central Valley grew out of a reporting assignment for a San Francisco newspaper—but which he could not get into major East Coast publications when he tried to use the material to draw national attention to the workers' plight. *Life*, for example, would not run his account of the Visalia floods in 1938 that were so devastating to migrant camps because the magazine's editors considered the material too politically charged, and he only was able to publish it in the local *Monterey Trader*. Steinbeck never forgave the national press for its disinterest in the workers' plight, which he called "the most heartbreaking thing in the world." Famously, Steinbeck channeled that anger into his classic novel *The Grapes of Wrath* (where he incorporated the Visalia flood material into the final chapters). Steinbeck—who had outfitted an old bread truck for his first trip to the camps in 1936—experienced such anguish from talking with the migrants, attending their camp meetings, and witnessing the miserable living conditions that he found himself drinking heavily afterward and so agitated that he could not concentrate on his fiction-writing projects. But after the publication of his seven-article series, "The Harvest Gypsies," for the *San Francisco News*, his next novel began to take shape in his mind—including his recognition that he wanted to build it around a family he had seen living in a residence of tree branches, flattened cans, and torn-up cardboard boxes. In the spirit of Defoe, Steinbeck discovered that his fictional portrayal of the migrants' plight in *The Grapes of Wrath* succeeded in galvanizing attention in ways that his nonfictional efforts had not. Still, Steinbeck continued to use journalistic-style research and investigation as the basis for fictional and nonfictional projects. "What can I say about journalism?" he said. "It has the greatest virtue and the greatest evil. . . . It is the mother of literature and the perpetrator of crap. . . . But over a long period of time . . . it is perhaps the purest thing we have. Honesty has a way of creeping in even when it was not intended."[28]

The nature of the traumatization of Agee's experience connected to *Fortune* magazine's rejection of his project that would become *Let Us Now Praise Famous Men* is a complex one, and it occurred in stages throughout the research, completion, and eventual publication of the book. Agee decided at the outset that he was going to write about impoverished Alabama tenant farmers as he saw fit and not worry about the magazine's formulas and restrictions. Yet, the job of portraying the sharecroppers as truthfully as his conscience dictated seemed so vast a task that Agee—who spent eight weeks in Alabama with photographer Walker Evans in the summer of 1936—grew paralyzed by the grandiose goals of his writing scheme. Agee battled an overpowering sense of guilt and a terrible self-consciousness about the project's impact on the lives of the Depression-ravaged farmers. "It seems to me curious, not to say obscene and thoroughly terrifying . . . to pry intimately into the lives of an undefended and appallingly damaged group of human beings . . . for the purpose of parading the nakedness, disadvantage and humiliation of these lives . . . in the name of . . . 'honest journalism,'" he said. When the series that he produced—idiosyncratic, elaborately crafted, and built around Agee as a character in the story with his subjective feelings and misgivings—was spurned by Henry Luce's *Fortune* magazine, where he was employed, Agee seemed outwardly nonplussed. However, inwardly he was highly distressed at what he saw as a repudiation of a sympathetic realism that he believed virtually embodied the sharecroppers and their lives. As he worked to expand the material into a book, Agee came to see the project as neither journalistic nor invented but as a hybrid product that would allow him to incorporate his anguished conscience into the text. Although critics have complained that Agee's experimental and eclectic mix of writing styles and his self-involvement in the story overshadow his portrait of the farmers, the book's publication by Houghton Mifflin in 1941 compensated for Agee's feeling "weak, sick, vindictive, powerless and guilty" after the article's earlier rejection. The book soon grew into a cult classic—and particularly so in the 1960s after Agee's death, when he took on the posthumous mystique of a tortured artist-genius with a James Dean–like quality about his memory.

Agee's effort at artistic perfection as an atonement ritual for his and society's failings has left him with a romantic but tragic legacy as a figure who symbolized the way that the attempt by a writer to capture the meaning of traumatic experiences can undermine mental health even as he pursues writing for its healing possibilities.[29]

For a number of the journalist-literary figures who were transformed by the circumstances of the Depression into leftist radicals, socialists, and communists in some cases (Agee, Anderson, Caldwell, Orwell, Wilson, Wright, Hughes, Carl Sandburg, John Dos Passos, J. B. Priestley), their journalism, often in radical and reform-oriented publications, reinforced their views about political and social inequity by propelling them into the coverage of events with traumatic overtones. Although some leftist-oriented journalist-literary figures—including Dreiser, Orwell, Wilson, and Sinclair Lewis—were pugnacious in their defense of their political beliefs, others were shaken by the backlash against their political viewpoints when the national mood changed during World War II and the coming of the Cold War. Anderson, who suffered from depression and anxiety in his later career, precipitated to a great degree by the decline of his writing reputation, found a new vitality in his social activism during the Depression, including offering his personal support to textile strikes throughout the South, writing a series of magazine articles that were assembled into a book about the plight of out-of-work laborers and economically devastated people (*Puzzled America*), and publicly endorsing the communist candidate for president in 1932. Anderson's radicalism was genuine but naïve, based as it was largely on a native sympathy for people who were suffering, and he was increasingly out-of-place with party ideologues, the editors he wrote for at *New Masses* magazine, and his fellow participants in seminars about "How I Came to Communism." Anderson was mortified when he was attacked in *Scribner's* magazine for joining other radical intellectuals in abandoning the freethinking principles of artistic independence for party doctrine. In his apologetic reply to the article—"It may be that I got reckless. After all . . . you have to trust someone. I am not a politically-minded man"—Anderson began the backpedaling that happened with other radical artists who came to recognize the seriousness of the charges that they had become fellow travelers. Anderson died before the United States' entry into World War II and the coming of the Red Scare, and he never faced serious repercussions for his involvement with communism, but his qualms from the experience stayed with him, as did the growing fear of political retaliation that came to grip those in the artistic community who realized that they might be forced to pay a price for their dalliance with left-wing politics during the 1930s.[30]

Trauma and the Journalist's Job

American and British news organizations have had the dubious distinction of having fired or forced out of a job some of the most prominent names in journalism who have gone on to notable literary careers. The journalist-literary figures who were dismissed or walked out because their work was censored or before they were fired from journalism jobs include Harte, Dreiser, Orwell, Steinbeck, Lewis, Parker, Benchley, Hemingway, Mark Twain, Stephen Crane, George Kaufman, Heywood Broun, Edna Ferber, Raymond Chandler, John O'Hara, V. S. Pritchett, E. B. White, and Truman Capote. In some cases, they were fired because of their protests over professional restrictions that were placed on them; in other cases, they were let go because of things they wrote that offended their audience or their editors. Often it was the stories that could not be told, and the perspectives that could not be put into print, that created the tensions that led to their exits. In other instances, stories that were spurned by a news organization ended up as the basis for celebrated works of art, as was the case with Agee's *Let Us Now Praise Famous Men* and Greene's articles warning Americans not to follow the French into the quagmire of Vietnam, also rejected by Luce's *Life* magazine, which proved to be a prescient theme in Greene's 1955 novel, *The Quiet American*. Researchers have found that employment circumstances can in themselves cause traumatic stress—and particularly so when a story that a journalist feels is vitally important to the community (or one where he or she took a life risk to get it) is not published. Trauma researcher Elana Newman has described what can happen to a journalist who wants to tell a story but is not allowed to do so as "vicarious traumatization." Patrice Keats—in a study of Canadian journalists—found that the failure to be able to tell a story proved to be a "big issue" with the journalists that she interviewed, and she termed it "assignment stress injury."[31]

The peripatetic reporter Dreiser was fired from his last job in newspapering at the *World* when he was viewed as too much a feature writer who could not master the art of the quickly reported, once-over-lightly, scoop-oriented journalism of the paper. This was the final blow in a series of negative experiences at newspapers for Dreiser, who was discouraged by the *World*'s sensationalistic practices and wrote in his memoirs that the grim material he covered often dropped him into depression. "Never again, if I died in the fight, would I condescend to be a reporter on any paper. I might starve, but if so—I would starve," he wrote. Dreiser's sometimes depressive, sometimes manic moods (at one point, he described the "undoubtedly semi-neurasthenic . . . disease-demonized soul" Pulitzer as something of a kindred spirit—"fighting an almost insane battle with life itself [and] trying to be omnipotent and what not else"—and life at the *World* as "immense . . . terrific") were only inflamed in the world of novel writing. Dreiser's nervous breakdown in 1903 after *Sister Carrie's* initial difficulties with the critics, many of whom deemed it immoral and an affront to Victorian sexual mores, was the first of a number of episodes where he demonstrated erratic behavior in the face of publishing disappointments (he reportedly began his post–*Sister Carrie* recovery when, on the way to New York City's East River, presumably to throw himself in, he encountered a gleefully drunken Scotsman who flipped up his coattails, did a jig for Dreiser's benefit, and told him: "Ah, we're feeling verra low today, but we'll be better by and by"). Although sometimes jarringly candid in his memoirs, Dreiser did not engage in complex psychological diagnosis or let on to the world the extent of his emotional fragility, nor did his fictional characters demonstrate great introspective powers (as Dreiser also did not). For Dreiser, the importance of Freudian theory tended to be limited to reinforcing Dreiser's lifelong obsession with female conquest. ("Sex, sex, sex. . . . The dark flower of passion that glorifies and terrifies the world. . . . Books—Freud—life!," as Dreiser put it in *Dawn*.)[32]

Orwell is a prime example of how traumatic emotions connected to journalism experience could work their effects slowly into a writer's conscience, build to a climax, and then come out in themes of fiction. In Orwell's youth and early adult life, he had experiences with institutional structures and bureaucracies that were traumatic in a low-level way—but which critics see as foundational to his vision of a surveillance-filled future in *1984* and the vicious barnyard politicking in his allegorical novel, *Animal Farm*. In his memoirs, Orwell discussed his hatred for his boarding school and what he claimed were the sadistic practices of the couple who ran it; this was followed by his resentment at working in the colonial police in Burma, where he found the repression of the natives and the rigidity of the bureaucracy maddening and intrusive to his independent-minded personality ("When the white man turns tyrant it is his own freedom that he destroys," Orwell wrote in his essay, "Shooting an Elephant"). His resentment of organizational life came to a climax when he joined the Republican forces fighting in the Spanish Civil War, was seriously wounded in the fighting, and then, in the midst of his recovery, narrowly escaped a purge during the in-fighting of the communist factions. This experience reinforced his innate suspicion of a host of things: political ideology and ideologues, institutional structures that tried to control people's lives, censorship and attempts to limit and dictate people's speech and even their thoughts. Orwell's traumatized emotions continued to dictate the course of his writings—and particularly so after his World War II experiences as a journalist at the British Broadcasting Company (BBC) exposed him to censorship, surveillance, and punishment for not towing the agency's political line. At his BBC job, Orwell could not say anything over the air that had not been screened by censors, and he was reprimanded on a number of occasions for not sticking to the chain of command. The ominous nature of this experience—where he came to believe that a person's psychology was heavily influenced by trying not to say anything that might conflict with the rules of authority—was transposed into the themes of *1984*, his novel about a sinister, Big Brother bureaucracy, which forever ties journalistic management practices into one of the great literary statements about the dangers of collective thinking, monolithic administration, invasion of privacy, and the emotional effects of thought policing. As one of his biographers, Michael Shelden said, Orwell never got over his bitterness at attempts to keep him from saying what he thought—and intellectual honesty became for him a release from his traumatized emotions.[33]

Perhaps because he was a humorist, Benchley was able to bounce back from a series of resignations from periodical posts, including at *Vanity Fair* magazine, where he quit as a sympathetic gesture in the wake of the firing of his good friend, Parker, who was jettisoned for her too astringent play reviews. Benchley also embroiled himself in employment trouble when, as a picture editor at the *New York Tribune*, he was overruled after trying to juxtapose a photograph of a regiment of black American soldiers fighting in World War I with a picture of a black man in Georgia being murdered by a crowd of whites. Ernest Gruening, Benchley's managing editor, defended him to the newspaper's top management, including after another incident where Benchley unsuccessfully tried to run a picture of a German U-boat picking up shipwreck survivors. When the *Tribune* executives, suspecting Gruening of pro-German leanings, learned that he lived in an apartment building where a man had been arrested for running a German-owned newspaper, Gruening was dismissed. Benchley, his funny man reputation belying his strong social conscience, wrote to his superiors: "Without any rational proof that Dr. Gruening was guilty of the burlesque charges made against him . . . you took steps, which on the slightest examination could have been proven unwarranted, to smirch the character and newspaper career of the first man in three years who has been able to make the *Tribune* look like a newspaper. I haven't the slightest idea who is boss of this sheet, so I am sending this resignation to three whom I suspect."[34]

With the writer's byline adopted and copy desks established at many urban newspapers, the avenues for personal expression or anonymous or pseudonymous commentary became restricted by the latter years of the nineteenth century. Many factors came to constrain robust expression in the industrialized newspapers of the era, as well as any discussion of topics that might have made a writer or columnist look aggrieved or an employer look bad. These included the submergence of the writer's voice into the wire service and telegraph dispatches that filled the news columns, the priority put on the employment of journalists whose consciences were not troubled by the use of opportunistic approaches to finding stories of crime and violence, and the ease of replacing workers who had mastered the hackwork formulas for reporting about the "concrete jungle" of urban life. Women journalists, in particular, often have been hampered from open expression by the nature of the relatively narrow range of jobs and opportunities available to them. As a result, a number of journalist-literary figures found that fiction writing provided them with a cover for discussing past workplace issues, including ones that could be considered traumatic in nature.

Jan Whitt has argued that a number of female journalists who have gone on to acclaimed novel-writing careers later disparaged the newspaper business in their fiction, at least in part, because of their resentment of the treatment they received at the hands of male journalists. Katherine Anne Porter, whose journalism career was limited largely to writing what was then considered fit domain for women (wedding notices, obituaries, and cultural activities), was circumspect in her criticism but expressed her views more openly in her fiction. Her short novel, *Pale Horse, Pale Rider*, offered Porter the chance to comment on news work through her protagonist, Miranda, who is banished along with a fellow woman reporter to the theater and society beats after they were sent to cover a "scandalous" aborted elopement but decided to suppress the story when the recaptured girl tearfully pled with them not to publicize her debasement. It was in the fictionalization of a real-life event—Porter nearly dying during the flu epidemic of 1918 while working for the *Rocky Mountain News* in Denver—that the difference between journalism and fiction as her preferred venue to convey traumatic experience was illustrated in dramatic fashion. In a later interview, Porter described how the newspaper had just about given up on her ("The paper had my obit set in type") when she miraculously survived. However, it was only in Porter's fictionalized version of the event—where her real-life lover, like Miranda's fictionalized lover, dies—in which she conveyed the full tragedy of her experience. In the novel, Porter dramatized Miranda's near-death experience in spiritual terms that are described in a manner far beyond the scope of conventional journalism—as well as the devastation that overcame Miranda in learning that her lover, who had nursed her through the worst period of her illness, died of the flu as she recovered. That Porter chose fiction to illustrate the impact of the events on her was made clear in a 1956 interview. "It's in the story," she told the interviewer tearfully. "He died. . . . It's a true story. . . . It seems to me true that I died then, I died once, and I have never feared death since." (In another interview, she added, "I had what the Christians call the 'beatific vision,' and the Greeks called the 'happy day,' the happy vision just before death. Now if you have had that, and survived it, come back from it, you are no longer like other people, and there's no deceiving yourself that you are.")[35]

One can make a case that in Hemingway's situation—and that of other journalist-literary figures raised in dysfunctional environments with family secrets and fragile parental emotions dominating their upbringing—the passion for finding the "truth" of life was what drew them to a journalistic career and then upset them when they found their truth-telling strategies thwarted in newspaper employment. Hemingway's lack of trust in and skepticism of the motives of others grew out of an upbringing where so much seemed false and hidden to him and where honesty could not be tolerated by his troubled parents. The emotional release in devoting one's life to what is "authentic" and "genuine" about life—as Hemingway believed that he did, despite his psychological incapacity to fully live the role of a person of integrity—very likely played a part in his proselytizing for a form of writing that cut through the subterfuges of social discourse and his disillusionment (as he experienced in conventional journalism) when this mission was compromised. Hemingway's animus was shared by writers such as Bierce, Dreiser, Gilman, Parker, Orwell, Wright, Mark Twain, Charles Bukowski, and Hunter S. Thompson whose anger at the shams and evasions of society was turned onto their employers when they did not live up to the truth-seeking pretensions of the journalism profession. Twain—who produced a novel (*Huckleberry Finn*) that Hemingway once called the source of all American literature—also had in common with Hemingway this impulse (a hatred of phoniness, pretense, and the disingenuous practices of newspapers) based in part on a family history of distrust and dissembling. Like Hemingway's,

Twain's mother was beautiful but mentally unstable, and her suspicion of Twain's father right up to his death (she ordered an autopsy—a rare request at the time—very possibly because she believed his cause of death to be venereal disease contracted on his business trips) left Twain wounded from a home atmosphere of parental coldness toward each other, tension over his father's financial failures, and family secrets (his mother, who married Twain's father to spite a former lover, apparently never got over her prior devotion). One can argue—at least, within the emotional transference theory of Freud—that Twain's outsized resentment at the falseness of much newspaper discourse may have been rooted at least in part in his family history. (In fact, one could speculate that journalists' cynicism and mistrust of authority figures reflect the same impulses of Twain's and Hemingway's—thus making journalism particularly appealing for people with early life experiences that severed their faith in the world as a trustworthy place.)[36]

It is remarkable how often the U.K. and U.S. literary figures most associated with social and political protest and reform were connected with journalism in one way or another. In some cases, they were able to cultivate their viewpoints as they continued in journalism jobs; more often, they found a more effective forum by blending their reformer's message into their fictional works. Conventional journalism—in hailing no-fear-or-favor-expression but in owing its greatest loyalty to the marketplace—was both friendly and hostile to these venturesome writers in the nurturing of their reform spirits. Whatever the outcome of their days in journalism, the profession has attracted more than its share of personalities who had been traumatized—or were willing to be traumatized—in dealing with the social justice issues of life. One certainly does not have to look far to find trauma's spur to reform behind a credo such as Orwell's in his essay, "Why I Write": "My starting point is always a feeling of partisanship, a sense of injustice. When I sit down to write a book, I do not say to myself, 'I am going to produce a work of art.' I write it because there is some lie that I want to expose, some fact to which I want to draw attention."[37]

3

Trauma in War, Trauma in Life

The Pose of the "Heroic" Battlefield Correspondent

"I think Vietnam was what we had instead of happy childhoods."
—Michael Herr

As a war correspondent in the Spanish-American War, Stephen Crane covered the story for both the Hearst and Pulitzer newspapers, as well as serving as the subject of continuous press coverage himself. As perhaps the second most famous writer reporting on the war in Cuba, Crane cut a romantic figure trying to outdo Richard Harding Davis, the dapper prototype of the nineteenth-century war correspondent (and the most famous writer there). Riding on a pinto horse in a gleaming white rain coat, Crane would gallop along with the American regiments and head off with scouting parties, rushing to the scene when he came to any fighting (he reportedly followed the Rough Riders during their actions on San Juan Hill). At one point, Davis ordered Crane, theatrically indifferent to his life, off an embankment as bullets whistled by. The other correspondents, both awed and perplexed by his risk-taking behavior and his cool in combat conditions, were as apt to report on the feats of Crane as they were the activities of the soldiers. "There was no fear in him," one fellow correspondent reported, "so far as battle, murder, or sudden death was concerned."[1]

Yet, beneath Crane's bravado posture, was the body of a very sick man, already in serious decline from the tuberculosis that would kill him in a matter of months at age twenty-eight. There are those who believe that Crane's "grim flippancy" in the face of danger was his way of dealing with an even greater trauma concerning his own health. Some biographers think Crane knew that he was dying before he left to cover the Greco-Turkish War in

1897, and that his later Spanish-American War coverage reflected the actions of a man who understood that his death would soon be at hand one way or another. This meant that Crane's diffidence, his willingness to put himself in harm's way, and his tendency to withdraw and retreat into reverie after battle may have been as much a reaction to his awareness of his fatal affliction as it was courage under fire.[2]

Contrast this picture with that of Ambrose Bierce, the misanthropic jour-nalist-humorist–short story writer who was contemptuous of the patriotic war coverage by Crane and his fellow correspondents, called the conflict the "Yanko-Spanko War," and did not bother to ask to cover the campaign even though he was one of the top journalists for Hearst at the time. Un-like Crane, who wrote about combat in his Civil War novel, *The Red Badge of Courage*, before he ever witnessed it, Bierce's view of war was profoundly shaped by his experiences as a Union Army combatant in some of the most grisly conflicts of the U.S. Civil War, in which he was recognized for bravery and almost fatally wounded by a bullet to the head.

Some historians now speculate that Bierce very likely suffered from the ef-fects of post-traumatic stress disorder (PTSD), and they have interpreted his lifelong cynicism and his darkly scoffing writings—as well as his reluctance to go back to the scene of military conflict—as a function of the psychologi-cal stress of dealing with his Civil War experiences.[3] Bierce's handling of the trauma of warfare may have been very different than Crane's methods for dealing with the dangers of combat—but both men, considered among the great literary commentators on war, were examples of the dramatic impact of military conflict on the human psyche in eras before people talked about shell shock or PTSD or had much understanding of how the stress of the battlefield could affect one's psychological condition.

Trauma has played out in complex, and sometimes seemingly contradic-tory, ways in the life histories of the fifty-six journalist-literary figures in this study who experienced the consequences of war in up close fashion. Although Crane lacked firsthand experience in the military (he was not born until six years after the Civil War ended), he is the one who is considered to have written the great Civil War novel and to have played a prominent role in producing the jingoistic war coverage associated with the Spanish-American and Greco-Turkish wars. Crane's celebrity, his eagerness to cover the wartime conflicts of his day, and his willingness to portray combat romantically left Bierce looking with a jaundiced eye at the young writer who Bierce believed (somewhat enviously) should not get such great credit for describing battle when he had never experienced its true ferocity. In fact, the only romantic thing that Bierce ever did was to head off through the South as a melancholy seventy-one-year-old writer to tour many of his old Civil War battlefield sites before vanishing into Mexico, where his disappearance amid the violence of the Mexican Revolution has made the circumstances of his death one of the great literary mysteries of all time.[4]

One is tempted to look for evidence of PTSD in the lives of the figures in this study who witnessed terrible things as soldiers, war correspondents, medical aides, prisoners of war, or revolutionary fighters. Though a sense of shock, psychological distress, and numbed feelings can be found in the biographical accounts of their lives, it is important to note the multifaceted way that their experiences with battle influenced their emotional world and the personal philosophies that they developed to deal with those feelings. Hemingway's biographers, for example, tell of a stunned, alienated, and emotionally withdrawn young man who returned to the United States to recover from the serious shrapnel wound he suffered as an ambulance driver on the Italian front in World War I. For a long time, critics saw his novel about a disenchanted soldier in World War I, *A Farewell to Arms*, as an antiwar statement, and even a pacifist novel. In addition, there is a school of critical thought among Hemingway scholars (known as the "wound theory") that the author's life and art were indelibly shaped by the trauma of his war injury. However, by the time of World War II, Hemingway had articulated his "code" for dealing with battlefield stress ("grace under pressure"), volunteered to use his fishing boat in Cuba to watch out for German submarines, enthusiastically headed off to cover the war in Europe as a journalist, and involved himself in adventures with the troops. An irony of Hemingway's World War II reporting exploits is that it showed him to be anything but the writer of honest and authentic journalistic prose that his novels had made famous. In his journalism from the European front, Hemingway was an unreliable correspondent who told exaggerated stories about his own role in military operations, served as the source of self-aggrandizing accounts that he passed on to other reporters, and violated press conduct codes with his participation in combat activities.[5]

In recent years, psychological researchers have examined the relationship of general traumatic life experience (e.g., death of a parent while a youth, childhood abandonment, growing up with an alcoholic or mentally ill parent) and the tendency of a journalist to suffer later psychological distress or to choose a high-risk profession and/or lifestyle as a way to deal with inner psychic tension. Trauma researcher Anthony Feinstein has explored this issue in a study of twins, one of whom chose to be a war reporter and one of whom did not. Although stressing that more research needs to be done in this area, Feinstein said his study indicated that the twin who chose to be a war reporter had neurotransmitters that operated differently and measured higher levels of dopamine than her genetically identical twin who chose to stay near home and work as a law clerk. This, Feinstein said, could mean that environmental circumstances may have modified genetic predisposition, thus leading to the twins—who both showed evidence of psychic stress (the war journalist twin demonstrating elevated levels of anxiety on a trauma history questionnaire, whereas the law clerk twin described some symptoms of depression during interview questions)—responding in different ways to external stimuli and taking different approaches in their choice of career opportunities despite their similar genetic makeup.[6]

Feinstein's research is suggestive of a pattern that can be found among a number of the journalist-literary figures who chose different ways to deal with similar psychological symptoms that grew out of traumatic childhood and early life experiences. Among those in this study who covered war as journalists, many were already struggling with emotional issues linked to early life trauma—including Crane, Hemingway, Richard Harding Davis, Jack London, John Dos Passos, Graham Greene, and Michael Herr—and were positively attracted to the stimulation of frontline danger. On the other hand, others of the journalist-literary figures who suffered from youthful traumas and depression, including Philip Freneau, William Dean Howells, and Theodore Dreiser, found their coverage of violence in civilian life or encounters with military conflict so unsettling that they turned away from trauma as a focus of their journalistic careers. Feinstein notes that people are wired differently, and that one has to be cautious before trying to predict how people burdened with psychological troubles may respond to stressful life circumstances. Although there is strong evidence that some of the journalist-literary figures who were exposed to combat or coverage of violent events suffered at least some form of PTSD based on an already fragile psychological disposition, others appeared to handle it without manifesting major emotional symptoms. Some journalist-literary figures—Hemingway and Greene, for example—might have profited from heading to counseling rather than to war zones. But their war experiences did not appear to exacerbate their troubled psyches beyond what they were already experiencing. Among those who were wounded in combat situations (Bierce, Hemingway, George Orwell, J. B. Priestley, Philip Caputo), it is interesting that Hemingway, Orwell, and Caputo were happy to try to return to war zones after their recoveries whereas Bierce and Priestley were not.[7]

The likelihood that a journalist working in a war zone or suffering from PTSD will try to mask the symptoms of anxiety and stress with alcohol and/or drug use has been documented by Feinstein and other researchers, and this pattern holds up with a number of journalist-literary figures whose lives were touched by violence and war. Sigmund Freud noted that humans tend to become fixated on moments of psychological trauma and to try to gain mastery over the internal pain, but the emotional consequences can often be too big to overcome. Some of the journalist-literary figures who experienced war and engaged in serious drinking during that period—including Crane, London, Hemingway, Priestley, Greene, John Steinbeck, Evelyn Waugh, A. J. Liebling—also were heavy drinkers (and/or drug users) before and after their experiences with armed conflict and cannot blame their excessive use of substances entirely on the stress of combat.[8] Sadly, Feinstein says that other factors, including happy marriages and good personal relationships, can make journalists more emotionally resilient when they cover war or violence, but—in looking at the problematic personal and family lives of many of these figures—one can speculate that their human support system may not have been much help to them.[9]

It is striking how often journalist-literary figures that have experienced combat or traumatic events associated with warfare have adopted strategies—both in their personal lives and in the way they presented the behaviors of their war-traumatized literary characters—that reflect what trauma researchers say are typical of people coping with trauma-inducing experiences. In such literary works as Crane's *The Open Boat*, Hemingway's *The Sun Also Rises* and *A Farewell to Arms*, Dos Passos's *Three Soldiers*, Greene's *The Quiet American*, Caputo's *Del Corso's Gallery*, Martha Gellhorn's *The Stricken Field*, Elie Wiesel's *Night*, Kurt Vonnegut's *Slaughterhouse-Five*, Norman Mailer's *The Naked and the Dead*, Gloria Emerson's *Loving Graham Greene*, Tim O'Brien's *The Things They Carried*, and Bierce's short stories, one can see the main characters demonstrating at least some of the symptoms of PTSD or find indications that the authors were using the story to help them cope with the stress of overpowering feelings connected to war-related experiences. Some of their characters' strategies and behaviors—struggling to cope with intrusive memories, grappling with guilt, experiencing agitated and disrupted sleep, adopting fatalistic views, finding support and higher meaning in comradeship, looking to personal relationships and social support structures to prop up morale—are similar to ones Nigel Hunt and his colleagues found in asking a group of Korean War and World War II veterans about how they managed the aftermath of their wartime experiences. Critics have even interpreted a number of O'Brien's Vietnam War–era writings as "rewritten" texts that mimic some of Hemingway's passages about war stress (an assessment that O'Brien, in describing his writings as containing "echoes of Hemingway," to some degree has acknowledged).[10]

When examining the backgrounds of the fifty-six writers in this study who experienced armed conflict as journalists and/or participated in the military or military-related activities, just under 60 percent also suffered some form of childhood trauma (e.g., a lost parent, childhood abandonment, being raised by an alcoholic or emotionally ill parent) and more than three-quarters personally struggled with emotional and/or substance abuse difficulties at points during their adult lives. (See table 1 in the appendix.) In total, almost 90 percent were included in one or more of the categories involving childhood abandonment, mental health problems, addictions, and substance abuse. One cannot perform medical evaluations on historical figures or subject them to contemporary psychological testing, and thus it is generally not possible to say in diagnostic or research terms what was the "cause" of their psychological symptoms or their decision to expose themselves to the environment of war. But the biographical evidence warrants paying attention to the links that can be found between stressful early lives, problematic lifestyles, and journalist-literary figures' choices to become involved in military activity and to put themselves in a position to experience the circumstances of combat.

At its least complicated level, Crane and Bierce represent the polar wings of the well-known journalist-literary figures who have experienced war but came away from it with very different feelings. In Crane's case, his amalgam of poses as a war correspondent illustrates the role that war has played within the commercial press in the United States and the United Kingdom and journalists' identification with their countries' military campaigns around the globe. In much of his reporting about the Spanish-American War, Crane tended to embrace war and his country's cause in ways that also can be found in the writings of Davis, London, Rudyard Kipling, Frank Norris, and some of the later journalism of Hemingway and Steinbeck. A sizeable number of the journalist-literary figures who have known war as journalists have operated in the role of the patriot and have clearly fallen in love with the intensity of combat. It was those who sought out overseas war correspondents' jobs—often after they were already established writers and famous—who typically were most willing to give up their journalistic independence and to involve themselves directly in the combat operations that they were covering. Bierce, on the other hand, represented a second strain of journalistic reaction that can be found with writers who often reflected conflicted and skeptical views of warfare—and sometimes even antiwar and/or pacifist feelings. Interestingly, the journalist-literary figures who have viewed war in the most critical terms have tended to be those who had experienced some sort of traumatic, combat related event—a wounding, participation in intense conflict, the witnessing of civilian casualties, and/or up close involvement in caring for or transporting the injured victims of battle.[11]

The most cynical about war (as he was of most things), Bierce shared London's and Kipling's Anglophile views but not their jingoist imperialist outlook (in Kipling's case) or the blend of imperialist and leftist ideology (in the case of the socialist London). Bierce's jaundiced view of American expansionist ambitions and his refusal to glorify war were influenced by his Civil War experiences, including his involvement in the battles of Shiloh (where more Americans were killed than in the entire Revolutionary War), Chattanooga (where Bierce participated in the charge up Missionary Ridge when a Union Army company operating without orders defeated the Confederate forces), Pickett's Mill (where he participated in a gruesome frontal assault on the Confederate lines), and Kennesaw Mountain (where he was shot in the head behind the left ear, requiring months of recovery). Bierce's background has given additional force to his caustic comments about military conflict, including: "War is God's way of teaching Americans geography," and "Patriotism is fierce as fever, pitiless as the grave, blind as a stone and irrational as a headless hen."[12]

At the same time, Crane and Bierce demonstrated anything but a one-dimensional view of the role of military conflict in human affairs. Along with his journalism that conformed to the patriotic story line of Hearst and Pulitzer, Crane also wrote philosophical passages about military action that did not shirk from pointing out the senselessness of conflict. In this, Crane maintained at least some consistency in his inverse way of portraying war, writing first about combat in his critically acclaimed 1895 novel, *The Red Badge of Courage*, which was built around a young soldier-protagonist's stunned and numbed reactions to the disorienting events of battle, before Crane decided that he wanted to see battle for himself. (Crane was reported to have informed a fellow reporter on the way to covering the Greco-Turkish War that "he was off to Crete because, having written so much about war, he thought it high time he should see a little fighting"; then having seen the action, he told novelist

Joseph Conrad that *The Red Badge of Courage* was "all right.") When Crane covered war as a correspondent in Greece in 1897 and Cuba in 1898–1899, he—like his model, Davis—viewed the situation one-sidedly and was willing to frame his accounts in the pro-American and pro-Greek rhetoric that could be found in the American newspapers of the time. However, with his ironic view of life, he would punctuate this with the occasional portrayal of what he saw as the futility of combat in vivid but detached terms that helped cement his reputation as one of the great literary "naturalists."[13]

The bitterly irreverent Bierce, too, was anything but a pacifist liberal in outlook, and he mixed into his antiwar stances racist commentary about the American campaign to come to the defense of the insurgents in Cuba, which he described as "a great war to save a swamp full of anthropoid mongrels in mad reliance on the power of our Jingoes to make the crime our own." Bierce mocked the heroic ethos of soldierdom, as he did many of the pretenses attached to the patriotic position. However, as an ex-soldier, he had a highly developed sense of honor, and he drew a distinction between the soldier fulfilling a duty and an act of special bravery. He wrote of James Garfield, the Civil War general turned presidential candidate, who once retreated then returned to fight in another attack, that "there was no great heroism in it. That is what every man should have done, including the commander of the army. I did so myself, and have never felt that it ought to make me president." Bierce's impressions of the grisly side of battle—conveyed so vividly in his Civil War short fiction, which often was first printed in the newspapers where he worked—left a lifetime mark on his emotional condition and pervaded the deep, almost anarchic, debunking of public pieties that constituted his writings as an attack journalist and his stories of the shocking and the supernatural.[14]

An important manifestation of this fascination by the famous journalist-literary figures with experience in combat and/or as war correspondents was the development of the "code"—a set of personal, professional, and literary principles that went beyond simple guidelines of conduct to become a life stance, a nexus of values, and a philosophical statement about the meaning of existence in a world shorn of transcendent meaning. With its sources in a mix of Protestant and Calvinistic principles about morality and duty, British public school notions of character building, Greek stoical philosophy, and traditional military standards for conduct under fire, the "code" can be seen as incorporating the heroic and patriotic values that are identified with military training and the concept of putting one's life on the line for one's country. It also includes implicit instructions for how a person in combat conditions should be expected to deal with trauma and the experience of violence as a way for preparing to sacrifice one's self to a cause.

As reflected in the heroic (or antiheroic) characters in the writings of the famous journalist-literary figures who covered the military conflicts, often with colonial and imperialist overtones, that embroiled the United Kingdom and/or the United States during the last three centuries, elements of the code can be seen running backward and forward in time: back to Daniel Defoe's principled pirate figure, Captain Singleton, and Thomas Paine's rhetorical exhortations to the American Revolutionary troops in the eighteenth century, through Mark Twain's satire of romantic values of honor in *A Connecticut Yankee in King Arthur's Court* and Bret Harte's honorable gold miners and gentlemanly saloon gamblers in the nineteenth century, and forward to H. H. Munro's and Orwell's journalism and other writings about the noble military cause in the twentieth century. It is interesting, for example, that James Joyce once identified elements of the code in Defoe's *Robinson Crusoe*, which Joyce called the "embodiment" of British imperialism: "persistence, manly independence, slow yet efficient intelligence, well-balanced religiousness, calculating taciturnity, unconscious cruelty."[15] But it was during the latter half of the nineteenth century when British and American notions of manifest destiny and the strenuous life modeled by Teddy Roosevelt had captured the popular imagination that journalist-literary figures led the way in the creation of a heroic mythology for war correspondents and the fictional protagonists that they forged from their experiences in witnessing war.

Although journalists who were politically conservative and strong supporters of a nationalistic foreign policy have tended to be identified with the code, it also has been subscribed to in various and modified forms by journalist-literary figures who were seen in their day as liberals and even leftist radicals, as well as by those whose political views were kept under wraps or expressed in idiosyncratic and often inconsistent ways. It is interesting how often it was international warfare that brought out the chauvinistic tendencies in some of the liberal-, leftist-, or once-pacifist-oriented of the well-known journalist-literary figures. In a sense, one can see these writers as mirroring the press organizations for which they worked, and which often were politically moderate, even liberal, in their editorial page views on domestic matters but nationalists when it came to their country's overseas military role.

The influence of trauma and psychological stress has operated within elements of the code in both direct and indirect ways. Because soldiers, war correspondents, and other military ancillary personnel know the implications of the life-and-death circumstances they face, the code has come to offer models for how to deal with physical suffering, psychological stress, and dangerous situations that require the taking of action. Scholars have been influenced by Philip Young's theory that Hemingway's repeated creation of literary characters who demonstrate honor and courage under the stress of war was his way of trying to master the trauma of his own youthful wounding. At the same time, Hemingway's advocacy of stoicism in the face of mortality also has been interpreted as an act of repression on his part and as evidence that he lived much of his life in denial and avoided directly dealing with psychological pain. This has left some analysts to speculate that his heroic philosophy and his seeking out of high-risk experiences were really attempts to compensate for a profound sense of inadequacy. O'Brien, for example, has said that he never put much store in what he felt was the posturing element of Hemingway's definition of courage. O'Brien's experiences as a soldier in the Vietnam War, with all the moral ambiguities that came to be attached to it, led him instead to define courage as trying to do the right thing in the midst of evil. Courage, O'Brien added, "is the endurance of the soul in spite of fear—wisely."[16]

Psychologists also would look for other motives in those who seek out risky and emotionally intense experiences. For a person such as Hemingway, who was troubled by anxiety and psychological stress, life could be especially difficult when he experienced those symptoms at times when there was no direct reason or source for the feelings. Sometimes this kind of person will seek out situations that are stressful to counterbalance the emptiness and despair that can set in if life is not being lived at heightened levels of intensity. When this happens, the theory goes, a person will feel most comfortable in his or her skin—and sometimes the most so when there is the greatest hazard to personal safety (thus fulfilling an acknowledged or unacknowledged death wish, as Freudian theory would imply).

The War Traumatized

Bierce was not the first journalist-literary figure to have seen warfare up close and to find that it left a lasting impression on his conscience and emotions. Tobias Smollett's accounts of the brutality of naval life in his 1748 novel, *Roderick Random*, have been criticized as exaggerations that fit into Smollett's tendency to use caricature and extreme personalities in his fiction. However, one critic has noted that—in his accounts of naval warfare, at least—Smollett, who served as a British navy ship's surgeon, was very probably not overstating the horrific conditions aboard a man-of-war of the time. Douglas Jerrold, one of the founders of *Punch* magazine in 1841, had gone to sea at ten, and as a midshipman, he saw floggings and the terrible injuries of battle. These experiences dismayed him, and—like Bierce—he claimed never to have been fooled during his journalistic career by glorious descriptions of war. Freneau was a third mate on an American ship that was captured by the British in 1780. He was placed in a prison ship where he was treated harshly, kept below decks for days with other prisoners in heat and stench, and then transferred to a hospital ship where the conditions were not much better. "I expected to die before morning," he said at one point. "But human nature can bear more than one would first suppose." The mistreatment became a shaping force for his political views (he came to hate all things British while also harboring a revulsion against war and violence), as well as his journalism and his poetry. In scores of visits that he made to wounded Union Army soldiers in hospitals, Walt Whitman was exposed to poignant scenes of trauma and suffering, and his encounters triggered the poetic sensitivities of someone who saw beyond the terrible wounds and maiming to a higher spiritual meaning, but who nonetheless experienced anguish in the empathy he felt for the dying soldiers.[17]

Throughout his life, Whitman alternated between a gentle advocacy of peace-loving principles and a nationalistic fervor for war, which was reflected in jingoistic editorials he wrote for the *Brooklyn Eagle* in support of American entry into the Mexican-American War. Concerned at the news of the wounding of his brother, George, as a Union soldier at Fredericksburg in December 1862, Whitman searched him out in a military hospital, where he saw others whose wounds were much worse than what turned out to be the relatively mild injury of his brother's. This led Whitman to volunteer as a nurse at Washington, D.C., war hospitals, where he sat for hours at the bedsides of the wounded soldiers. Although Whitman had mixed feelings about the taking up of arms in the Union cause, he came to believe that the Civil War helped to purify America by laying out the case for abolition openly, and he reacted to the recovery room scene in intensely mystical ways. For Whitman, soldierly sacrifice became akin to Christian brotherhood; he would refer to battles as crucifixion day; and he ultimately found his work in the hospitals to be soul restoring. Critics have commonly seen Whitman's spiritual response to the soldiers' conditions as necessary for him to preserve his idealism and to deal with the psychic strain of working amid the maiming and loss. ("Poor youth, so handsome, athletic, with profuse beautiful shining hair," Whitman said of one young soldier. "One time as I sat looking at him while he lay asleep, he suddenly, without the least start, awaken'd, open'd his eyes, gave me a long steady look, turning his face very slightly to gaze easier—one long, clear, silent look—a slight sigh—then turn'd back and went into his doze again. Little he knew, poor death-stricken boy, the heart of the stranger that hover'd near.")[18]

Yet, it also was not unusual to find Whitman—the exuberant, romantic poet—discussing his reactions to the injured soldiers in straightforward and unemotional terms in *Specimen Days*, his journalistic diary of his nursing experience ("I notice a heap of amputated feet, legs, arms, hands . . . a full load for a one-horse cart . . . I go around from one case to another. I do not see that I do much good to these wounded and dying; but I cannot leave them"). Whitman's training as a journalist in the early nineteenth century— and the profession's encouragement to tell a story sometimes in the sparest of prose, sometimes in rhetorically elevated terms—is evident in the muted prose manner in which he often described the scene compared with the passionate and unrestrainedly optimistic poetry of *Leaves of Grass*, which was published only a few years before the war's outbreak. One can say that the coming of the Civil War shattered the mood of romantic idealism and faith in American destiny that Whitman represented as a poetic figure, and this may account for the somber tone *of Specimen Days*. However, Whitman's choice to deal with his nursing experience largely in prose rather than poetic form also may signal that he believed more prosaic journalistic writing to be the appropriate way to respond to the depth of the human trauma he witnessed— although on occasion he could not help expressing emotion. ("There they lie . . . in an open space in the woods, from 200 to 300 poor fellows—the groans and screams—the odor of blood, mixed with the fresh scent of the night, the grass, the trees—that slaughter-house!") Yet, no matter how awful the suffering that he saw, Whitman's fundamentally romantic outlook on the war—and the expression of his support for the Union cause—was unaffected. ("It was a pronouncedly warlike and gay show; the sabers clank'd, the men look'd young and healthy and strong . . . the gallant bearing, fine seat, and bright faced appearance of a thousand and more handsome young American men, were so good to see," he wrote of one military parade.)[19]

Although he considered himself a critic of the school of literary realism, Bierce was intensely realistic in his portrayal of the carnage of the Civil War battlefields—to such a degree that H. L. Mencken called him "the first writer of fiction ever to treat war realistically" and the only major American writer who knew firsthand what the Civil War had meant to the soldiers on the battlefield. Angered throughout his life by glorified portrayals of war, Bierce battled "the gilded hypocrisy" and the "aggressive heroizing" of his time with his witty, sardonic, and polemical columns that lashed out against the U.S. imperialist ventures in Cuba and the Philippines. But, even more memorably, he wrote fictional short stories, which often were penned in parallel with nonfictional, journalistic accounts that portrayed in stark and vivid fashion the traumas experienced by the individual soldier as Bierce had witnessed them in some of the Civil War's most harrowing battles: at Girard Hill, where he carried off a fallen comrade in open view of Confederate riflemen who sprayed bullets at him, and Stone's River, where he rescued a wounded officer (which led to one of the fifteen commendations that he earned for bravery under fire), as well as overseeing two military executions and surviving a lead ball to the skull at Kennesaw Mountain. Even though he praised soldiers who showed heroism on the battlefield and commanders whose intelligence and tactical skills he respected, Bierce built his writing career around his uncompromising descriptions of the fighting, the psychological impact of battlefield stress, and his blunt assessments of the emotions that truly motivated a soldier (fear that he would be left behind, embarrassment at being called a coward). Like Edgar Allan Poe, Bierce tended to build his stories around a single horrific incident and the feelings of an isolated combatant who was facing the moment of mortality. Many of Bierce's scenes in his Civil War short stories are more shocking to the sensibilities than anything that he wrote in his equally famous tales of the macabre and the paranormal: a small child who climbs on a wounded soldier's back, thinking he is playing horsey, only to have the man turn a shattered face on the boy; a wounded soldier, caught under the timbers of a building collapsed by a mortar shell, working methodically to position his pinned rifle so he can point it to his temple and pull the trigger; an officer with his intestine looping outside his stomach wound, begging with his eyes to have a fellow officer thrust his sword into him and end his misery. Even though there were those who complained, Bierce never shirked from portraying graphically those incidents that he said were "too dreadful to describe." It "commonly occurs that in my poor little battle-yarns the incidents that come in for special reprobation by the critics as 'improbable' and even 'impossible' are transcripts from memory—things that actually occurred before my eyes," Bierce said.[20]

In reversing the techniques of the yellow journalism of his day, Bierce's accounts of battle were invariably as vivid and unvarnished as the sensationalistic techniques that the tabloid press used to illustrate the details of crime and deviance. But Bierce applied the principle equally to military conflict and eschewed the heroic and patriotic framework that a publisher such as

William Randolph Hearst used to present American imperialistic ventures. In the journalistic versions of his Civil War reminiscences (many published in Hearst's *San Francisco Examiner*), Bierce described a wounded sergeant, laying "face upward, taking in his breath in convulsive, rattling snorts, and blowing it out in sputters of froth which crawled creamily down his checks." In a Confederate charge "the forest seemed all at once to flame up and disappear with a crash like that of a great wave upon the beach—a crash that expired in hot hissings, and the sickening 'spat' of lead against flesh. A dozen of my brave fellows tumbled over like ten-pins." One can compare these scenes to his fictional battlefield accounts in "An Affair of Outposts" ("The sound of the conflict was a clatter like that of the interlocking horns of battling bulls—now and then the [b]ash of a crushed skull, an oath, or a grunt caused by the impact of a rifle's muzzle against the abdomen transfixed by its bayonet") and "One Officer, One Man" ("Captain Graffenreid lay alongside the dead man, from beneath whose breast flowed a little rill of blood. It had a faint, sweetish odor that sickened him. . . . Nothing suggested the glory of a soldier's death nor mitigated the loathsomeness of the incident"). When Bierce deviated from the relentless verisimilitude of his accounts, he laced his stories with irony and sarcasm (a governor visiting the front lines who is foolishly caught up in an attack—"This is beastly!" he says to himself. "Where is the charm of it all? Where are the elevated sentiments, the devotion, the heroism"—and then finds himself next to the corpse of the captain who had rescued him. "It was so near that the great man could have laid his hand upon it, but he did not," Bierce wrote. "He may have feared that it would bleed").[21]

Bierce wielded his commitment to honesty like a sword throughout his career, and he seemed to take personally every effort by people to dress up issues of war and peace in glorifying and romantic terms. ("There never was a war in which both or all the tribes engaged did not believe that their fighters showed themselves wonderfully courageous—never one in which the noncombatants did not beslubber the soldiery with silly adulation for qualities which are the common heritage of mankind.") Yet, beneath his polemics was Bierce the veteran soldier who never forgot the trauma that he had experienced and whose anger was palpable at the injury done to him. "We are backing our men to win, but in our secret hearts . . . we keep a muttering disappointment that resents the facile triumphs of the American arms," he wrote during the Spanish-American War. "We want harder fighting, more gore. . . . Who of us does not experience an honest, patriotic satisfaction when shown by irrefutable figures that Chickamauga was the bloodiest battle of modern times, that at Spotsylvania the trenches had repeatedly to be cleared of the dead?" It is even possible to see his stories of the supernatural as fundamentally realistic, at least in Bierce's mind, in the sense that he sometimes would describe his experiences of combat conditions as almost "supernatural" in feeling. Bierce's short story, "An Occurrence at Owl Creek Bridge"—in its confusion of fact with fantasy in the telling of a story of the hanging of a Confederate sympathizer who imagines the rope breaks as he plunges to his death—communicated something of the surreal quality that Bierce found both in the nature of warfare and in his personal feelings of disassociation and emotional alienation as he labored to hold together his shell-shocked personality through the rest of his life.[22]

As much as Bierce found emotional release in his literary recreations of his combat memories, others of the journalist-literary figures who were injured or involved in war preferred not to discuss their experiences—or, if they did, they often applied imagination to their portrayals as a way to filter what they had personally experienced. Priestley served with British forces in the trenches in France in World War I where he was wounded and deafened for a time when a shell crashed near him. After a lengthy convalescence, he returned to the front, only to be declared unfit for combat after inhaling mustard gas that leaked through his mask. Although he wrote upon first hearing the guns at the front that "flesh and blood had no place in this factory of destruction," he did not like talking about his combat experiences later in life. However, biographers have noted that after he was taken out of service and given a clerk's job, he sustained himself with bottles of Guinness that he could buy at one franc a bottle. He also came to dislike traveling on the underground throughout his later civilian life for fear that the earth would close in around him (as it did when he was buried by the explosion that injured him in the trenches). As an ambulance driver at the German front in World War I, Dos Passos described the difficulties of bringing back the wounded as a mixture of "boredom" and "desolation." "I cannot find words to translate my impressions," he wrote. "Hell cannot be so terrible. Men are mad!" Although battlefield experience is not the focus of his novel, *Three Soldiers*, Dos Passos's imagined scenes of trauma laid the groundwork for the main plot line (his most important character, John Andrews, decides to go AWOL). Dos Passos clearly drew from his ambulance experiences in his scenes of the infantryman Andrews being transported back to the medical facility after suffering a shrapnel wound (he realized his "legs were on fire. He tried to move them; everything went black again in a sudden agony of pain. . . . His mind became entirely taken up in the curious rhythm of his groans. The only parts of his body that existed were his legs and something in his throat that groaned and groaned"), as well as his encounters with soldiers suffering from PTSD in describing a recovering Andrews thinking about not going back to his military post ("Andrews was telling himself that the war was over, and that in a few months he would be free in any case. . . . But the same thoughts were swept recklessly away in the blind panic that was like a stampede of wild steers within him. There was no arguing. His spirit was contorted with revolt so that his flesh twitched and dark splotches danced before his eyes. He wondered vaguely whether he had gone mad"). Still, Dos Passos also found that his politics (which changed from left to right during his lifetime) tended to frame his literary portrayals of war throughout his career—and which was captured in his ambivalent comments even as a young leftist. "Curiously enough I adore la vie militaire, apart from my convictions," he said.[23]

Vera Brittain's traumatic experiences providing medical care for British troops in Malta during World War I—combined with the loss of her fiancé, her brother, and two of his close friends while in the military—was life shaping in its emotional impact on her. In chronicling in her antiwar memoir, *Testament of Youth*, her evolution from provincial young woman who signed up to be a volunteer nurse to demonstrate her support for the war into a feminist, socialist, and pacifist, Brittain acknowledged the role of traumatic emotions in refashioning her worldview. "I am often asked when I first became a pacifist," Brittain wrote. "It is always difficult to recall the exact moment of 'conversion.'" But Brittain told of a day when she had just finished "the gruesome and complicated dressing of a desperately wounded prisoner" and her thinking, "Wasn't it somehow odd that I . . . should be trying to save the life of a man whom my brother . . . had perhaps done his best to kill?"[24]

For much of her nursing period in Malta and in England from 1914 to1919, Brittain described herself as a "complete automaton" existing in a state of "numb disillusion." First, she received the news of the death of her fiancé, Roland Leighton, who died as a combatant in France in 1915. "The worst of the whole thing is that I get so very depressed," she wrote. "I haven't the energy to write much and reading for long at a time tires my eyes . . . so I lie for hours & think about Roland & go over & over in my mind all the times I saw Him & all the details of His death until there seems nothing worth having left in the future at all." Although she struggled with her urges to give up nursing, she stayed at it—including through the numbness of grief that she experienced at the deaths of two close friends of her brother, Edward. Edward's death in action in June 1918, left Brittain and her family devastated (her father, Arthur, fell into a deep depression that lasted until his suicide in 1935 and that, in combination with the memory of her brother's death, contributed to a deep and pervasive sadness experienced by both Brittain and her mother for the rest of their lives). "Now there were no more disasters to dread and no friends left to wait for," Brittain wrote. "With the ending of apprehension had come a deep, nullifying blankness, a sense of walking in a thick mist which hid all sights and muffled all sounds. I had no further experience to gain from the war; nothing remained except to endure it."[25]

Although he was not a soldier, John Hersey's stark accounts that grew out of his reporting during and after World War II dealt in acute fashion with trauma—those of some of the most horrific and violent events in human history, including his research among the survivors of the Jewish Holocaust and the atomic bombing of Hiroshima, and his own trauma in facing up to the devastating emotional implications of what had happened during the war. After covering a number of World War II campaigns for *Time* magazine and sustaining injuries in a plane crash while working as a correspondent on Guadalcanal, Hersey based his postwar novel, *A Bell for Adano*, on his observations of General George Patton and the American administration of the Italian front. However, Hersey's most traumatic experiences came as he chronicled what the world did not fully know about the Holocaust or Hiroshima. In his nonfictional *Hiroshima* and his fictional novel about the Holocaust, *The Wall*, Hersey played a frontline role in revealing to the public the full story of humankind's capacity for inflicting inhumanity on its fellows. Although both books were notable for the detached manner in which Hersey told the stories, Hersey acknowledged the profound impact on his emotional state. "I wish I could convey how shocking, how life-changing, that story was to me in my unknowing state at that time," he said of his interviews with the survivors of the Nazi death camps.[26]

In *Hiroshima*, Hersey deliberately adopted a flat style to let the words of the survivors speak for themselves, and he let his straightforward prose convey the ghastly scene (one local doctor working in a Red Cross hospital, he wrote, realized that there were so many burned and lacerated victims that he began to "pass up the lightly wounded; he decided that all he could hope to do was to stop people from bleeding to death. Before long, patients lay and crouched on the floors of the ward and laboratories and all the other rooms, and in the corridors, and on the stairs, and in the front hall, and under the porte-cochere, and on the stone front steps, and in the driveway and courtyard, and for blocks each way in the streets outside"; a Catholic priest, in trying to help injured people in a park, came across twenty wounded men, probably anti-aircraft personnel, whose "faces were wholly burned, their eyesockets were hollow, the fluid from their melted eyes had run down their cheeks"). Often seen as an early example of the "new journalism," *Hiroshima* is still widely recognized as an iconic work in the establishment of the field of memory research and the art of interviewing as methods for recognizing the impact of trauma in life. It also is a work that can be viewed in the context of "secondary traumatization"—and teachers who have assigned it to their students have suggested that the possibility that it might prove to be highly disturbing should be recognized and accounted for in school use of the book.[27]

Kurt Vonnegut produced his literary antiwar statement, *Slaughterhouse-Five*, in what he implied became an almost obligatory effort to "write out" the trauma of his witnessing of the American fire bombing of Dresden while he was a prisoner of war in Germany during World War II. Vonnegut has described his struggles trying to write his "famous Dresden book" until he hit on a strategy that allowed him to complete it more than twenty years after his detainment. It became a story about Billy Pilgrim, a passive and diffident optometrist, who remembers his war experiences through the filter of a postwar nervous breakdown where he oscillates between memories of Dresden and hallucinations that he has been kidnapped by space aliens from the planet, Tralfamadore. With satire and black humor as the means for keeping his distance from his traumatic memories, Vonnegut used a variety of literary devices to convey his moral message ("Now, when I hear that somebody is dead, I simply shrug and say what the Tralfamadorians say about dead people, which is 'So it goes'"). The novel contains a number of scenes that describe what Vonnegut might have witnessed as a prisoner who—after surviving the bombing locked up in a slaughterhouse converted into a prison—was pressed into service by the Germans excavating bodies from the rubble. He describes a fellow prisoner who dies from violent dry heaves after being sent below ground where bodies have rotted and liquefied; in another scene, prisoners in a below-ground meat locker receive reports from a guard about what the explosives were doing to the city (the extent of the firebombing, one of the book's characters notes, was kept secret from the American public until well after the end of World War II "for fear that a lot of bleeding hearts might not think it was such a wonderful thing to do"). Meanwhile, as Vonnegut reported as he was writing the book, which was published in 1969, "every day my government gives me a count of corpses created by military science in Vietnam." Vonnegut then conceded that his novel "is a failure, and had to be, since it was written by a pillar of salt." People "aren't supposed to look back," he added. "I'm certainly not going to do it anymore. I've finished my war book now. The next one I write is going to be fun."[28]

One can only imagine what it was like for Vonnegut to deal with his Dresden experience only months after the events of his mother's suicide, and it is a logical interpretation to see him commenting on the insanity and dysfunction that underlay not only American military policy but also the surface of a family life. With a father who was severely depressed (at least partly connected to the loss of family wealth in the Great Depression) and a neurotic mother who killed herself with an overdose of sleeping pills while Vonnegut was home on leave in May 1944, Vonnegut was in a frail mental state when his unit was cut off from his American combat battalion during the Rhineland campaign, and he was captured by the Germans and imprisoned in December of the same year. His cataloguing of the absurdities of his war experiences (he received his Purple Heart for a "ludicrously negligible wound"—frostbite; his character, Edgar Derby in *Slaughterhouse-Five*, dies by firing squad when the Germans catch him with a teapot he took as a souvenir while digging in the catacombs of Dresden) put him in the ranks of other mordant fictionists with experience with both wartime incarceration and in the journalism business (including P. G. Wodehouse, whose *The Swoop!*, his 1909 satire of the pre–World War I German invasion novel, prefigured his own World War II experience, when he was arrested by the Germans in France where he had a country home and then bitterly criticized back in England for a series of light-hearted broadcasts that he agreed to make for the Germans while in detainment). The multiple levels of Vonnegut's trauma can be seen within the framework of *Slaughterhouse-Five*, where the "hidden" stories—of what really happened in Dresden, of what lay below the "moonscape" that the bombing left behind, of the real picture of his family's emotional distress and its impact on him—are illuminated through his sardonic commentary mixed with his darkly satirical recounting of Pilgrim's surrealistic memories. Vonnegut's method for describing the "madness" of warfare and the moral contradictions of American cultural and political life only grew in popularity as American military causes grew less popular, and his novel about World War II as a statement about the Vietnam War was embraced by the war protesting left of the 1970s. Interestingly, Vonnegut—who worked briefly as a reporter for a Chicago news bureau after he returned from Germany—presented journalism as one of those frameworks that packages life in ways that made no sense to a war-traumatized veteran. In the nonfictional portion of the novel, Vonnegut described how he was asked to break the news to a woman whose husband had been crushed and killed when his ring finger caught in an elevator door. When Vonnegut returned after getting his comment from her, an employee in the news bureau asked him (while she was eating a Three Musketeers candy bar) what the squashed guy had looked like, and if it had bothered him. "'Heck, no, Nancy,' I said. 'I've seen lots worse than that in the war.'"[29]

With Hersey and Vonnegut as bridge figures, the incorporation of trauma into their awareness and their willingness to be candid about war's impact on the psyche became the hallmark of war journalists and novelists of the 1960s and beyond. The Vietnam War generation of journalist-literary figures reflected in their emotional lives, as did the United States as a whole, the shock, pain, and the moral ambiguities of the first lost war in the nation's history. The war writings of Herr, Caputo, O'Brien, and Emerson depart in important ways from much earlier American war literature in the intensely personal and graphically realistic ways that they portrayed battle and in the antiheroical manner in which they compared the so-called glories of war with its real terror and ghastliness. The Vietnam War has been said to have shorn Americans of their illusions about the romance of warfare and their sense of idealistic mission in the world, and the fictional, nonfictional, and semifictional writings of this group are notable for dealing vividly with the folly of the American military strategy in Vietnam, as well as the mind-altering intensity of modern jungle warfare and the pressures on American soldiers of fighting an indigenous enemy in a conflict with no clear moral or strategic demarcations.

Herr, in particular, conveyed the countercultural attitudes of the young people who looked askance at the war while spending a year as a freelance journalist in the war's early stages. His highly personal, surrealistically textured accounts of his on-the-ground combat observations reflected his own fragile emotional state both before and after he went to Vietnam. Agoraphobic and a heavy marijuana user, Herr observed the battlefield through a heightened (and often drug overloaded) sensory system that captured in his impressionistic style of countercultural writing the crazy-making nature of guerilla counterinsurgency warfare and the alienated mood of the times. "Maybe you couldn't love the war and hate it inside the same instant, but sometimes those feelings alternated so rapidly that they spun together in a strobic wheel rolling all the way up until you were literally High On War. . . . Coming off a jag like that could really make a mess out of you,"[30] he wrote.

After returning from Vietnam, Herr suffered what he called a "massive collapse" and described in interviews the anguish of his existence holed up in a Greenwich Village apartment. "I couldn't wait to get stoned every day, not high, stoned, unconscious," he said. "The terror I felt, it was worse than Vietnam." What kept him going was the hope that he could expand the Vietnam reporting he did for *Esquire* magazine into something that would redeem the experience for him. "Sometimes I was crazy in a very public way, and after I crashed, I was crazy in a very private way. Except . . . I always believed that there was another door on the other side of me that I could go through and come out of with a book under my arm," he said. In his much-praised account of his experiences, *Dispatches*, which was published in 1977 (more than seven years after his return from Vietnam), Herr both recognized the conventional journalistic limits in covering this kind of warfare and the psychological cost of reporting the "death face" of jungle combat. "I went to cover the war and the war covered me. . . . The problem was that you didn't always know what you were seeing until later, maybe years later, that a lot of it never made it in at all, it just stayed stored there in your eyes," Herr wrote. "Time and information, rock and roll, life itself, the information isn't frozen, you are." Later Herr told of how he continued to get queries from editors who hoped that he would be interested in covering a new war. "Every time there's a shot fired around the world, I get a call from some magazine to go," he said. "I don't want to see it ever again. I don't want to, man."[31]

Emerson's Vietnam War journalistic and book-length accounts focused less on the war itself than on the effect of the violence on both the American and the Vietnamese people. She wrote particularly movingly about the impact of advanced American military bombing technology on the lives of the Vietnamese people and how the impersonal slaughter of the civilian population insulated the war's consequences from the conscience of Americans. "For fifteen years it was a country that haunted me and held me," said Emerson of her reporting on the war for the *New York Times*. "It still does. I do not expect to recover." Emerson's struggles growing up with an alcoholic father; her reporting about conflicts in Northern Ireland, Algeria, Gaza, and Central America; and her fascination with the moral quandaries and writing exploits of Greene (as reflected in her novel, *Loving Graham Greene*, with its naively good-hearted heroine trying to help out journalists caught up in the dangers of the Algerian conflict), left Emerson with a reputation (reinforced by her suicide in 2004) as one of the first female prototypes of the restless journalist seeking out overseas assignments as a way to deal with a conflicted conscience and a troubled inner life. Caputo, who served both as a military combatant in Vietnam in 1965–1966 and then a correspondent for the *Chicago Tribune* during the fall of Saigon in the mid-1970s, described in his Vietnam War memoir, *A Rumor of War*, how he felt guilty after he left the frontline ranks and was given a clerk's job recording combat deaths as if they were "numbers" on a scorecard. "One of its symptoms is a hatred for everything and everyone around you; now I hated myself as well, plunging into morbid depressions and thinking about committing suicide in some socially acceptable way—say, by throwing myself on an enemy grenade." Like Tracy Kidder—who, as a first lieutenant in Army Intelligence from 1967 to 1969, conveyed some of the same themes of despair and disillusionment, and also implied that he considered suicide during his lowest points in Vietnam—Caputo was particularly vivid in describing the grief and anxiety of the soldiers that could set off fits of morbidity and rage. "I had begun to see almost everyone as they would look in death, including myself," he wrote. "Shaving in the mirror in the morning, I could see myself dead, and there were moments when I not only saw my own corpse, but other people looking at it." Away from the action, Caputo described emotions that are associated with PTSD, "a feeling of being afraid when there was no reason to be. And this unreasoning fear quickly produced the sensation I had often had in action: of watching myself in a movie. . . . My sensations were those of a man actually under fire . . . I was outwardly normal, if a little edgier than usual; but inside, I was full of turbulent emotions and disordered thoughts." It is notable that Caputo's stressed response to his soldiering experience in Vietnam did not keep him from returning to Vietnam and going to other global hot spots as a war correspondent for the *Tribune*—including Lebanon, where he was wounded and held as a hostage while covering the civil war (and which, along with his Vietnam reporting, served as the backdrop for his novel about overseas newspaper journalists, *Del Corso's Gallery*). However, Caputo's fiction—while highly realistic in its picture of battle zones—is less forthcoming in discussing the consequences of trauma on the psyche than is the case in his journalistic memoir. In the novel, Caputo alludes to the ways that the effects of trauma can leak out—particularly in Del Corso's relationship with his long-suffering wife and the comparison of Del Corso to Greene ("he [Greene] was miserable inside . . . he was afraid of what he might do if he ever stopped moving. . . . It was like wars and traveling were a drug to him"). But the hard-bitten war photographer–protagonist, Del Corso, who dies in Beirut covering the civil war, is typically close-to-the-vest in never fully revealing why it was that he (like his creator, Caputo, who has followed in Greene's footsteps by reporting on and setting his fiction in such global conflict zones as Afghanistan, Sudan, the Horn of Africa, the Mexican-U.S. border, as well as Lebanon and Vietnam) has found it irresistible to keep returning to the scene of trauma and war.[32]

In the ultimate sense, the most traumatized of the journalist-literary figures involved in war was Munro, who died of a sniper's bullet while serving with the British forces at the front in World War I. The son of a career military officer who served in the military police in Burma, Munro was a strong believer in the code of heroic conduct and a proud supporter of British military imperialism. While establishing his reputation as a short-story writer, Munro also worked in the Balkans, Poland, and Russia as a correspondent for the London *Morning Post* and covered the Bloody Sunday uprising in St. Petersburg in 1905. Described as selfless, sincere, and honorable after volunteering as a soldier in France in 1915–1916, his last words at the front line were reportedly "put that bloody cigarette out." A German sniper heard the shout, and in a moment, he was dead. Earlier, in his philosophizing about war in the *Morning Post*, Munro had written, "Somehow, in spite of its horrors, there seems to be something in it different to anything else in the world, something a little bit finer. . . . The thrill that those far-off things call forth in us may be ethically indefensible, but it comes in the first place from something too deep to be driven out."[33]

The Subscribers to the Code and Those Who Did Not Want to See Themselves as Traumatized

One cannot disconnect the experiences of journalist-literary figures from the historical circumstances of their ages, and the late nineteenth and early twentieth centuries were periods when the colonial ambitions of the world's great powers were peaking and military conflicts were breaking out in many parts of the globe. Press organizations played an important role in these conflicts—both in terms of covering them and, in certain cases, promoting them. Most commonly, American and British newspapers reported on the conflicts with the newly emergent standards of "objectivity"—but an objectivity that was defined such that war was largely presented from a sometimes conscious and sometimes unconscious sympathy for the American and English military and diplomatic standpoint. In its most extreme form, newspapers of this period were blamed for fomenting war—as was the case leading up to the Spanish-American War when Joseph Pulitzer's *New York World* and Hearst's *New York Journal* outdid each other with scare headlines and sensationalized stories of alleged Spanish atrocities in Cuba. A favorite tactic of the newspapers of this period was to employ celebrity writers and journalists to go beyond plain battlefield accounts and to cover the conflicts with color and personality. Over the years, big name journalist-literary figures who were hired to report on war included Davis, Crane, Kipling, London, Hemingway, Steinbeck, Greene, Mencken, Liebling, Frank Norris, Evelyn Waugh, Langston Hughes, and Edna Ferber. A number (such as Mencken, Kipling, Ferber, and Waugh) never witnessed much real battlefield action and got their material mostly by hanging out with other war correspondents at hotel bars or making the rounds speaking to military officers, government officials, and soldiers when they were not at the front. But others—such as Davis and Crane in the Spanish-American War, London in the Russo-Japanese War, Hemingway and Steinbeck in World War II, and Greene and Steinbeck in Vietnam—put themselves in real danger in order to do their jobs.[34]

Phillip Knightley, in his history of war correspondents from the Crimean to the Vietnam wars, calls 1865 to 1914—when Kipling, Crane, and Hemingway all developed or were developing their professional values and their journalistic ethos—the "golden age" of war correspondents. Knightley described the scribes of this period as frustrated soldiers whose main motivation was to fulfill "a thirst for battle and adventure." A physically brave, slightly disreputable, and highly colorful crew, they showed "little humanity and no historical perspective," Knightley said, nor did they have the "hearing ear and the seeing eye" to discern the deeper implications of combat. "They pandered to the blood thirsty tastes of the age. . . . War, for most of them was a highly profitable game, and they became thrill purveyors. . . . [Few] felt sufficiently concerned over what they witnessed to write in protest against the conduct of war, to be partisans for truth and compassion rather than adventure or glory," Knightley wrote.[35]

The powerful pull of the image of the heroic journalist can be seen even in the lives of journalists who were skeptics of colonialism and foreign wars carried on in the name of colonialism. The socialist Orwell—whose politics could not have been more diametrically opposed to Kipling's—nonetheless was a defender of the great imperialist, not the least because as a fellow child brought up in Asia by parents working within the British colonial system they shared the same stoical and dutiful view of life and human responsibility. (Orwell, who criticized Kipling for his tolerance of brutality and his moral insensitivity to the ills of colonialism, nonetheless wrote, "Every enlightened person has despised him, [but] at the end of that time nine-tenths of those enlightened persons are forgotten and Kipling is in some sense still there.")[36]

The manner in which Hemingway's heroic ideal loomed over his generation and generations since can be seen in the lineup of other prominent journalist-literary figures—including Steinbeck, Dos Passos, O'Brien, John O'Hara, Wallace Stevens, Dorothy Parker, Richard Wright, Norman Mailer, Hunter S. Thompson, Pete Hamill—who spent considerable energy focusing on Hemingway and evaluating their experiences against his ideal of bravery, adventuring, and risk-taking as the measure of life. (Parker's *New*

Yorker profile of him was a major factor in establishing Hemingway's saga; the famous phrase—"grace under pressure"—was elicited from Hemingway when Parker, who liked to see herself as one of the boys who viewed life as he did, asked him to define *guts*.) Kipling and Crane, too, exercised an enormous influence on their contemporaries and journalist-literary figures who came after them—with Hemingway, who read both avidly, acknowledging a great debt to each. These expanding circles of influence—with journalist-literary figures who embraced the notion of the valorous journalist in turn influencing other journalist-literary figures—can be explained by the tremendous resonance that the heroic code has had throughout journalistic history. Whether it was Paine in the eighteenth century ("The glow of hope, courage, and fortitude will, in a little time, supply the place of every inferior passion, and kindle the whole heart into heroism"), Norris in the nineteenth century (he could not wait to see "the correspondent in all his glory, leaping from a dispatch boat . . . dashing ashore in all the panoply of pith helmet, Norfolk jacket, and field glasses, a bundle of dispatches in one hand, racing his fellows to the telegraph office"), or Munro in the twentieth century ("I have always looked forward to the romance of a European war"), the heroic ideal has come to define the nobility of the journalistic mission and to infuse the journalistic credo with a romantic glow that (while satirized by journalist-literary figures as often as it has been seriously advanced) has left a deep mark on the profession. Yet, beneath the heroic code—as one can learn from exploring the emotional wounds of its great proponents—lurk deeper questions of human psychology and of the way human beings deal (or do not deal directly) with the pain of traumatic experience.[37]

As expressed by Crane, Kipling, and Hemingway—the three most prominent promulgators of the ideal of the heroic modern journalist—the code of courageous journalistic conduct can be summarized in some or all of the following ways: Life is all that we have, and it should be experienced to the hilt; one's identity is best discovered in action and by testing one's mettle in circumstances that try a person's bravery, endurance, and life skills; looking squarely at death can be the ultimate test of life and risking death for the sake of one's beliefs can have transcendent value and give meaning to life in a world where little else may make sense; endorsing the values of human fellowship and the willingness to sacrifice for the sake of others is a great virtue (and the only value from traditional Christian teachings that can truly be affirmed). At the same time, thoroughly committing oneself to a radically independent life is the proper stance to retain one's integrity in a corrupt and compromised world; maintaining a stoical outlook and bravely facing up to life's essential tragedy are the proper responses for the modern hero (or courageous antihero); recognizing that traditional codes of conduct—the British gentleman's code, the soldier's code, the code of the frontier—have important messages to convey, particularly as they emphasize responsibility, sacrifice, duty, and humility; knowing how things "work" and mastering the craft of one's profession are the essentials to living a life of accomplishment; being a part of an inner circle—a group "in the know"—is an important element in the satisfaction of feeling one's personal superiority to the rest of humankind; appreciating the cultures and belief systems of peoples different from oneself is the key to a worldly and sophisticated viewpoint on life, all the while affirming the essential superiority of one's own heritage as the measure of civilized achievement. Finally, embracing these principles can serve as a secular substitute for God or religious meaning, even to the point of imbuing them with "mystical" significance and allowing them to operate as an alternate faith system.

The code comes from many sources, and within each of its major journalist-literary figure proponents the genesis is different, although in a certain fashion linked, because they were such strong influences on each other. In its evolution, the code offers a preferred professional response to the impact of trauma and psychological stress, although a rigid one, and, given the later life psychological condition of many of those who subscribed to it, one must question its effectiveness as a way for the body and the mind to process traumatic experience. However, in measuring the code's powerful hold over so many famous journalists and journalistic writers throughout history, one can see the challenges faced by those who want to help contemporary journalists deal with stress and psychological trauma in overcoming an inherited viewpoint that encourages a "stiffer upper lip" approach to handling the consequences of human tragedy, no matter how much repression of feeling is required in the process.

Crane's conception of the code—as reflected in his journalistic and his fictional writings, as well as the biographical accounts of his conduct in combat conditions—was built around courage, dignity, and an ironic view of life. Heroism to Crane was a humble act and should always be carried out with the recognition that life inevitably ends in futility and tragedy. In pointing toward a philosophy quite similar to twentieth-century existentialism, Crane felt that the "excellence of human conduct" involved an acknowledgment of humankind's freedom to exercise free will and defy institutional imperatives and social expectations but also an acceptance that this usually led to some form of personal sacrifice and suffering. Crane once wrote to a friend that he confronted life with "desperate resolution. There is not even much hope in my attitude. I do not even expect to do good. But I expect to make a sincere, desperate, lonely battle to remain true to my conception of life the way it should be lived, and if this plan can accomplish anything, it shall be accomplished. It is not a fine prospect."[38]

Crane's application of the code to the American scene was rooted in his family and religious values, as well as his experiences as a journalist that reinforced parts of his religious heritage while leading him to reject others. While eschewing the piety of his Methodist preacher father's and evangelist mother's beliefs, Crane retained his faith in certain moral fundamentals: the importance of individual responsibility, the value of duty and commitment to others, the need for fortitude and perseverance in the face of bad odds, the sense that there is an animating spirit in people that allows for human bonding and elevates life experience to something beyond the mundane. Crane also imbibed the aura of romanticism that was becoming attached to the role of the reporter by his time, and he offered up his life and his career as a romantic statement about finding transcendent meaning in a world shorn of traditional religious comforts. Throughout his life, Crane projected an aloofness and lack of emotional response to life's stresses that grew out of what he saw as radical independence and a determination never to be tainted by life's compromises, but which others have interpreted as compensatory behavior for a person with limited capacity for, rather than great resilience in, dealing with the distress caused by traumatic experience. Crane's rebellion from the evangelical religion of his parents and his embrace instead of journalism and its carpe diem lifestyle can be interpreted in the context of the death of his preacher-father when he was a boy; his sangfroid and his self-possession, as demonstrated in his casual reaction to his firing from his reporting job at the *New York Tribune* in 1892; and his apparent equanimity under the pressures of combat reporting. Some critics have viewed these as the life stances of a sickly young man who—at some point, in realizing that he was dying—had decided to adopt a fatalistic, naturalist's pose and not to reveal his feelings while awaiting his fate.[39]

It is worth noting that the journalist-literary figures who most glorified war have tended to be those who, like Crane, had gained their literary fame through writing about people in action, military or otherwise, but who had not been members of the military or experienced war as soldiers. Crane was sensitive to critics who wondered how someone who had not yet been born at the time of the Civil War could write about it with such sensitivity for the texture and feel of combat. With his great war novel already written, Crane came to Greece in 1897 as a man determined to show that the reputation he had gained at the scribbler's bench could be lived out in real life. (In this Crane set the tone for future journalist-literary figures, such as Hemingway, Dos Passos, Greene, and Mailer, who as aspiring writers headed off to war zones with at least one motivating factor being the desire to get material for their writing—or as Mailer's first wife reportedly said of his going "into combat so he'd be able to write the Great American Novel.") In Cuba, Crane and three reporters carried supplies from the coast to a Marine encampment; later Crane and four Marine signalmen lay belly down in a trench, taking turns jumping up to send messages by lantern amid fire from Spanish marksmen; in another encounter, when he saw an American company out of water and surrounded by Spaniards, he climbed the hill with a dozen water bottles attached to him; and he even served as a temporary aide to an American military captain who was short of subordinates. Of course, Crane was hardly alone among the American correspondents in showing his patriotic colors; at one newspaper encampment, the reporters raised the flag of the anti-Spanish Cuban insurgents and the flag of the *New York World*. Still, it is telling how a number of his fellow correspondents—despite sharing Crane's fundamental views about their role in the conflict and admiring him for his indifference to combat danger—conveyed a sense of unease about Crane's frequently curious behavior and appeared to be nagged by questions of whether there might not be something more than courage that explained his actions. Davis, for example, called Crane "the coolest man, whether army officer or civilian, that I saw under fire at any time" during the Spanish-American War, although he added that Crane was "annoyingly cool, with the assurance of a fatalist."[40]

At least some of the complaints about the predictable and jingoistic war coverage of American foreign correspondents during the Spanish-American War can be laid at the feet of Crane, who knew what he was doing, adopted a cynical attitude about it, but was happy to profit from the situation. If a cruiser fired a single shot, "the world heard of it, you bet," Crane wrote. "We were not idle men. We had come to report the war and we did it. Our good names and our salaries depended on it." Although Crane sometimes demonstrated in his war journalism the spare, bleak, naturalistic prose style that he has become known for in his fiction, he framed it in subjective terms that met the needs of his jingoistic employers, and he never hesitated to emphasize the superior fighting skills of the American or the Greek soldier (who he sided with against the "insane and almost wicked" Turk squadrons). In Greece, he portrayed the Greeks as "good fighters and long fighters and stayers," even though they were often retreating during his coverage of the campaign. His unwillingness to acknowledge this led him to write what at times must be termed laughable military analysis ("Back fell the Greek army, wrathful, sullen, fierce as any victorious army would be when commanded to retreat before the enemy it had defeated," he began one dispatch). At least as problematically, Crane did not hesitate to portray war in a romantic context in his war journalism when he knew (and much of his fiction and his memoirlike accounts reflect) that he saw it in much more ambivalent terms. ("The roll of musketry fire was tremendous. . . . It was a beautiful sound; beautiful as had never been dreamed. . . . It was the most beautiful sound of my experience, barring no symphony," he wrote for Hearst's *New York Journal* in May 1897. "The crash of it was ideal," before he added, "This is one point of view. The other might be taken from the men who died there.") However, his one-sided view of the Greek and Turkish conflict cannot be compared to his reporting from Cuba, where his pro-American sentiments were undisguised (and virtually mandated by his bosses). "Nothing of the enemy was visible to our men, who displayed much gallantry," he wrote in a June 1898 account for Pulitzer's *World*. "In fact, their bearing was superb, and couldn't have been finer," which he bested in a later dispatch, "Their performance was grand! Oh, but never mind—it was only the regulars. They fought gallantly of course. . . . Have they ever been known to fail?" Occasionally Crane detailed in direct journalistic terms the hobbled and bleeding soldiers, some with their faces shot off, and the stretchers of dying being transported back to the medical facilities. But in his deadline journalism, Crane portrayed this as another manifestation of the American soldiers' gallantry. Repeatedly in his newspaper journalism, Crane carried out Pulitzer's and Hearst's task, which was to line up their coverage with U.S. foreign policy aims and to make sure that the war was portrayed in the terms that would justify their early stories that helped to foment the conflict.[41]

Crane's vainglorious journalistic picture of the American military campaign in Cuba took a very different shape in his series of short stories, *Wounds in the Rain*, which was published in 1900, the year of his death. Compare, for example, this passage from "An Episode of War" with the requisite valorous accounts that made up the staple of his newspaper stories: "A wound gives strange dignity to him who bears it. Well men shy from this new and terrible majesty. It is as if the wounded man's hand is upon the curtain which hangs before the revelations of all existence—the meaning of ants, potentates, war, cities, sunshine, snow, a feather dropped from a bird's wing; and the power of it sheds radiance upon a bloody form, and makes the other men understand sometimes that they are little." Crane, in fact, was adept at manipulating writing genres to his purposes, including a journalistic form, which he cynically would acknowledge was meant to serve the demands of his employers, and a fictional form, where ironically (because fiction is considered to be less "truthful" than journalism by many) he would write in a moving and high literary style that expressed his troubled reactions to the traumas that he witnessed. "A number of people got killed very courteously, tacitly absolving the rest of us from any care in the matter," he wrote in *Wounds in the Rain*. "A man fell; he turned blue; his face took on an expression of deep sorrow; and then his immediate friends worried about him, if he had friends"; and "I looked down into a miserable huddle at Bloody Bend, a huddle of hurt men, dying men, dead men . . . I doubt if many of us learned how to speak to our own wounded. In the first place, one had to play that the wound was nothing; oh, a mere nothing; a casual interference with movement, perhaps, but nothing more; oh, really, nothing more. . . . As a result I think most of us bungled and stammered in the presence of our wounded friends." Crane's deftness at exploiting the line between journalism and fiction (or perhaps one should say semifiction, as it is not always clear how many and how much of the accounts are imaginatively embellished) is on masterful display in *Wounds in the Rain*. However, though one cannot help but be impressed with Crane's abilities as a writer, the same cannot always be said for his cynicism in holding back his deepest feelings about warfare for his fictional and literary as opposed to his newspaper writings.[42]

In this, Crane showed again that he was a protean figure when it came to portraying war romantically in his last fictional novel, *Active Service*. One is unsure with Crane of how much ironic distance to read into his portrayal of Rufus Coleman, his journalist-protagonist, who Crane described as a "solemn and knightly joy of this adventure" and compared to "an armour-encased young gentleman of medieval poetry" as he reached the battlefield of the Greco-Turkish War. Given the postures that Crane reflected as a war correspondent, it is hard not to see self-commentary in his description of Coleman as someone who "regarded himself cynically in most affairs, but he could not be cynical of war, because he had seen none of it." In fact, Crane was caught between the imperialist and romantic worldview of the Victorian Age and the coming of the twentieth-century literary landscape of antiheroes, portrayals of human disillusionment, and relativistic notions about human moral conduct in the face of trauma. Crane's ready experimentation with many literary forms—and his sometimes seemingly contradictory views about the "meaning" of life in his naturalist's "indifferent universe"—have left him an ambiguous figure when it comes to determining how he felt about the impact of trauma, both in his own life and in his view of the sufferings of soldiers in war. His stoicism that merged into opportunism at points in his life—as well as his "modest" view of himself as someone whose "weak mental machinery" left him willing to acknowledge his moral and literary failings ("There was born into an unsuspecting world a certain novel called 'Active Service,' full and complete in its shame," he said at the book's publication)—makes his commitment to an honest portrayal of life as it is, though worthy of admiration in much of his literature, something that was not always consistently applied when his own journalistic self-interest came into play.[43]

Not surprisingly perhaps, Kipling shared certain personal, family, and religious traits with Crane, and his expression of the British variation of the code had many similarities with Crane's (although it was Crane—in once referring to his early writing as done in the "Rudyard Kipling style"—who was largely influenced by Kipling, rather than vice versa). Kipling believed that it was his business to serve the "God of Things as They are," which led him to write, "First a man must suffer, then he must learn his work, and the self-respect that that knowledge brings." Like Crane, Kipling retained a residue of the Methodist outlook of his family (one set of grandparents were strict Methodists); also like Crane, he turned away from the Christian orthodoxy of Methodist doctrine but retained its moral spirit in his writings and his view of upright individual conduct. One can find the vestiges of Methodist attitudes about human sin, the potential for human perfection, the importance of individual conscience, the values of social duty, and the sense of life rooted in an essential spirituality in his advocacy of the "law" of the jungle in *The Jungle Book* and his rebel's rules of behavior in *Stalky and Company*. Kipling was ambivalent about the idea of following one's duty to authority and, again like Crane, he resisted a strict "letter of the law" enforcement of formal rules of conduct, as his thinly autobiographical *Stalky* dramatized. The high jinks of Stalky and his cohort of boarding school miscreants conveyed their own subversive, tough-minded, and sometimes cruel code that revolved around loyalty to an in-group, irreverence toward institutional dictates, and intolerance for cant and hypocrisy. ("Softness," Kipling once wrote, "is for slaves and beasts, for minstrels and useless persons.") Kipling went so far as to present his interpretation of the unofficial "honor code" that he had embraced in a boarding school setting as a pragmatic and bare-knuckled creed for the maintenance of the British Empire. In this way, Kipling came to be seen as the poetic inspiration for the far-flung British administrators, soldiers, and engineers who were the "doers" and the "cogs" of the colonial system, and whose steadfastness, practical flexibility, and technical skills Kipling celebrated ("The seaman's duty to the ship is the measure of his manhood," was how he put it in his novel, *Captains Courageous*).[44]

Kipling's early experiences as a journalist on newspapers in India were as influential on his life view as Crane's journalistic experiences were to him. Journalism deepened Kipling's belief in the importance of life lived in action, the value of absorbing an understanding of humanity in its full array of beliefs and cultures, and the power of observation to unlock the secrets of how individuals keep the human enterprise afloat. Kipling's notions of battlefield valor were revealed to Crane through Kipling's fantasies of the artist-journalist in combat in his 1891 novel, *The Light That Failed*. In it, Kipling painted an impressionistic picture of a battle where his blinded protagonist dies during British military operations in the Sudan. Critics have noted the ways in which Crane borrowed and then improved on Kipling's metaphors (such as Kipling's "wrathful red disc" in *The Light That Failed* that turned into Crane's "blood-red wafer" in *The Red Badge of Courage*). The irony is that Crane was taking his cues about the battlefield from another "realist" who also had never personally experienced war before penning his war novel.[45]

Like the youthful Crane, Kipling gained literary stature by writing about military people and military action without seeing any of it himself—and he never was a member of the military. However, unlike Crane, Kipling never experienced the danger of combat as a journalist, and he never considered becoming a frontline war correspondent, even late in his career. Kipling's talent as a journalist made him a brilliant armchair patriot, and he used his masterful reporting skills—where he interviewed military people, hung out in soldier's quarters, and voraciously read military history—to produce stories and poems that gave the impression that he was intimately acquainted with the experience of military life. ("I am seeking a poet," he wrote at one point, who shall "compose the greatest song of all—The Saga of the Anglo-Saxon all around the earth—a paean that shall combine the terrible slow swing of the Battle Hymn of the Republic with Britannia needs no Bulwarks, the skirl of the British Grenadiers with that perfect quickstep, Marching through Georgia, and at the end the wail of the Dead March. Will any one take the contract?") In reality, the closest Kipling came to military action was in his work as a volunteer journalist for a British Army newspaper during the Boer War. His admirers might have been surprised to learn that Kipling's only encounter with the whiff of grapeshot was when he briefly came under fire while visiting British troops; it was an experience that "exhilarated" him, he later said, and "stirred his pulse." In fact, Kipling—like other writers raised in the repressive atmosphere of Victorian society—kept the gap between his inner life and his outward profile well concealed, and his emotional debilitations (his anxiety, his depressions, his mistrust of people, his insecurity, his tendency toward reclusiveness) indicated a disposition that was anything but sanguine in the manner in which it manifested the effects of trauma in his life.[46]

Kipling's heroic view of war often does not come through in his fiction to the degree that it does in his patriotic poetry, his often bombastic public statements supporting the cause of British imperialism, and in his sometimes strident journalistic writings. As a fiction writer, Kipling operated in the same model as Crane in which he portrayed life circumstances—including the experience of war—in more ambiguous, nuanced, and less romantic terms than were reflected in his political expression. When a despairing Dick Heldar of *The Light That Failed* heads off to the Sudan to essentially commit suicide by throwing himself into the frontline action, he is described by Kipling as a "blind, bewildered vagabond" and, in a far from heroic encounter, finds himself in a dawn attack as he rides a camel heedlessly forward, while saying to himself, "What luck! What stupendous and imperial luck! . . . Oh, God has been most good to me!" with Kipling adding that, "His luck had held to the last, even to the crowning mercy of a kindly bullet through his head." Although one can see Heldar's actions as self-destructively romantic—even to the point of bathos, as some critics have claimed—there is nothing in Kipling's fictional account of battle in *The Light That Failed* that has any glorious elements to it.[47]

The model of Crane, rather than Kipling, became the animating factor in the decision of a number of the journalist-literary figures to become war correspondents after they had attained literary fame. When London—already famous for his naturalistic stories with mythic and primal heroes—signed up to cover the Russo-Japanese War for Hearst in the winter of 1904, he missed a ship that was going to take him from Japan to Korea to the scene of the fighting. After chartering a junk with a crew of Koreans, he landed in Korea with frostbite, then hired pack ponies, grooms, a manservant, and an interpreter. Although his determination led him farther north than any other reporters, his rivals in the press—unimpressed with his efforts to imitate the Davis ideal—complained about his access to the fighting, and he was brought back from the front to Japan and made to wait behind the lines like the other correspondents. Even more than Crane, London's experiences as a war correspondent seemed driven by the desire to live out the larger-than-life profile that he had created for the characters in his fiction and to live up to his image of himself as a Teddy Roosevelt–style man-of-action. (Ironically, Roosevelt, who entertained great suspicions about London, once got into a public dispute with him over Roosevelt's allegations that London distorted the realities of canine life in his dog stories about Alaska.) London, who like

Crane died at a young age (in the drug-addicted London's case, at age forty, from an overdose of morphine), also has been credited, again like Crane, with harboring a death wish amid his manly poses, and his psychological condition combined with his substance addictions present the picture of a fragile personality living out a grandiose life story. London's views about white Aryan superiority, his preference for the Russian cause versus what he called the "militant yellow peril" of the Japanese side, and his flag-waving support of American imperialism endeared him to his jingoistic Hearst editors. "One tingled at the sight, and the hot blood rushed backward through all the generations of culture and civilization to things primordial and naked," he once wrote for Hearst when the SS *Oregon* returned to San Francisco after service in the Spanish-American War. However, at other times, he would say that the hope of socialism was all that kept him alive, that war was a "silly, non-intellectual function," and that nothing could stop him from clinging to his faith in the brotherhood of man. These were all signs that his seriously fractured personality could not settle on an image of himself as a victim of the social order and his early life traumas or as a rugged individualist who had conquered the world and his past.[48]

Fittingly, it was the romantic icon Davis who, on a number of occasions, bailed out both Crane and London from predicaments of their making. Besides trying to rescue Crane from his recklessness in Cuba, Davis once helped London—who had grown impatient waiting for permission to chronicle the fighting—get back a camera that had been confiscated by Japanese authorities after London tried to take pictures without authorization. Davis's intervention saved London from a military trial after Roosevelt, at Davis's behest, negotiated an agreement where charges were dropped in return for London leaving Japan. There were signs (most noticeably in the fiction he wrote satirizing the stereotypical journalistic character) that the dapper Davis grew cynical about the consequences of his posturing at the point when he saw his younger imitators trying to one-up him (his colleagues returned the disdain; he was often referred to by them as "Richard the Lion Harding"). Davis's private life, too—where he wrestled with depressive episodes, tried in letters to calm the obsessive worrying of his mother about his well-being, and was fixated on gaining her approval throughout his life—reflected the gap between the affectations of journalists in a romantic and imperialistic era and the real nature of their psychic lives.[49]

London's overheated rhetoric was matched by Norris's in his description of the heroic ethos that a fledging journalist found in reporting about the Spanish-American War. "You want to see excitement, turmoil, activity, the marching and countermarching of troops," Norris wrote in explaining his desire to cover the conflict. Perhaps it is no surprise to learn how willingly someone of Norris's inflamed romantic temperament and hyperventilating prose flourishes (he once described a journalistic character in his autobiographical novel, *Blix*, as suffering "an almost fatal attack of Harding Davis") gave up the stance of the independent journalist in his first overseas reporting assignment. In South Africa, in 1895, to cover the preliminaries of the Boer War for a San Francisco newspaper, Norris rushed off to secure a pair of hunting rifles and a horse in the hopes of joining an insurrection of British citizens against the Boer leaders of the Transvaal province. In Cuba, in 1898, on assignment for *McClure's* magazine, he traveled with American troops who were ordered to clear a town of Spanish soldiers. With pistol cocked, Norris went from building to building, where he captured two soldiers that he marched back in front of him. The incidents illustrated the contradictions in Norris's real life and his writing philosophy. Norris subscribed to the then-fashionable, Kipling-esque notion of advanced societies leading lesser peoples out of their primitivism; at the same time, he reflected from his reading of the European naturalistic fiction of Emile Zola and Honoré de Balzac the stance that the mature view of the Darwinian struggle meant that a person should uncomplainingly embrace the indifferent and deterministic forces at the heart of the universe. For example, Norris wrote ecstatically of the Spanish-American War that Cuba was "ours, ours, by the sword we had acquired, we, Americans, with no one to help—and the Anglo-Saxon blood of us, the blood of the race . . . conquering and conquering and conquering, on to the westward, the race whose blood instinct is the acquiring of land." But he also wrote, "that no one could be a writer, until he could regard life and people, and the world in general, from the objective point of view—until he could remain detached, outside, maintain the unswerving attitude of the observer." In this case, it was his romantic impulses—not his naturalistic cool—that most colored his war-reporting experiences.[50]

Hemingway treasured his tough guy image and his man-of-action reputation, and little about him (from hunting big game in Africa to romanticizing the gory spectacle of bullfighting in Spain) indicated a peace-loving temperament, despite his reputation (based largely on his World War I semi-autobiographical novel, *A Farewell to Arms*) as an antiwar author. During World War II, when patriotism was running high, he became an enthusiastic partisan before deciding to cover the action himself. While living in Cuba, he set up a counterintelligence group in Havana (made up of fishermen, jai alai players, and refugee noblemen from Spain) in cooperation with the

American embassy and the Cuban government. Even more ridiculously, he cruised off the Cuban coast looking for German submarines in his fishing boat, the "Pilar," which he had stocked with government bazookas and machine guns, and a number of the cruises turned into fishing trips with grenades hurled into the sea as drunken sport. Hemingway's patriotism (and his need to burnish the Hemingway myth) also led him to jump into the job of war correspondent with such gusto that (à la Crane and others) he did not let his role as journalist stop him from crossing the line into direct military involvement. When a shell landed outside the mess where Hemingway and American officers were eating during the Allied invasion of France in World War II, all the officers hit the floor except Hemingway who sat calmly and continued to eat his meal. At least some of the accounts of Hemingway's derring-do as a World War II correspondent have to be taken with a measure of suspicion, however, as the source was often Hemingway himself. *True* magazine carried an article about Hemingway assuming command of a combat unit that was under fire from German gunners, helping the group to safety, and then crawling back to relay the information to the beach commander—an account, it turned out, with Hemingway as its source. Still, witnesses have indicated that Hemingway showed considerable battlefield bravery at times. At one point, he was driven in a jeep for a day and a half through an area with armed Germans to reach a task force commanded by an American colonel who had sent Hemingway a note taunting him for missing an important military assault. He organized and directed patrols scouting for counterattacks, and Reuters once reported that he had captured six German soldiers. However, Hemingway's combat involvement clearly violated Geneva Convention principles for journalists. But when the U.S. Army later investigated him, he beat the "rap," as he put it.[51]

Hemingway's support of leftist causes in the 1930s and his sympathy for the Republican forces in Spain, combined with *A Farewell to Arms*, which captures the despair and apathy that the shock of a terrible wounding had visited on him, have left Hemingway with a divided legacy on the great questions of war and peace. One can view the disillusioned Frederic Henry in *A Farewell to Arms* and the emotionally and physically crippled Jake Barnes in *The Sun Also Rises* as embodiments of the symptoms of PTSD raised to the level of literary characterization. Yet, Hemingway never lost his attraction to the Kipling ideal—and his moving back and forth between the pose of the psychologically troubled witness to war and the foreign correspondent who happily joined with his country's cause can be seen as reflections of the ambivalence of a journalism industry that believes in "telling it like it is" but

seldom does so when it comes to fully and graphically describing the consequences of war or in fully and honestly facing up to the potential effects of
trauma on journalists' emotional state.[52]

The clipped, laconic dialogue of Hemingway's novels often has been associated with his training in journalism. But the no-affect style of his fictional
conversation equally can be seen as a manifestation in his literature (whether
consciously or unconsciously) of the symptoms of PTSD, which Hemingway
showed signs of—particularly when he came home after his World War I
European rehabilitation. When Frederic Henry is asked about his travels on
his leave, he says, "'I went everywhere. Milan, Florence, Rome, Naples, Villa
San Giovanni, Messina, Taormina. . . . ' 'You talk like a time-table,'" responds
another soldier. There are places in the novel where Hemingway reflected
great insight into a soldier's disillusionment with war, including in dialogue
that can be seen as conveying muted anger, emotional numbness, apathy,
detachment, and feelings of meaninglessness—all signs of PTSD. "I watched
for awhile and then went to sleep," Henry recounts at one point. "I slept
heavily except once I woke sweating and scared and then went back to sleep
trying to stay outside of my dream." After Henry's nurse-lover, Catherine
Barclay, gives birth to their dead son (and soon dies herself), Hemingway
portrayed Henry as acting stoically in the face of the trauma. "Now Catherine
would die," Henry says to himself. "That was what you did. You died. You did
not know what it was about. You never had time to learn. . . . Stay around
and they would kill you." Hemingway's repeated use of the phrase "the hell
with . . ." and his conveyance of the nihilistic attitudes that can be produced
by war were hammered through in message after message throughout the
novel—including, at times, in ways that can sound stilted and overwrought
in his reach for symbolic effect. "I'm afraid of the rain because sometimes
I see me dead in it. . . . And sometimes I see you dead in it," says Catherine
Barclay to Henry at one point. After Henry tries to reassure her, she adds,
"It's all nonsense. It's only nonsense. I'm not afraid of the rain. I'm not afraid
of the rain. Oh, oh, God, I wish I wasn't." Henry then says, "She was crying.
I comforted her and she stopped crying. But outside it kept on raining."[53]

As he developed as a fiction writer, Hemingway found novels a wonderful place to maintain his bravura front—and his commitment to the heroic
code—while expressing his real feelings through characters that he could keep
(at least technically) at arm's length from himself. Although many readers and
critics have presumed that Henry and Barnes were his alter egos, Hemingway,
in promoting his own myth of himself as an heroic literary figure, implied in
numerous ways to the world that in real life he had matters all worked out, and

it was only his fictional male protagonists—tough and impenetrable on the outside, while plaintive and emotionally wounded on the inside—who were struggling to get through life. Hemingway's sentimentalism—which reached cloying levels in *A Farewell to Arms*—was often most dramatically expressed in his female figures who as some critics have observed are much more clinging and passive than the most important women figures that Hemingway himself was involved with (and married to) in real life. Catherine Barclay, in particular, is so emotionally needy in her relationship with Henry that one wonders if she may not be Hemingway's alter ego as much as his self-contained male characters. Jake Barnes, with his war wound that has left him emasculated, does cry over the unattainable Lady Brett Ashley during an interior monologue in *The Sun Also Rises*—but demonstrations of vulnerability are unusual among the male protagonists of Hemingway's fiction. Given this dynamic in Hemingway's upbringing and in his psychology (his mother dressing him in girl's clothes; his father countering this by educating him in macho outdoor activities), it is easy to speculate that Hemingway's access to his painful and unresolved feelings could best be dealt with when he could put them in the mouths of characters that were not him, but were him, at the same time. Still, this strategy—as one can see in his compulsions, dysfunctions, and the self-destructive behavior in his own life—hardly proved to be the solution for a happy existence.[54]

By World War II, the overall quality of Hemingway's fiction was in decline and his critical reputation was being assailed—and this was reflected in his journalism, too. As a celebrity writing figure, Hemingway's prose had begun to come across as a self-parody of his famous dictums for writing authentically, and his war journalism took on the aura of posturing that critics complained had come to permeate such works as his nonfictional *Green Hills of Africa* and his novel *To Have and Have Not*. The increasingly solipsistic nature of Hemingway's writing was evident in his first-person accounts for *Collier's* magazine from the European front, where he put himself at the center of the action, portrayed himself as memorizing maps and strategic plans and giving suggestions to military officers, and implied that things would have gone better if they had taken his advice. ("As we came roaring in on the beach, I sat high on the stern to see what we were up against. . . . Coming in I had spotted two machine-gun nests. . . . 'That's where he [the commander] wants to go,' Andy [the landing boat's top officer] said. . . . 'It isn't any good,' I said. 'I've seen both those guns open up. . . . Talk to him and get it straight.'") In places, Hemingway's dispatches contained echoes of the "knowing insider" Jake Barnes discussing bullfighting or trout fishing—but with Hemingway as the protagonist of his (supposedly) nonfictional account. ("At the regimental command post I was informed there was heavy fighting outside of Rambouillet. I knew the country and the roads around Epernon, Rambouillet, Trappes and Versailles well. . . . I was the only person at the outpost who spoke French"); in other places, Hemingway described himself as taking charge of French guerilla forces against the Germans (even though he acknowledged that "war correspondents are forbidden to command troops").[55]

More than her husband, Gellhorn (who was Hemingway's third wife) was the picture of the selfless and detached foreign correspondent, and her moving chronicles of her reporting experiences—both in her periodical journalism and in her novels—are of growing fascination to scholars. Whereas Hemingway would add self-aggrandizing touches to his journalistic accounts of battle, Gellhorn is known for the dispassionate and vividly realistic way she captured the real effect of war, and her seeing-through-the-glass-clearly approach in her reporting is today viewed by many as the more honest and effective way to convey the actual nature of military action. The lack of distance between the combatants, the reporters, and the civilian population was powerfully captured in Gellhorn's journalistic and fictional prose, as were the terrible consequences incurred by innocent victims of war. Her reporting for *Collier's*, claims Gellhorn biographer Carl Rollyson, is better than Hemingway's because it is "so direct, so concrete, and so deeply felt." Like the characters in a number of her novels, Gellhorn experienced real pain when she could not do more to help the victims of war, and she struggled with maintaining the detached and objective position that journalism required. In her own journalistic accounts, Gellhorn often used understatement and indirect allusions to deeper emotion in the way Hemingway did in his fiction (but less so in his later journalism), and her prose lacked the self-referential glibness that Hemingway-the-public-personality came to display in his war reporting. At the same time, Gellhorn's own psychology did not particularly suffer under these burdens, and she—like Hemingway—seemed to thrive in the atmosphere of danger and risk-taking. Still, Gellhorn carried an additional burden. After the breakup of their troubled marriage, she discovered that her writing career was always discussed in the context of Hemingway's, and the price she paid for once wanting to be like Hemingway (scholars have noted this trait in Gellhorn, Parker, and other women writers of his time) was to have discovered in marrying him how much psychological dysfunction lay beneath the surface of the hero's pose.[56]

More than other journalist-literary figures who operated in the heroic model, Gellhorn's journalism and her fiction were virtually inseparable in their treatment of war and trauma. Her novels, *A Stricken Field* (1940) and *The Wine of Astonishment* (1948), deal with World War II events, and she drew heavily from her reporting, at times literally lifting material verbatim from her reportage. In the same way that Gellhorn's presence was unobtrusive but conscience-driven in her reporting, her reporter-character, Mary Douglas, in *A Stricken Field*, explores the dilemma of working as a correspondent as she tries to make the suffering of what she sees visible to her readers, including her decision to step outside the journalist's professional credo and to get involved in helping out refugees in Czechoslovakia who were uprooted by Hitler's invasion of Sudetenland in 1938. Gellhorn's fictional correspondents are not torn between sentimentality and cynicism as is so typical in fiction written by journalists (including by her husband, Hemingway). The women among her journalistic characters may be jaded, but they remain committed to social ideals through their reporting. Although Gellhorn once said, "Fiction is much harder than journalism; so naturally I respect it more," she used both genres to portray the suffering and the resilience of ordinary people in wartime and to convey a sense of moral urgency in addressing the trauma visited on the innocent victims of military conflict.[57]

The poet-journalist Hughes also sought out and spent time with Hemingway when he went to Spain in 1937 to report on the civil war for a group of African American newspapers. Hughes traveled throughout the countryside amid shelling and sniper fire, wrote straightforward accounts of bombings and air raids, and interviewed black soldiers involved in the war through the lens of his left-leaning politics (one article was headlined, "Hughes Finds Moors Used as Pawns by Fascists in Spain"). However, Hughes only once ventured near the front lines during live combat, and even then, he spent most of the time in a tent near the trenches waiting to interview a returning unit. Hughes, according to biographer Faith Berry, wrote little that was highly personal about his experiences ("like an elephant, he could remember everything he wanted to; he could also conveniently 'forget' anything he preferred not to divulge"), and he was like other idealists among his generation of journalist-literary figures when he said that the longer in stayed in Madrid, "the more I liked it," and that Spain was "a thrilling and poetic place to be at that moment."[58]

Although both were huge names in the literary world, Steinbeck, too, was fixated on Hemingway (as a writer, Steinbeck admired Hemingway but resented those who saw Steinbeck's own style and literary approach as imitative of Hemingway's; before their only meeting, Steinbeck fretted about what Hemingway thought of him and was disappointed when they never seemed to connect during their conversation in a way that Steinbeck viewed as meaningful). When he got a chance to cover the American invasion of Italy for the *New York Herald Tribune* during World War II, he relished the opportunity as much as Hemingway did—and Steinbeck demonstrated the same eagerness to jump into the action. He would wait on the landing boat until there were few witnesses, and an extra tommy gun would be brought up so he could carry it. "John, to his everlasting glory and our everlasting respect, would take his foreign correspondent badge off his arm and join in the raid. . . . We had great admiration for him," said the boat's commander, Douglas Fairbanks Jr. In 1966, Steinbeck went to South Vietnam to cover the war for *Newsday*, and he traveled with the troops by helicopter throughout the country often under dangerous circumstances. The comments he made about the war ("I wish I could tell you about these pilots. They make me sick with envy. They ride their vehicles the way a man controls a fine, well-trained quarter horse") projected a "super hawk image" and upset people in the antiwar left who had assumed that Steinbeck was one of them. In one column, he wrote about "the shiver of shame I sometimes feel at home when I see the Vietnicks, dirty clothes, dirty minds, sour smelling wastelings. . . . Their shuffling, drag-ass protests that they are conscience-bound not to kill people are a little silly. They're not in danger of that. Hell, they couldn't hit anybody." Steinbeck's views about the Vietnam War as a reporter—his faith in the character and motives of the American soldier, his interest in weapons and tactics, his general enthusiasm for the venture—showed that even a writer who was once a strong social critic of his country and who demonstrated great empathy for those who suffered the trauma of the Dust Bowl and Depression-era poverty in the 1930s could turn patriotic and embrace the heroic ideal under the right circumstances.[59]

The Satirical and the Ambivalent in the Face of War

Orwell, too, was filled with contradictions when it came to questions of war and peace. He had experienced many things that made him deeply suspicious of warfare and military solutions to world affairs, including the dissembling and callousness that he encountered while working in a militarylike colonial police hierarchy in Burma and his terrible wounding and escape during his combat service in the Spanish Civil War. While fighting with Republican forces in Spain, Orwell was struck by a sniper's bullet that missed a carotid artery by about a millimeter. However, Orwell's even greater trauma came when he learned how near he was to becoming a victim of the violent political infighting among the communist factions. After escaping Spain, he and his wife tried to rest on the Mediterranean Coast but to no avail. "We ought to have felt profoundly relieved and thankful," he wrote. "We felt nothing of the kind. The things we had seen in Spain did not recede and fall into proportion now that we were away from them; instead they rushed back upon us and were far more vivid than before. We thought, talked, dreamed incessantly of Spain." Yet, Orwell never let this experience undermine his general idealism, his leftist sympathies, or his faith in human beings, and he spent much of the rest of his life writing as a socialist about what had gone wrong in Soviet Russia and other communist regimes.[60]

In *Homage to Catalonia*, his much-admired account of his Spanish Civil War experiences, he spoke of his wounding this way: "Roughly speaking it was the sensation of being *at the centre of* an explosion. There seemed to be a loud bang and a blinding flash of light all round me, and I felt a tremendous shock—no pain, only a violent shock, such as you get from an electric terminal; with it a sense of utter weakness, a feeling of being stricken and shriveled up to nothing." On the stretcher, as soon as he heard the bullet had gone through his neck, he assumed he "was done for. . . . The blood was dribbling out of the corner of my mouth. 'The artery's gone,' I thought. I wondered how long you last when your carotid artery is cut." His first thought was for his wife, he said; his second was "a violent resentment at having to leave this world which, when all is said and done, suits me so well." The week he spent in a hospital with others with "frightful" wounds left him even more shaken and disturbed. During his recovery, his wife described him as "violently depressed," and he later wrote that he "had an overwhelming desire to get away from it all." But Orwell had a deep-seated love of life, which sustained him through the ordeal. His strong psychological disposition also meant that he experienced fewer long-term emotional effects than his wife, who was troubled by lingering anxiety from their Spanish travails.[61]

Despite his reputation as a skeptic of war, Orwell never came close to becoming a pacifist, and his willingness to suffer for a principle led him never to foreclose the possibility of taking up arms in the right cause. Even though some of his socialist colleagues were critical of him, he joined the Home Guard during World War II and took a job furthering the Allied cause in the BBC (his bad lungs kept him out of active military service, even though he registered himself as eligible). As a sergeant in the Home Guard, his job was to defend England in case of an invasion, and he kept his home filled with homemade explosives and other weapons. ("I can put up with bombs on the mantlepiece," his wife said at one point, "but I will not have a machine gun under the bed.") Although Orwell, like Crane, suffered the emotional stress of dealing with a chronic lung ailment that would lead to his death at age forty-six, he did not alter his workaholic dedication to social and political advocacy or back away from the many unpopular political stands that he championed in his writing. Orwell's stoical and uncomplaining life philosophy came straight out of his upbringing in the family of a dutiful British colonial official ("On balance life is suffering," he once said, "and only the very young or very foolish imagine otherwise"). In his final months, as he worked furiously to finish *1984* before death's deadline, he clung to life with a tenacity and stalwartness that reflected the principled toughness that many have come to admire about him.[62]

Greene's authoring of *The Quiet American*, which grew out of his Vietnam reporting experiences and helped to burnish his reputation as a critic of American foreign policy and a prescient observer who predicted the United States' entry into the Vietnam quagmire, leaves a misleading impression if one sees it as his definitive statement about colonial warfare. Few people have paid as much attention to Greene's reporting a few years earlier when he portrayed favorably the British government's successful campaign to eradicate a communist uprising in Malaysia. Greene's reporting for *Life* magazine has been called "pure propaganda" for its sympathetic depiction of the white planters, its admiring account of the British propaganda campaign, and for making no attempt to question the savage tactics of the British troops. In fact, Greene relished his role as an opportunistic correspondent in colonial wars—working as a British spy in Vietnam (and compromising his role as a journalist in doing it), traveling with troops in dangerous circumstances (which some have seen as Greene's death wish in action), and using opium and large amounts of alcohol along the way. Greene's greatest pleasure—which could be called a mixture of the hero's and antihero's code—was to engage in acts of deception and intrigue as a way to confound the world's opinion of him and to burnish his image as a gadfly activist with no loyalty but to himself. Greene's machinating nature, his psychological complexity, and his duplicity of motives must always be taken into account when trying to gauge the impact of trauma—both personal and as a witness to war—in his life and writings. In fact, Greene's propensity for opening himself up to and chronicling the traumatic events of the human psyche—experiences in war, religious crises, suicide, alcoholism and drug abuse, adventuring in danger zones, and death wishes—place him at the head of a list of twentieth-century authors who realized that writing about traumatic experience made for good book sales. But that propensity has left critics pondering exactly how it was that trauma really worked in his own life.[63]

Evelyn Waugh's novel *Scoop*, which converted his experiences as a foreign correspondent into a literary spoof, was transformed into a case of life imitating a father's art when his son, Auberon, accidentally wounded himself with his own machine gun while serving in Cyprus with the British Royal House Guards. Like his protagonist in *Scoop*, William Booth, Evelyn never experienced up-close combat during his time covering the prelude to the Italian invasion of Abyssinia in 1936, and his own farcical encounters with the military and his newspaper's bureaucracy made up the bulk of his experiences in Ethiopia, as did his interactions with the pack of foreign correspondents assembled there that he took delight in skewering in the novel. Interestingly, Evelyn's jaundiced and ironical view of war reporting (as well as most everything else) became the stance of Auberon, who took up his father's mantle of the contrarian, debunking conservative in his own journalism and fiction. Auberon's machine gun incident—where he lost a lung, spleen, and finger and spent nine months recovering in the hospital after accidentally triggering the gun while it was pointed at himself—never struck him as funny, but it may have helped to set the tone for the "affectless" way he treated shocking events in his fiction writing. Auberon's inheritance of his father's acidic view of the human enterprise can be seen as the cynic's form of expressing trauma and anger, and in much of the writings and autobiographical accounts of both men, there clearly is much deeper and more serious psychological material than they were willing to explore in direct or earnest fashion.[64]

Like Waugh, a number of women journalist-literary figures journeyed to battlefronts while witnessing virtually no real military combat. But this often was because—as women—they were denied access to the front lines. Margaret Fuller, Lillie Devereux Blake, Rebecca West, Dorothy Thompson, and Edna Ferber all wrote about military affairs from a close—but safely "protected"—proximity to it. However, none worked harder than Gellhorn to get to the action (one can find satiric references to Gellhorn's strategies to outfox her military overseers in her dramatic comedy, *Love Goes to Press*, that she cowrote with fellow war correspondent, Virginia Cowles), and they did involve themselves in highly disturbing events connected to armed conflict. Fuller reported secondhand accounts of the violence associated with the Italian revolution while she was an Italian correspondent for Horace

Greeley's *New York Tribune* (she, her young child, and her new Italian husband died in a shipwreck returning to the United States from Italy); Thompson interviewed Hitler (and wrote a book about it) and traveled to Russia to investigate the consequences of the Bolshevik revolution; West covered post–World War II treason trials for the *New Yorker;* and Ferber visited the European front in World War II and interviewed soldiers and officers from behind the front lines. In fact, just because they were not in the line of fire did not mean that they were free from the effects of trauma. Fuller, for example, nursed wounded fighters in Rome as they resisted the siege of the city by French forces in 1849, and her husband took part in the fighting, whereas Thompson helped war and political refugees both during her years as a European correspondent and back in the United States. As an early figure in the movement of women into military defense reporting, Blake covered war department matters as a Washington, D.C., correspondent for a Philadelphia and two New York City newspapers in the 1860s, and the carnage of the Civil War—while not witnessed directly in her role as journalist—was reflected in themes of violence intruding into the domestic realm that showed up in her fiction. Psychological repression and hidden, violent emotions were a fascination for Blake—and her frustrations with the restraints imposed on Victorian women, the trauma of suffering her husband's suicide after he had lost her inherited fortune, and her advocacy of women acknowledging their sexual needs culminated in the themes of her novel, *Fettered for Life.* One can see her feminist advocacy—for women's suffrage, protections against discrimination, and meaningful employment opportunities—as precursors to both Margaret Mitchell's historical fiction romance (*Gone with the Wind*) with its independent but war-traumatized woman protagonist and Charlotte Perkins Gilman's novels imagining an ideal world where women's work and domestic difficulties were resolved.[65]

In the tradition of Hemingway, Mailer, by his own self-referential accounts of his exploits within the anti–Vietnam War movement, tried to have it both ways when he offered himself up as a war veteran–turned-countercultural participant in the protest years of the 1960s and 1970s. Mailer's experience in the military and his spare, naturalistic account of the World War II Pacific front in his novel, *The Naked and the Dead* (which was based, in good part, on the notes to his wife that he made when he would slip out of sight of his unit to write, and which led one of his unit comrades to comment after reading the novel, "Here they are, dammit. Those are the guys from basic") always loomed in the background of his autobiographical tales of his involvement with the radicals of the antiwar left in *Armies of the Night* and *Miami and the Siege of Chicago.* It has been difficult for some to accept Mailer's exhibitionist, in-your-face approach to life, his celebrated feuds, and his history of domestic abuse as the actions of a peace-loving person. Nonetheless, Mailer's hyperkinetic probing of the gun-loving mindset in *Why Are We in Vietnam?* is an impressive portrayal of the cultural aggressiveness of Americans that Mailer understood deeply. As a great admirer of Hemingway, Mailer was a master at submerging his inner life beneath grandiose performances of the self-promoting celebrity and the experimental stylist. However, despite his robust displays of ego, one can find glimpses of a troubled man in both his fiction and his nonfiction. Mailer's cultivation of the image of the artist living on the edge of violence and deviance—which he then transformed into a new image of himself as war protester and an opponent of militarism—has left him with a suspect legacy (at least, with the peace movement) and a reputation as a far from fully reliable commentator on the perennial question of whether war is an inevitable expression of fundamental human nature.[66]

With the changing nature of warfare, today's literary journalists are framing their themes of battlefield trauma in more inconclusive, paradox-filled, and professionally detached circumstances that reflect the nature of anti-insurgency combat fought by volunteer forces against indigenous foes in seemingly permanent campaigns of nation-building. Like the professional troops they traveled with in Afghanistan and/or Iraq, journalists such as Dexter Filkins, David Finkel, and Sebastian Junger have chronicled what Filkins described as the "ambiguity, the heartbreak, the fear and the joy" of American efforts to impose a military solution to the problems of terrorism, tribal division, poverty, religious polarity, and competition for natural resources in the Middle East. In their respective books, *The Forever War, The Good Soldiers*, and *War*, Filkins, Finkel, and Junger have presented themselves as neutral journalism professionals who offer no policy solutions while providing a ground-level view of the troops that fight in circumstances where death is more likely to come from a roadside bomb than frontline combat. However, they also have given glimpses of the cost of this experience to the human nervous system. In his eight months embedded with an American battalion in Iraq, Finkel said the dangers of roadside explosives meant that he was always thinking, "Is this the moment? Is this the moment?" Filkins— who has described everything in Iraq as "murky and gray and uncertain and possibly lethal"—said he would regularly go jogging in the streets of Baghdad, even though it was "crazy. . . . It was reckless, but I needed to do it to stay sane. . . . When I ran, I felt free." After he returned home, Filkins said he experienced the weddings and picnics the same way as "everything had been in Iraq, silent and slow and heavy and dead." When another reporter mentioned that he could not talk about Iraq with anyone who had not been there, Filkins responded: "I couldn't have a conversation with anyone who hadn't been there about anything at all."[67]

The journalist-literary figures' ambivalent feelings about war were on display in a poignant scene in Paris in 1939 where Hemingway, the Spanish Civil War idealist, and James Thurber were trying to persuade Ring Lardner's son, James, to go fight in Spain as a soldier (Hemingway's position) or "go as a reporter, if he must" (as Thurber was pleading). Lardner—who Thurber said just gave him "the old Lardner smile"—joined up and was killed, leaving Thurber in the lonely role of arguing that writers should write and not participate as partisans. "This is one of the greatest menaces there is," Thurber said ". . . How can these bastards hope to get hold of what's the matter with the world" when they are so "Spanish war stricken" that they have lost all "balance and values?"[68]

If there were contradictions, vacillations, and turnabouts in the attitudes about war and peace among the journalist-literary figures who have experienced military conflict firsthand, they have tended to be consistent when it came to one uniting attribute—their general recognition of the violent consequences of warfare and the suffering it has caused for participants and those caught up in the violence. How much they recognized the impact of trauma on themselves is another question, however. As independent-minded, adventurous, and often idiosyncratic figures, each had his or her own way of personally dealing with what they had seen, heard, and felt in battlefield circumstances, and the emotional impact of witnessing combat was sometimes near the surface and sometimes buried beneath a tough outer shell constructed around a code of personal honor. However, even among those most swept up in the military mood, one can find examples of writings where the intensity and the cruelty of warfare are the dominant elements, and where the trauma of the experience is conveyed vividly to the reader. Whether or not they themselves demonstrated the symptoms of PTSD—and even if they proved to have little interest in exploring this in their journalism or other writings—the journalist-literary figures who knew military conflict firsthand have played an important role in disseminating the journalistic material and the literary themes that have given the world an intimate picture of the assault that warfare can be on the human psyche.

4

Depression, Drink, and Dissipation

Dysfunctional Lifestyles and Art as the Ultimate Stimulant

> "Words are, of course, the most powerful drug used by mankind."
>
> —Rudyard Kipling

There is a photograph of an aging "Papa" Hemingway at the height of his fame—bulky, puffy faced, his hair combed over his balding forehead, hoisting a bottle of Spanish wine to his lips at a bullfight in the summer of 1959. Hemingway had gone to Pamplona to relive the glory days of his youth that provided the setting for the critically acclaimed *The Sun Also Rises*. In the 1926 novel, drink played a vital role for the collection of expatriate friends who form the social circle in which Hemingway sets his psychological drama. Alcohol acts as an aphrodisiac, an energy stimulator, and a truth serum for the expatriates, fueling their partying, their sexual exploits, their repartee, and their witty but often ugly honesty with each other. After the book was published, young people and college students all over America were infatuated with it, and took to imitating the style, the mannerisms, the dialogue—and the drinking—of Hemingway's characters.[1]

Hemingway's romanticizing of drinking in the most celebrated novel of his youth provides a tragic counterpoint to the story of his last years—that of a depressed and despairing writer suffering from alcoholic psychosis, trying vainly to rediscover his lost talent, and ultimately committing suicide when he found himself unable to cope with the collapse of his body and mind. The biggest burden for the aging Hemingway (who made a series of secret trips to the Mayo Clinic where he unsuccessfully sought help) was to maintain the Hemingway myth—of machoism, of risk-taking, of the pursuit of danger and excitement, of hedonism and living for the day, of the worship of vitality and youth—against the reality of a burned-out life. An existence undermined by the very drinking that he so celebrated is demonstrated by the list of ailments he suffered in his waning years: paranoia and psychological disassociation, major depression, morbid anxiety, cirrhosis of the liver, diabetes, hypertension, kidney disease, high blood urea, edema of the ankles, cramps, chronic sleeplessness, episodes of sexual impotence, disfiguring skin problems, and obsession with suicide. As early as 1936, when he was in his mid-thirties, Hemingway—faced with a serious depression after many critics panned *Green Hills of Africa*—confessed that he thought he was "facing impotence, inability to write, insomnia and was going to blow my lousy head off." When older, he was said to be "merrier, more lovable, more bullshitty" while drunk; otherwise, he was "morose, silent, depressed."[2]

Hemingway was in the front row of a gallery of journalist-literary figures who have battled the bottle and/or drugs, struggled with depression and psychological episodes, and often lived lives of incredible dissipation and sexual self-indulgence. Drinking and drugs often were used to ease the pain of psychological distress and mask the symptoms that can grow out of traumatic experiences; sexual antics and other compulsive behaviors compensated for feelings of inadequacy mixed with narcissistic self-images and grandiose delusions. Art itself can serve as the ultimate stimulant and an escape mechanism for those trying to deal with inner turbulence. Depression, in particular, with its painful experience of a loss of meaning in life, combined with the adoption of manic defenses as a way to stimulate oneself out of low moods and to deal with the anxiety that depression always lurked behind life's ordinary events, has provoked many artists into embracing the intensity of writing as a method for restoring and retaining emotional equilibrium, no matter how fragile or short-lived. ("What a born melancholic I am!," Virginia Woolf declared at one point. "The only way I keep afloat is by working.") Still, psychologists have noted that any singular activity pursued with great fervor can prove to have an unbalancing impact on a healthy psychological foundation, and literary achievement often came as compensation for unhealed emotions and broken lives. As Graham Greene, one of the legendary drinkers, drug takers, and womanizers among the journalist-literary figures, put it: "Writing is a form of therapy; sometimes I wonder how all those who do not write, compose or paint can manage to escape the madness, the melancholia, the panic fear which is inherent in the human situation."[3]

For many of the literary figures in the United States and the British Isles who began their careers as journalists, substance abuse—traditionally alcohol, although throughout the years, drug taking, too—was something to lean on during their working years. Journalism is perhaps the only profession where drinking has been glorified and where the image of the hard-drinking journalist has been embraced and perpetuated in the lore and legend of the business. Journalists often have blamed their affinity for alcohol on deadline pressures, a footloose and transient work culture, and the demands of a professional activity that tends to put the needs of the present above concerns about the future. Booze also can serve as insulation for people who routinely are involved in chronicling traumatic events, as well as a method to regulate the traumas to the nervous system that can come with overwhelming experiences of anxiety and depression. Whether journalism creates alcoholic personalities or whether people with addictive tendencies are attracted to the business can be debated endlessly. But one thing is certain—up until recent years, when health considerations and public campaigns against drinking and substance abuse came to the front—journalists have tended to be proud of the way that drinking and the role of alcohol helped to define the profession, and they have accepted its use as a strategy for managing the psychic stresses and strains connected to traumatic experience.

The stereotype of the hard-drinking journalist is rife throughout the literature that has been written by journalists to both celebrate and condemn the lifestyle of the journalistic personality. In their play, *The Front Page*, Charles MacArthur and Ben Hecht, both ex-daily journalists themselves, referred to their main character, Hildy Johnson, as "of a vanishing type—the lusty, hoodlumesque, half-drunken caballero that was the newspaperman of our youth."[4] Throughout the decades, well-known journalist-literary figures have embellished this stereotype with such comments as: "A man is never happy for the present, but when he is drunk" (Samuel Johnson); "The drinking man is never less himself than during his sober moments" (Charles Lamb); "Abstainer, n. A weak person who yields to the temptation of denying himself a pleasure" (Ambrose Bierce); "Alcohol is nicissary f'r a man so that now an' thin he can have a good opinion iv himself, ondisturbed be th' facts" (Mister Dooley/Finley Peter Dunne); "I've made it a rule to never drink by daylight, and never to refuse a drink after dark" (H. L. Mencken); "An alcoholic is someone you don't like who drinks as much as you do" (Dylan Thomas); and finally, "Anybody can be a non-drunk. It takes a special talent to be a drunk. It takes endurance. Endurance is more important than truth" (Charles Bukowski).[5]

In his memoir, *A Drinking Life*, New York City journalist-literary figure Pete Hamill discussed the myth of the hard-drinking reporter and said that he appropriated it for himself by never thinking of himself as "a drunk; I was I thought, like many others—a drinker. I certainly didn't think I was an alcoholic." From Hemingway, Hamill said, he stole the "guise of the stoic drinker," and he was deeply influenced by the romance of Hemingway's hard-drinking characters in *The Sun Also Rises* and other novels. But when Hamill had to put together his newspaper's account of Hemingway's suicide, he said he was stunned by the experience. "His writing, his life, his courage, his drinking, were all part of the heroic image," Hamill said. "Suicide was not." No one that he knew in journalism knew the extent of how terrible Hemingway's final years were, Hamill said, even though the story he was assembling showed it "right there on the pages. I just didn't choose to see it."[6]

Modern psychology and family systems theory has tended to view alcoholism, drug abuse, and other compulsive and addictive behaviors as reflections of deeper emotional conflicts—including ones that can be triggered by traumatic events and traumatized feelings. In this perspective, one's ability to handle troubling emotional symptoms is less a test of strength, will, and character than it is an acknowledgment of the problem and a willingness to try to do something about it (whether in psychological counseling, alcoholics anonymous programs, antidepression and antianxiety medications, or a mixture of these). In the days before therapies and legal pharmaceutical alternatives existed—as was the case with many of the journalist-literary figures discussed in this study—the person with the troubled psyche and turbulent emotional life often found relief in a range of compensating behaviors such as drinking, pill popping, philandering, or simply succumbing to self-annihilating behavior. In fact, contemporary research about antianxiety medications indicates that untreated patients tend to turn most often to alcohol as an alternative.[7]

One set of researchers has suggested that the journalism profession per se should undergo psychotherapy treatment. They have postulated (based on personality tests given to a group of journalists, as well as journalism graduate students at Columbia University) that journalists tend to project their inner struggles onto the outside world, and that this has been the basis for much of the energy behind investigative reporting and the adversarial tradition of journalists at odds with government and leadership. S. Robert Lichter, Stanley Rothman, and Linda S. Lichter have argued that unhealthy psychological tensions have led to a range of characteristics in the profession, including narcissism and grandiosity, an addiction to stimulation and heightened experience, and the desire for social reform as a way to alleviate psychic tension. Although Lichters' and Rothman's research is best known for its conservative orientation, they have applied Freudian psychological concepts to the journalistic psyche in ways that mirror what some biographers have said about their journalist-literary figure subjects. (For example, one biographer of the muckraker Lincoln Steffens has implied that it was depression and psychic tension that, at least in part, fueled Steffens's investigative zeal, and that self-recriminations over past behaviors led him to believe that "he had finally succeeded in muckraking himself. . . . But, like muckraking as he had practiced it, exposure of this sort led to no structural changes, did not alter in the least the laws of his personality"; at the same time, fellow muckraker, Ida Tarbell, was clearly motivated in her expose, *The History of the Standard Oil Company*, by the family trauma she experienced when the Rockefeller cartel cornered the oil market in Pennsylvania where her father was trying to compete.)[8]

Still, there has not been a large body of quantitative research about journalists and their emotional troubles and problems with substance abuse—and none about the literary figures who have started out in journalism per se. However, there have been studies about the effect of job dissatisfaction and burnout on journalists.[9] Also, a number of research findings have shown substantial degrees of alcohol use and psychological disorders in journalists involved in covering war.[10]

Depression, Anxiety, Aberrant Behavior, and the Journalist-Literary Figure

Although the lives of the best-known journalist-literary figures cannot be presumed to be a reflection of their involvement in journalism alone, it is difficult not to notice how many exhibited damaging psychological compulsions and mental health symptoms at rates that appear to be much higher than in the public at large.[11] Of the 150 writers identified as journalist-literary figures in this study, more than two-thirds have been identified by biographers, critics, or scholars as having suffered from major mood swings, serious depression and/or anxiety, manic-depressive behavior, nervous breakdowns, or other psychological disorders. (See table 1 in the appendix.) Even though one cannot make statistical comparisons from a selected population or draw scientifically meaningful conclusions about earlier historical eras, it is worth noting that this figure compares to the roughly 15 percent of the general adult population that the U.S. Surgeon General has estimated suffers today from some kind of mental health problem. Although the stereotype of the journalist as a mentally troubled figure is not as commonplace as the type-cast of the hard-drinking journalist, there are journalists, such as one-time *New York Times* reporter and novelist Anna Quindlen, who have noticed the phenomenon. "Being a reporter is as much a diagnosis as a job description," she once wise-cracked.[12]

The connections between emotional trauma and psychological stress suffered in early life is well documented by researchers, and a number of the journalist-literary figures recognized their mental health problems, destructive behaviors, and aberrational lifestyles as rooted in earlier traumatic and stressful experience (or, if they did not, their biographers and critics have made the connections). Djuna Barnes, who experienced childhood traumas growing up with an amoral and philandering father, suffered in her adult years from depression, alcoholism, suicidal impulses, and myriad physical ailments, as well as engaging in multiple bisexual affairs and being institutionalized for a time. She once summarized her life this way: "I have suffered shock, betrayal, disenchantment, outrage, the perpetual anxiety of small and uncertain money, and ill health." Others gave names to their internal tormentors that tell something of the pain that rested beneath their lives. James Boswell called his affliction "hypochondria"—a profound melancholy and the compulsive sexual antics that often grew out of it—and "the foul fiend" that would grip him episodically. The rotund William Thackeray described his depression as "fits of blue devils" and joked, "Despair is perfectly compatible with a good dinner, I promise you." Hemingway would complain about having a "bad head," and E. B. White talked about having "mice in the subconscious." G. K. Chesterton experienced free-floating anxiety waiting to attach itself to a target, and as a youth was fixated on the idea that the world was not real and was only a projection of his own mind. Theodore Dreiser's "nervous" disease as he sometimes described his condition led to a host of anxious broodings, imagined ailments, and periodic breakdowns throughout his life, and he would take refuge in sexual escapades and heavy drinking. A famous hypochondriac, Heywood Broun was tormented by the idea that he was going to suffer a heart attack, despite doctors finding no evidence of it. (White joked how Broun "once bought me a drink and kept taking his pulse to see whether he was still alive.")[13]

Only on the rarest of occasions, however, was a journalist-literary figure willing to discuss his or her psychological travails in an open public forum. One of the few who did was Boswell, who said his purpose in writing his "Hypochondriack" column in *London Magazine* was to divert melancholy readers from "dwelling on their uneasiness" by finding "satisfaction [from] those who have felt the same distresses . . . the fretfulness, the gloom, and the despair that can torment a thinking being." Although written anonymously, the column was widely known to be Boswell's, and he persisted in publishing it despite what many readers of his time believed were far too intimate reflections about his inner life. A hypochondriac "dies many times before his death. . . . When one has found relief by any remedy, however accidental, it is humane to mention it to others," Boswell wrote. Many of his essays involved a cataloguing of the miseries he experienced—including dealing with "an extreme degree of irritability" that makes a person "liable to be hurt by every thing that approaches him" and ruminating "upon all the evils that can happen" such that one never has "a moment's tranquility." For Boswell, religion provided some sustenance ("How blessed is the relief which he may have . . . from the comforts of God . . . who graciously hears the prayers of the afflicted")—although it was writing that proved to be the best therapy. "While writing this paper, I have by some gracious influence been sensibly relieved from the distress under which I laboured when I began it," he wrote.[14]

Edgar Allan Poe was a literary innovator—in the development of the detective novel, in the application of poetic rhythms to prose writing—but his most memorable contribution to the literary tradition may be in the way that he perfected the eerie, disturbed tone of the survivor of traumatizing experience in narrating stories of the bizarre and the macabre. Poe's mastery of the technique of the psychologically unhinged personality as the chilling storyteller grew out of his familiarity with the "horror story" formulas of folk tales and the tradition of Gothic writing. But Poe's own bouts of "madness" and his strange relationships—particularly with his cousin and sickly child bride, Virginia (she was thirteen years old when she married the twenty-seven-year-old Poe in 1836 and twenty-five when she died of consumption)—have led critics and readers to make inexorable connections between his own life and the themes of morbidity and terror that he used to titillate his audience. In his story "Berenice"—where a deranged and grieving narrator finds the teeth of his recently deceased cousin-fiancée (over which he has obsessed throughout the story as she deteriorated from an unnamed disease) in a box by his bed—Poe attributed to his narrator many of the syndromes (obsessive-compulsiveness, hypersensitivity to things around him, and extreme anxiety) that Poe suffered from in his own life. His technique of dramatizing the psychological effects of traumatic feelings and experiences—also made famous in his stories, "The Tell-Tale Heart," with its narrator driven to murder by his obsession with an old man's "vulture-like eye," and "The Fall of the House of

Usher," in which an overwrought man entombs alive his twin sister who is prone to cataleptic and deathlike trances—was so effective that Poe as both the model for and the creator of the narrator revealing his or her own insanity has been imitated in movies, television dramas, and popular literature ever since, and Poe's image as the archetype of the emotionally tortured but brilliant artist has become enshrined in the popular understanding of how traumatic experience can overwhelm the mind and the nervous system.[15]

Charlotte Perkins Gilman's *The Yellow Wallpaper*, published in 1899, is Poe-like in its unfolding horror in telling the tale (based on Gilman's own experience) of a woman going mad inside a suffocating marriage. "You see he does not believe I am sick?" says the bedridden narrator of the story. "And what can one do? If a physician of high standing, and one's own husband, assures friends and relatives that there is really nothing the matter with one but temporary nervous depression—a slight hysterical tendency—what is one to do?" Elaine R. Hedges has noted that in Gilman's time most people did not see a connection between insanity and sex role, and Gilman's tale shocked even advocates for women's rights. When the narrator imagines patterns in the wallpaper and wants to repaper her room, she says her husband tells her that "with my imaginative power and habit of story-making, a nervous weakness like mine is sure to lead to all manner of excited fancies, and that I ought to use my will and good sense to check the tendency. So I try." The shocking ending—where after seeing creeping women in the wallpaper, the narrator is discovered by her husband to be completely mad and creeping on her knees around her bedroom—is matched by Gilman's personal story of suffering a nervous breakdown during her marriage, becoming a "mental wreck" after the birth of her daughter, and then being pilloried in the press for divorcing her husband and leaving her daughter in his custody.[16]

Sari Edelstein has argued that the *Yellow Wallpaper* should be seen as a symbolic protest against yellow journalism, as well as a protest against patriarchal oppression and the rise of the consumer culture that pushed women to identify their lives with mass-produced products. Gilman engaged in a famous feud with Ambrose Bierce who loved to tussle with women's rights advocates and wrote in his "Prattle" column, "With rare exceptions, women who write . . . are moral idiots." Gilman had been interviewed by a Hearst reporter and asked that he keep details of her divorce out of the papers in respect to her dying mother. The story was written anyway, and, as she put it, her name "became a football" in the newspapers. With a father who had abandoned the family and a mother who taught her to never show weakness, Gilman craved paternal approval, and her vision of the "new woman," while challenging patriarchal culture, still demanded that men behave as gentlemen and have proper respect for women. "Attacks from the local press are meat and drink to him (Bierce)—he has plenty, and minds them not a whit," she wrote in a letter to an eastern professor. "Is there no way by which his literary conscience could be reached?" Most of her novels were utopian and didactic to the core, and she found that she could neatly resolve conflicts between the sexes in her fictional fantasies that eluded her in real life. As Shelley Fisher Fishkin has noted, many of Gilman's ideas to make life easier for women have become reality—day care, take-out food, home-cleaning services, child care professionals—even though she herself never fully recovered from her nervous breakdown and suffered from crying fits, depression, and fatigue throughout her life.[17]

Poe's notions of romance and madness—and the public's voyeuristic interest in the world of the insane that grew throughout the nineteenth century—were exemplified in the sensationalistic journalism of Nellie Bly and the way that she turned her encounters with trauma into performance art. Bly's stunt in getting herself committed to the infamous insane asylum on New York's Blackwell Island in 1887 was acceptable within the traditions of the city's lowbrow newspapers. But her account—where she adopted the manner of the "hysteric" female who was viewed as the typecast of the mad woman in her time—also served a subversive purpose in challenging the power of the predominantly male medical establishment and raising questions about how it treated disempowered women. Although the *New York World*'s handling of the story put the focus on the outrages endured by Bly, today's critics have suggested that the symptoms of hysteria might be blamed on Victorian society and its views about the fragility of female nature. By showing that she could convincingly act the role of the hysteric without being hysterical, Bly dramatized the fallacies of the expert tendency to pathologize differences of race, class, and gender and implicitly challenged narrowly drawn definitions of womanhood. Her success at "faking it" was made vivid by her claim that from the moment she entered the asylum, "I talked and acted just as I do in ordinary life. Yet strange to say, the more sanely I talked and acted, the crazier I was thought to be." The *World*'s use of Bly to exploit traumatic experience—done in the name of reform, but largely carried off to sell newspapers—was hardly above reproach, and Bly's actions were hardly what can be called an unalloyed blow for feminine advancement. But her stunt did open the hidden world of Victorian psychological treatment to public inspection and produced an investigative precedent that in the decades ahead would lead to important changes in psychiatric treatment within medical institutions.[18]

In reading the accounts of the women stunt reporters of the late nineteenth and early twentieth centuries—two of the most prominent being Bly and Barnes—one cannot help but wonder whether trauma played an underlying role in their attraction to public displays of the brave but vulnerable woman reporter willing to experience dangerous circumstances for the entertainment of sensation-seeking readers. Although by all accounts, Bly did not seek out the assignment that made her reputation, the theatrics that fooled police, judges, and hospital officials into committing her may have cut closer to the bone than readers of the *World* ever suspected. Her account in the *World* maintained the appropriate Victorian picture of a respectable young woman manufacturing hysterical symptoms in highly dubious circumstances (at one point she noted that she had never been near insane persons or had contact with people in the city's poverty zones; at others, she indicated that she had to repress her desire to slap doctors when they asked her if she had ever prostituted herself), but one wonders about the mental strain she must have experienced as a person who had suffered youthful trauma and would experience serious bouts of depression throughout her life. (One also has to entertain the question of whether the *World* itself was guilty of traumatizing Bly, as well as taking advantage of what it could ask an ambitious woman reporter to undertake in order to get ahead in a profession where women had few opportunities to make a name for themselves). Barnes, too, may be seen as a victim of double traumatization, given her traumatic childhood sexual experiences, when she became a famous New York newspaper stunt reporter who engaged in "seductive and ironic spectacle that courted the male gaze," in the words of one critic, and developed a fetishistic interest in people who involved themselves in lurid personal displays and dramatized their neuroses for public inspection. Even well into the twentieth century, there were sensationalist newspapers that followed in the tradition of asking traumatized women journalists to put themselves into dubious reporting situations—such as happened when Dorothy Day, already dealing with the effects of an abortion with a man who had left her and the birth of a child by another man who would soon leave her, was asked by the New Orleans *Item* to get a job as a taxi dancer on Canal Street and to write stories about the other dancers.[19]

The poignancy of early life traumas, and their influence in adult personal problems, can be seen in the confusing relationships a number of journalist-literary figures had with their parents in their early years. As Alice Miller has postulated, many gifted persons with neurotic, narcissistic parents grow up without any notion of their true selves and live with a hollow emotional core beneath a conforming outer self. A serious consequence of this early adaptation can be the difficulty of consciously experiencing certain feelings of one's own instead of responding to what a parent needs a child to feel. For example, J. M. Barrie's older brother's death when Barrie was six left his mother bedridden for much of the rest of her life. At one point, Barrie's older sister told him to go to their mother and say to her, "she still had another little boy." In the dark of her bedroom, Barrie's mother at first thought he was his dead brother. When Barrie told her, "No. It's no' him, it's just me," she let out a cry and held out her arms for him. From that day forward, Barrie would sit with her, listen to her tell stories of her childhood (which he borrowed from for the creation of his Peter Pan and Wendy characters), and try to make her forget his dead brother. Barrie's apparent desire to rest permanently in boyhood is commonly connected to his relationship with his invalid mother (who also has been interpreted as the inspiration for Barrie's 1887 article in the *Edinburgh Evening Dispatch*, in which he recounted a "ghastly nightmare" where he wrestles with a "heavy shapeless mass" of a female figure with a "mesmeric" power over him and whom he follows obediently even as she binds him in iron chains and "laughing horribly" drives him to a church to marry him). As biographer Lisa Chaney notes, Barrie, in his adult life, suffered from serious mood swings, a sense that he was incapable of deep feeling or real passion, and an unrelenting habit of observing himself outside of himself. He felt he must always be good, otherwise the risk was too great; life did not seem real to him, and he preferred to live in a state where he was waiting for it to begin; he took on prodigious tasks (such as artistic projects) as a defense against depression, which could only be warded off with increasing displays of brilliance. Simultaneously, Barrie exulted in trying to make women love him but would feel used and think that they only wanted him for their emotional satisfaction. Even though he ultimately married, Chaney said that the marriage was never consummated; Barrie once wrote in his notebook that the curse of his life was that he had never had sex with a woman. (Barrie's life mirrors other journalist-literary figures who suffered from "Peterpantheism"—H. G. Wells's term to describe his own resistance to growing up and accepting adult responsibilities and that also can be applied to James Russell Lowell, who was raised by a mother who had been insane for many years before she was committed when he was in his mid-twenties.)[20]

Wells's dynamism made him a popular public figure—including with the many "liberated" women (besides Rebecca West) that he both mentored and carried on affairs with. However, Wells suffered often in the shadows of his darker side: As a teenager, he threatened suicide to force his parents to let him resume his education; he was prone to feelings of claustrophobia, anxiety, and depression; and he experienced recurring emotional collapses throughout his life. The lonely circumstances of Wells's protagonists in *The Invisible Man* and *The Time Machine* have been interpreted as reflections of his sense of abandonment when his mother, a lady's assistant, thrust the fourteen-year-old Wells—in response to his storekeeper father's descent into squalor and bankruptcy—out into the world to work and care for himself. Wells explained that his ambition to rise above his working-class roots was fueled by anger at "the paltry sham of an education that had been fobbed off upon me. . . . I hated them (his parents) as only the young can hate, and it gave me the energy to struggle . . . for knowledge." However, when his exuberant approach to life (or what he came to call "the wild rush of Boomster") failed him, he would drop into fits of gloom (in the midst of which he once wrote a letter to a friend that concluded, "Damn, damn, damn, damn, damn, damn, God damn, God damn, God damn, God damn").[21]

Anxieties connected to youthful trauma also plagued Chesterton, who had an older sister who died when she was eight and Chesterton was three—and whose death was the only subject that his father would never discuss. Chesterton said that he did not remember his sister dying, but he did remember her falling off a rocking horse. "I always felt it as a tragic memory, as if she had been thrown by a real horse and killed. . . . This is the real difficulty about remembering anything; that we have remembered too much—for we have remembered too often," he wrote. Interestingly, in his autobiography, Chesterton did not tie his sister's death or his father's reaction to it to the period in Chesterton's teenage years when he described himself as full of "doubts" and "morbidities" and "temptations." During this period, Chesterton said he "did not very clearly distinguish between dreaming and waking; not only as a mood but as a metaphysical doubt. I felt as if everything might be a dream." Eventually, he said that he invented a "rudimentary and makeshift mystical theory" of his own and decided, "anything was magnificent as compared with nothing"—which laid the groundwork for his conversion to Roman Catholicism. As he expanded on this in his book, *Orthodoxy*, Chesterton said he found others who seemed to understand. "In this period of lunacy," he said, "I may have been a little useful to other lunatics." He said he decided that the curates of the church were wiser than anybody else was, and—with the debates about whether there was a God—"it was my experience that entering into the system even socially brought an ever-increasing certitude upon the original question." With this viewpoint, Chesterton's growing conservatism as he gravitated from his youthful socialist and agnostic beliefs into one of the most prominent intellectuals to publicly advocate for orthodox Christianity may account for his non-Freudian manner of interpreting his childhood experiences, as well as his increasing tendency to scoff at those who ignored "the solidity of Sin," as he put it, and preferred psychological explanations.[22]

Truman Capote's anxieties were as overwhelming as Poe's were, and they were intensified by painful experiences early in life that he saw as compounding the difficulties of his literary career. Capote once said, "Something in my life has done a terrible hurt to me, and it seems to be irrevocable." In talking as an adult about the times in his youth when his mother would abandon him in hotel rooms, Capote said, "That's when my claustrophobia and fear of abandonment began. She locked me up and I still can't get out. She was the cause of all my anxiety—'free-floating anxiety' is what all the psychiatrists say I have. If you've never had it, you don't know what it's like. . . . I live with it constantly. I'm never ever free from it. . . . You don't know what you're afraid of. Except something bad is going to happen, only you don't know what it is." Capote presented a desperate and pathetic picture of the person he became as an adult. "Every morning I wake up and in about two minutes I'm weeping. I just cry and cry. And every night the same thing happens. . . . The pain is not about any one thing; it's about a lot of things. I'm so unhappy." Capote easily and repeatedly acknowledged his alcoholism, as well as his dependency on cocaine, tranquillizers, and other drugs, which he said he was addicted to for the last two decades of his life. He tried to dry out on repeated occasions, but "the minute I get out I'll go back to my old ways," he said. "I know me. I'm just the person I am and I'm not going to be any different. I'm always going to drink. Undoubtedly it will kill me in the end." Although it was substance abuse that did kill him, he and others have pointed to the stress of completing *In Cold Blood* in painting a traumatic picture of the book's impact on his physical and mental decline. "He never really recovered from that book. . . . It was very destructive for him, especially when those boys wanted him to witness their hanging," said his friend Phyllis Cerf. "I don't know why he put himself through that, but he did. He thought that he was tougher than he was and that he could take it. But he couldn't."[23]

One of the more chilling events in Norman Mailer's life was his stabbing Adele Morales, the second of his six wives, in the stomach with a kitchen knife during an all-night party at their apartment in 1960. The efforts by his friends and supporters to minimize the impact of his brief institutionalization in a New York mental hospital reflected Mailer's anxiety that the antisocial themes of his writing might be taken less seriously if he was determined to be mentally ill (a worry that preoccupied him much more than his concern for Morales's recovery or the expression to her of any misgivings over the incident). Yet, five years later, his novel, *An American Dream*, presented the story of a husband, Steve Rojack, who murders his wife and goes unpunished despite his many perversities and lurid obsessions that are revealed throughout the narrative. In a radical act of self-revelation, Mailer's work virtually invites any reader to compare its themes with his own history of confrontational public spectacles and escapes from the consequences of his violent actions (as happened when Morales dropped the charges in the stabbing case). Mailer (who once predicted that his attack on his wife would be the first sentence of his obituary) told the *New York Times*, in 2000, it was the "one act I can look back on and regret for the rest of my life." However, his obsession with celebrity and his drive to make the public probing of his troubled psyche symptomatic of the sickness of his time have left scholars and critics debating whether Mailer's literary reputation will survive the passage of his outsized ego and his public theatrics (or what Kurt Vonnegut described as Mailer performing "in public what he had written") from the media stage.[24]

The power of depression and traumatic emotional collapse to infuse a writer's literary vision comes through repeatedly in Joan Didion's novels, where the bleak atmosphere and nihilistic moods of her protagonists reflect Didion's lifelong struggle with depression and profound feelings of meaninglessness. Didion's honesty in acknowledging her emotional struggles is demonstrated at the beginning of her book of essays, *The White Album*, in which she included a copy of a psychiatric outpatient examination of her in 1968 (where doctors indicated that she had a personality in "process of deterioration," "alienated herself almost entirely from the world of other human beings," and demonstrated "obviously and seriously impaired" reality contact and a worldview that was "fundamentally pessimistic, fatalistic, and depressive"). That Didion's novels have been best-sellers is a commentary not only on the literary mood of the age, but on the openness of authors in a post-Freudian era in displaying their own psychological maladjustments for a world that has supposedly lost its moral and philosophical bearings. In many respects, it is amazing that Didion, with her pervasive sadness and moods of withdrawal, her dependency and passivity, and her persistent migraine headaches, has been able to produce such a volume of fiction and literary journalism. Yet clearly her sense of cultural and psychological dissonance—combined with her precise and elegant prose that has long been admired by fans of literary journalism—has struck a chord with an audience that has become accustomed to literary themes of alienation and anomie. Although her marriage to

John Gregory Dunne did not lift her depression, it nonetheless provided her with strong personal support (the two were remarkably bonded and, despite some periods of disharmony, spent almost all their personal and working time together), and the intensity of her emotional episodes (sometimes causing her vertigo and nausea) never impaired her functioning as a writer.[25]

Didion's prolific creative production amid her chronic depression is a reminder of the studies that have shown depression's benefits in stimulating some of the creative and psychologically healing elements that can be found in the prose and the writing activities of many journalist-literary figures: a great ability to focus, the capacity to turn compulsive ruminations into creative products, the capability of managing emotional issues by writing about them, and the insight to see the world in realistic terms and to cut through society's evasions to the painful truth of things. The concept of depression as the body's adaptive response to affliction and trauma that can have positive benefits is gaining ground in some research quarters. However, as other researchers caution, one must be careful in too blithely presuming that emotional pain can be a beneficial thing. As Andrew Thomson points out, "To say that depression can be useful doesn't mean it's always going to be useful"; or, as Jonah Lehrer adds, "even if our pain is useful, the urge to escape from the pain remains the most powerful instinct of all." That so many journalist-literary figures put their emotional pain to creative use—but also adopted strategies to escape the pain that often led to tragic outcomes in their lives—is a sign that traumatic experience and its internalization are not something that can simply be written off as the sacrifices necessary to the production of art nor can they be understood without trying to recognize what the experience of that pain really meant.[26]

Drinking, Substance Abuse, and Dysfunctional Lives

Just under half of the journalist-literary figures in this study were viewed by biographers as engaging in excessive drinking and/or serious drug use at some point in their lives. (See table 1 in the appendix.) Again, although one cannot do a formal comparison between these selected journalist-artists and the general population of their eras, this is roughly twice the rate of today's population (25 percent) that the National Institutes of Health have estimated has some form of drinking and substance abuse problem.[27] A number of journalist-literary figures died earlier than they would have if it were not for the consequences of alcoholism or drug use whereas others managed to live out normal length and even relatively long lives but spent much of their time under the influence of alcohol or drugs.

By tradition, journalists are seldom people who are candid about their inner life or confide in each other about their problems when a drink is available as an alternative. To confess openly to emotional struggles, or to try to deal with them through therapy or counseling, does not typically fit with journalists' macho self-image or their stoical attitudes toward life. Since the editors of the Penny Press newspapers began to hire opportunistic young people as reporters in the early 1800s, journalists have been creating a public image of themselves as itinerants and journeymen, as people who run from their troubles, drift from job to job, and live for little but their work (and their play). Howard Good, in his examination of the image of the American journalist in fiction from 1890 to 1930, has noted that the "frowsy, allegedly bohemian drunken reporter" has become a prototype and has survived because it strikes a chord with the public.[28] Loren Ghiglione also has examined the phenomenon of the typecast of the journalistic character in literature, which included the "hard-living, fun-loving, irresponsible" reporter who Ghiglione said, "wears his rumpled fedora inside, keeps a whiskey flask in his bottom desk drawer, wisecracks out of one side of his mouth while smoking a dangling cigarette out of the other."[29]

Although the hard-drinking journalist-literary figures seldom went so far as to claim that their use of alcohol was medicinal or therapeutic in purpose and a method to curb overpowering emotions, a few of them did. For example, Conrad Aiken—who often downed a batch of martinis before lunch and dinner—defended drinking as "insulation" against the burden of consciousness and claimed that alcohol ministered to stress points in his psyche, numbing the pain inflicted by memory and a sensitive nature. Some have even suggested—such as happened when Eugene O'Neill quit drinking and did not write a Broadway play for a dozen years—that alcohol somehow may facilitate artistic production. Hutchins Hapgood also pointed to the use of alcohol, in combination with the professional demands and lifestyle of journalism, as "management" tools for depression, anxiety, and emotional turbulence. "Work takes one away from life, is a buffer between sensitive nerves and intensest experience," he said. "Strong natures who for some reason are dislocated . . . come too much in contact with life and often cannot bear it; it burns and palls at once." Hapgood (one of whose reminiscences, similar to Lamb's, Hamill's, and Susan Cheever's, was entitled "My Forty Years of Drink") often was immobilized by anxious introspection and a fatalistic response to his nervous debilitations; he said his psychological pain would only leave him in "moments of creative work, of great and satisfying love, of physical exertion in the face of Nature—but it was always there, in the background, lingering . . . waiting."[30]

By mid to later life, many of the journalist-literary figures were engaging in behavior that helped to make their legends—but which often was a disaster for the family and friends who cared for them. Thackeray, for example, refined his appetite for gambling, drinking, and prodigious eating in the "amiable but dissipated" company of journalists and other friends during his years writing for *Punch* and various London newspapers (during his life, he told a friend, he had drunk enough to float a seventy-four-gun battleship); as his health declined in his later years, he seemed gripped with lethargy and a sense of resignation to the effects of eating and drinking to excess. During his early years as a journalist in San Francisco, Bierce let his wife tend to their growing family while he slept half the day, wrote half the night, and drank around town with his friends. Ring Lardner took to drinking early, and by the time he was a young baseball writer, his alcohol consumption was enough to horrify his wife; at the height of his fame, Lardner was known for abandoning his family for days on end while he went on all-day-and-night drinking binges. James Agee spent hours boozing with journalists and Hollywood friends, wearing the same dirty clothes day after day as a screenwriter, and, in the words of one observer, living "in a fog of crapulous laundry, stale cigarette smoke, and dirty dishes, sans furniture or cleanliness" in fellow alcoholic Dorothy Parker's Los Angeles home. Robert Benchley and his friends became so drunkenly boisterous night after night in the motel where he lived as an L.A. actor and screenwriter that neighbors complained—but Benchley, already suffering from the effects of a wasted liver, could not contain his binges. Dreiser became a heavy drinker who would start strong on his writing projects in the morning, began to fade by noon, and then take off to buy whisky; one time he was missing for two days until the madam of a brothel called his home to report that Dreiser, drinking and quarrelsome, would not leave. Evelyn Waugh sounded personally nihilistic in his last years; the more he drank, the more he was prone to saying that he had lived longer than he wanted to and that he just did not care to go on anymore. (The way his father dealt with his habitual melancholy was by "relying on gin," said Auberon Waugh, "which is almost certainly not the best cure.") Three decades of this regimen left the elder Waugh suffering from arthritis, rheumatism, sciatica, rotting teeth, insomnia, hallucinating voices, and a fading memory by his mid-fifties.[31]

The stereotypical image of the drunken journalist sometimes has been perpetuated by journalist-literary figures in their own literature. For example,

O'Neill's besotted reporter character Sid, in the play *Ah, Wilderness!*, demonstrated that even a spectacular alcoholic writer could acknowledge the consequences of life lived out of a bottle. In real life, O'Neill, who linked the genesis of his drinking life with his professional life while he was a young reporter on the *New London Telegraph* (Connecticut), became the prototype of the "lush" writer who stays ensnared in a familial alcoholic pattern. O'Neill followed in the path of his father, whose heavy drinking was enabled by his life as a touring actor who socialized with other hard-drinking friends and colleagues. However, O'Neill's mother—the model for the neurotic family grand dame in his autobiographical play *Long Day's Journey into Night*—became the leading figure in O'Neill's own lifetime of alcoholism and emotional drama. After learning early in their marriage that another woman claimed to be married to his father and to have fathered a son with him, O'Neill's mother became a morphine addict following the birth of Eugene in 1888. In the play, O'Neill portrayed the character, Mary Tyrone, as saying to her son, "You were born afraid. Because I was so afraid to bring you into the world." Although O'Neill was at first shielded from the knowledge of his mother's addiction, he learned about it at age fourteen when she ran out of morphine and tried to throw herself off the family dock. It was at this point that O'Neill came to realize how his mother's addiction had affected every member of the family, which is what makes *Long Day's Journey into Night* one of the great dramatic and literary presentations of a dysfunctional family system case study.[32]

Others with family pattern alcohol problems—Poe, O. Henry, Capote, Damon Runyon, Jimmy Breslin, Mike Royko—demonstrated in artistic and journalistic venues the now well-accepted psychological theory that children of alcoholics have a greater tendency to become ones themselves. Cheever, the daughter of author John Cheever, has revealed in a variety of self-confessional writings and family exposés the many ways that the dysfunction of alcohol addiction is visited on children. In *Home before Dark*, she began what amounted to a publishing version of a recovery program by detailing what lay behind the façade of her father's life—his alcoholism, his troubled marriage, his failings as a parent, his confused sexual life where he came to act on his long-repressed homosexual feelings. In her next installment, *Note Found in a Bottle*, she examined her own life as a recovering alcoholic and tried to make amends for her behavior with friends, family, and lovers. Her third book, *As Good as I Could Be*, credited motherhood with helping to turn her life around, and—even though, as one critic said, the book should not be taken as a place to get parenting tips—she received praise in some critical quarters for her painfully honest self-examination.[33]

Agee's excruciating account of alcoholic thinking in the portrayal of his uncle in *A Death in the Family* presents a powerful picture of how an anguished drinker might feel during times of trauma—and one recognizes that Agee should know, given his own alcoholism and his experiences of trauma. As Agee told it in quasi-fictional form, his uncle Ralph's mixture of self-pity, self-loathing, and agonizing self-consciousness is triggered by the responsibility that he felt for unnecessarily summoning Agee's father, Jay, to their parents' house in the Tennessee mountains, after which Jay died in an auto crash on his way back home to Knoxville. As his uncle tries to comfort their mother after they have received the news, Agee writes how Ralph began "to feel that everyone else was watching him, and knew he was no use. . . . There was nothing to do, nothing to take charge of . . . and he began to think that he would burn up and die if he didn't have another drink." As Ralph escapes outside to satisfy "the ferocity of his thirst," he realizes that "he would never change, except for the worse. . . . He was just weak . . . like a chicken that comes out of the shell with a wry neck and grows on up like that . . . and he knew why he so often felt that she [his mother] did not really love him. It was because she was so sorry for him, and because she had never had and never possibly could have, any respect for him." Although Agee could not truly know what his uncle was thinking, the semifictionalized segment only slightly diminished Agee's goal of being true to the details surrounding his father's death as he remembered them. Agee's philosophy of writing about the past—that memory fused with subjective feeling and empathetic insight about others could produce a "truer" literary account than trying to extract some "objective" picture out of historical events—gives credibility to his "imagining" the way Ralph felt (and particularly so when the reader knows that Agee, as an out-of-control drinker himself, must have been highly familiar with the compulsive feelings that he imputes to his uncle—who, as Frank Agee in real life, showed up roaring drunk at Agee's father's funeral).[34]

Agee's insights into alcohol's grip on the personality follow the tradition of other journalist-literary figures writing in confessional mode about the blame they placed on alcohol or other substances for their troubles. An early variation of this—the temperance tract—was produced in 1842 by Walt Whitman in *Franklin Evans*, a propagandistic novel filled with emotional exhortations and moralistic language about the perils of drink. (Whitman liked to joke that he wrote the book for money in three days while under the influence of port, gin, and whisky.) In the novel, in which inebriation brings the protagonist to crime, causes the death of his wife, and leads to pain, mortification, and disgust with himself, Franklin Evans says of his first drink, "Oh, fatal pleasure! There and then was my first false step . . . I tremble now as I look back upon the results which have sprung from the conduct of that single night, as from one seed of evil." Whitman privately called the novel "damned rot—rot of the worst sort—not insincere, perhaps, but rot, nevertheless" and later took to disavowing it. His years as a journeyman journalist had taught Whitman how to use affected sentiment and exclamatory phrases in his editorial writings—but which (in ways that surprised his contemporaries) were beautifully transformed when he blended them into his free-verse poetry. (Interestingly, Whitman, a social drinker throughout much of his life, appears to have been offended less by the temperance message in the book—he had some sympathies for campaigns against drunkenness—than by the sloppy writing and the moralistic manner in which he framed the narrative. As the great sensualist and romantic advocate of passion and emotional freedom, Whitman was hardly puritanical in his view of human vices.)[35]

Whitman's novel quoted from Lamb's 1833 "Confessions of a Drunkard," a romantic's version of the temperance tract that was written in the confessional tradition that helped to establish the image of the artist as helpless before his or her compulsions and passionate attachments. In embracing the conflicted, irrational nature of the human personality, Lamb acknowledged that repentance and reform were unlikely to come easily to one who elegizes pain but does not always want to feel it. Lamb's picture of himself (he wrote his tract anonymously but was credited as the author by acquaintances as soon as it appeared) was both self-justifying and self-mortifying in that it asked readers to avoid what the author had not been able to help succumbing to—and did not intend to stop doing. ("What a dreary thing it is when a man shall feel himself going down a precipice with open eyes and a passive will,—to see his destruction and have no power to stop it. . . . But is there no middle way betwixt total abstinence and the excess which kills you? . . . With pain I must utter the dreadful truth, that there is none, none that I can find.") Unlike his friend, Thomas De Quincey, who, in *The Confessions of an English Opium Eater*, declared he had kicked his opium habit (which he had not), or London in *John Barleycorn* (who pretended that he could control a life of modest imbibing, which he could not), Lamb simply declared himself a failure at the task of abstaining. "Life itself, my waking life, has much of the confusion, the trouble, and obscure perplexity, of an ill dream. . . . I have told [the reader] what I am come to. Let him stop in time."[36]

In contrast to Whitman's temperance tract (which was filled with things he did not really believe) and Lamb's confessional (which was filled with things he believed but could not accomplish), De Quincey's memoir is a candid and nonmoralistic account of an opium addict's ambivalence about the pain as well as the positives that he found in his drug use. De Quincey's work—published anonymously at first, and then under his name—was unique for its time because he chose not to discuss the negative side of drug addiction without putting it within the context of the things that had attracted him to opium use—which he called "the accursed chain which fettered me" but also "this fascinating enthrallment." "What an apocalypse of the world within me!" he said of first ingesting the drug after he obtained it from a druggist. "That my pains had vanished was now a trifle in my eyes:—this negative effect was swallowed up in the immensity of those positive effects which had opened before me—in the abyss of divine enjoyment this suddenly revealed. Here was the panacea . . . for all human woes; here was the secret of happiness." At one point, he called himself the only member of "the true church on the subject of opium" and questioned those who focused only on the horror of opium use ("Lies! Lies! Lies!"). Opium made him feel "aloof from the uproar of life; as if the tumult, the fever, and the strife, were suspended; a respite granted from the secret burthens of the heart; a sabbath of repose; a resting from human labors." However, when he tried to reduce his opium intake, he could not stand the "unutterable irritation of stomach . . . accompanied by intense perspiration" that left him descending into "chasms and sunless abysses, depths below depths, from which it seemed hopeless that I could ever re-ascend." He claimed, however, that he had been able to "throw off" his addiction and that he was an example that opium use can be "renounced." (Yet, he acknowledged that, after four months without it, "think of me . . . still agitated, writhing, throbbing, palpitating, shattered"—and, as it would turn out, still addicted for life.)[37]

Greene's "whisky priest" in *The Power and the Glory* is another example of how an author's personal familiarity with substance abuse issues informed a portrayal of a tragically fated literary protagonist. Greene—whose tortured characters often mix religious longing, love gone awry, drug and alcohol use, and emotional health struggles into their angst-ridden lives—knew intimately about what he wrote, and his portrait of the doomed, fugitive priest during a Mexican government crackdown on the Catholic Church in the 1930s employed alcohol as both a metaphor for and the reality of the priest's empty spiritual life and the guilt he suffered. Greene portrayed the priest's well-known fondness for alcohol (as well as the daughter that he had fathered with a local peasant woman) as the mark of shame that he encountered in his dealings with the villagers that he hoped would hide him from the police. The priest's self loathing ("Wherever he went, whatever he did, he defiled God.

. . . He was a bad priest, he knew it") left him watched with contempt by his young daughter as he denied his identity while another man was taken as a hostage in his place, and the priest slinked away with a bottle of brandy in hand. The symbol of alcohol—as the substance of communion, the symptom of the priest's disgrace, and his insulation against the trauma of his impending execution after he is caught and jailed—suffused his final anguish (where he crouched on his cell floor with the empty brandy flask in his hand, saying, "Oh God, I am sorry and beg pardon for all my sins . . . crucified . . . worthy of Thy dreadful punishments . . . I have done nothing for anybody"). *The Power and the Glory* stands as a monument to Greene's recognition of the appeal of traumatic tales—and his brilliance at mixing the themes of religion, substance abuse, and tragic life experience—that grew out of his attraction to this formula in his own life, and his own inability (or unwillingness) to counter the power that intoxication of various kinds had over his personality and his writing career.[38]

Quite often, the hard-drinking journalist-literary figures bought into the image of the "good" and even the heroic drunk, and they seldom thought of their use of alcohol or drugs as compensating behavior for troubled inner lives. A common tendency among these figures was to romanticize drinking, even as they claimed (and probably believed) that they were expressing an antidrinking message. London's account, *John Barleycorn*, was written ostensibly to explain his support for Prohibition and his view that it was alcohol's accessibility—not human propensities—that led to alcohol abuse. "I was no hereditary alcoholic," he wrote. "I had been born with no organic, chemical predisposition toward alcohol. . . . I read back in my life and saw how the accessibility of alcohol had given me the taste for it." Whatever one thinks of London's argument, the overall effect of *John Barleycorn* was to turn London's story of taking to drink into an adventuresome account of the romantic escapades of his youth that he associated with alcohol, including drinking and fighting and intimidating competitors while illegally gathering oysters in San Francisco Bay and surviving a drunken plunge into the bay where he recognized his danger only when he had sobered up in the currents (interestingly, Bierce, like London, was rescued by a fishing boat in the same waters when he, too, fell off of a San Francisco ferry after a night of hard drinking). In reading London's account, it is hard not to draw the opposite conclusion from what he claims his antidrinking message to be ("Always the life was tied up with drinking. . . . It may be a cabaret in the Latin Quarter, a café in some obscure Italian village, a boozing-ken in sailor-town . . . but always it will be where John Barleycorn makes fellowship that I get immediately in touch, and meet, and know"). By personifying his drunkenness and blaming his situation on the availability of alcohol, London concluded by saying, "this is no tale of a reformed drunkard. I was never a drunkard, and I have not reformed." Yet, the specter of London's miserable last days and the overuse of drugs and alcohol that finally overwhelmed him hangs over his declaration in *John Barleycorn*, "I decided coolly and deliberately that I should continue to do what I had been trained to want to do. I would drink—but, oh, more skillfully, more discreetly, than ever before. Never again would I be a peripatetic conflagration. Never again would I invoke the White Logic. I had learned how not to invoke him."[39]

It was Hemingway, however, who was the master romanticizer of drinking, and it is remarkable how he became a hero to other heavy drinking journalist-literary figures who (in taking to heart Hemingway's comment that "Drinking . . . was as natural as eating and to me as necessary") saw him as a model for their imbibing lifestyle. As a fledgling writer, Hunter Thompson, like Hamill, was disconsolate at Hemingway's suicide, according to Thompson's friend and biographer, Paul Perry, who said that Thompson decided to declare his fiction projects dead and to shift his focus to narrative journalism. This included *The Rum Diary*, which he quit circulating to editors and agents (his only fiction novel to see print, it was resurrected and published in 1998 after Thompson had established his reputation as a "gonzo" journalist). However, Hemingway's fate did not keep Thompson from taking to the chemically stimulated life with even greater intensity. Even more than Hemingway, Thompson was a writer whose reputation is synonymous with drinking, drug use, and over-the-top antics (much of what he wrote is famous for being composed in high degrees of altered states; his mother, at one point, was quoted as saying that his family worried that he was killing himself with drugs). Although written in his youth and only published in his maturity, *The Rum Diary* drew on Thompson's experiences as a young newspaper reporter in Puerto Rico (though labeled a novel, it is probably not fictionalized to a much greater degree than many of his wildly subjective, journalistic screeds). The novel presents the world of the expatriate Caribbean journalist in the same decadent, romantic terms as Hemingway portrayed his hard-partying characters in *The Sun Also Rises*. Thompson's two major reporter characters are antiheroes surrounded by a cast of "drifters and dreamers," who, at best, are outlandish and unruly, and, at worst, "drunk, dirty, and no more dependable than goats." In pure Humphrey Bogart style, Thompson described the bar where his journalistic ne'er-do-wells hang out, "talking, drinking lazily, killing the time while a sad piano tinkled away inside. The notes floated out to the patio, giving the night a hopeless, melancholy tone that was almost pleasant." Ironically, Thompson did not hesitate to knock other hard-living journalist-literary figures, such as Mailer, whose routine of writing after a long evening of martinis, Thompson said, had turned Mailer into "the poor echo of some half-wit myth about Scott Fitzgerald" (which, as Perry noted, was the method that Thompson later adopted for himself). Thompson was more prophetic of his own fate in his analysis of Hemingway's waning writing powers in "What Lured Hemingway to Ketchum?," in which Thompson concluded that Hemingway had become bogged down in a crisis of conviction and a life of "trying to bring order out of chaos," which became "a superhuman task in a time when chaos is multiplying." Thompson's alcohol use and experimentation with a myriad of drugs led to a number of emergency room visits—including one where the doctor told him that if he kept it up he would be dead in a year. "I work a certain way and I can't give that up," Thompson reportedly responded. At the end, Thompson was sixty-seven, when, like his hero Hemingway, he shot himself in his home in Aspen, Colorado, in 2005. As with Hemingway and London, Thompson's suicide meant that some of his statements ("I hate to advocate drugs, alcohol, violence, or insanity to anyone, but they've always worked for me") needed to be reconsidered in the context of his foreshortened life.[40]

In his memoir, *A Drinking Life*, Hamill also illustrated how powerfully Hemingway's romantic ethos of drinking could influence a journalist, and for how many years it helped Hamill sustain his own out-of-control lifestyle. From Hemingway, Hamill said, he learned to become a drinker with endurance, and a portion of his memoir dealt with how he handled his Hemingway-fired imagination ("I could go to Paris. . . . Why not? I'd find the Café Bel Ami and sit at a table and order Fundador. . . . And absinthe. Of course"). However, in his real life, Hamill said he continued "the multiple routines of the drinking life. If I wrote a good column for the newspaper, I'd go to a bar and celebrate; if I wrote a poor column, I would drink away my regret. Then I'd go home, another dinner missed, another chance to play with the children gone, and in the morning, hung over, thick-tongued, and thick-fingered, I'd attempt through my disgust to make amends. That was a routine too."[41]

Other Out-of-Control Twentieth-Century Journalist-Literary Figures

Unfortunately, as with London, Hemingway, Agee, and others, the use of drink, drugs, and intense spells of work often became unmanageable and ultimately led to their physical and emotional demise. Their initiation into the journalistic lifestyle meant that many spent good amounts of time at favorite drinking hangouts, consumed large amounts of liquor, and let their bodies pay the price for their use of booze and other substances as a way to ease the tensions of writing, maintain connections with friends and sources in a sociable setting, and be voluble while carrying on a professional activity where much has to be held in. Because most did not write openly about their substance abuse, the chronicling of the painful circumstances and health horrors of their final days often was left for biographers and other observers. For example, the muckraker and abstainer, Upton Sinclair—in his anti-alcohol tract, *The Cup of Fury*—listed a roster of hard-drinking writers that he had known during his career who had started out with "vision and courage" but gave to the country a "sickness of mind and soul." Among the group whose genius, he said, was "distorted by alcohol poisoning" were a dozen among the journalist-literary figures in this study, including Bierce ("who had reached the stage of alcoholism where it is a torment to be alive"), Finley Peter Dunne ("a saloonkeepers' victim [who] retired from the literary world before his potential was half-realized"), Mencken ("I cannot help but wonder what [his contribution] would have been had [he] not been so occupied for so many years with the trivia of brands, vintages, and lagers"), and Thomas (his drinking life "a record of horror and catastrophe"). In particular, Sinclair lamented the demise of his friend and namesake, Sinclair Lewis, whose quart of brandy a day resulted in "shakes . . . the avoiding of friends . . . the decline in writing power and the final delirium. . . . Through a miracle of physical stamina [he] made it to the age of sixty-six. More tragic than any shortage of years was the loss of productivity, the absence of joy."[42]

Society's growing tolerance for the "walk-on-the-wild-side" artistic personality meant that the degree of dysfunction in the out-of-control writer could reach colossal proportions—as it did for Lewis, who became one of the most notorious public nuisance drunks in the annals of American literature. Alternately sullen, obnoxious, cruel, theatrical, rage-filled, fun-loving, and catatonic when in his cups, Lewis, at his best, entertained parties with lively impersonations of critics and artists (including sometimes those who were present) in a variety of languages and dialects, arrived with people he had picked up on the street or in taxi cabs, and once called a Catholic bishop from a dinner party to discuss ecclesiastical points about baptism while pretending to be another bishop. At his worst, he would grow petulant, lapse into obscenities and acts of childish insolence, and berate his audience, as he did at one writers' conference, where he swore through his speech, told the assemblage that it was impossible to teach creative writing, and called writers a bastard lot as human beings. He once hosted a party to celebrate the upcoming birth of a child, and then, drunk, drove his second wife, the journalist Dorothy Thompson, to the hospital after she experienced labor pains at the gathering. Of his drinking, Thompson wrote to him in a letter, "I suffer intensely from it as everyone about you does, because when you are drunk you act exactly like an insane person . . . I feel quite incapable . . . as though your drinking had become my phobia, a mania under which I will eventually crack"; while separated from Lewis, Thompson once went to rescue him in his apartment, where he drunkenly screamed at her in a parody of what he claimed she had often told him: "You've ruined your life, you're ruining mine! You've ruined your sons, you miserable creature! You're sick, sick, sick" and then demanded a divorce.[43]

It would be hard to decide who was the most astonishing alcoholic spectacle among such dedicated boozers, but Thomas certainly was among those in the front ranks. In his short story, "Old Garbo," Thomas detailed how, as a seventeen-year-old novice reporter on the *South Wales Daily Post*, an older reporter initiated him to the local low life by taking him on a pub crawl around Swansea, after which he ended up sick in "a wild bed" where "the wallpaper lakes converged and sucked" him down. His brief experience with the *Daily Post* in 1931–1932 gave him a regular wage that allowed him to "become drunk at least four nights a week," he wrote. However, he did not like reporting, and his choice in life at the time looked to be between a career in poetry or dissipation—"Muse or Mermaid" (one of his favorite pubs), as he put it. His short stint on the *Daily Post* proved "entertaining," as one editor said, "but a sore trial to the chief reporter" who supervised Thomas. In the days before his death at age thirty-nine, he chased a woman around a dance floor and treated her so violently that she reportedly suffered a concussion; he claimed to have drunk eighteen straight whiskeys (almost certainly an exaggeration, but perhaps not much); and he passed out drunk on the floor of a party in the middle of a dalliance with the hostess. As he was dying in a New York City hospital in November 1953, from fluid buildup on his brain caused by chronic alcoholic poisoning (compounded by heavy cigarette smoking and morphine use), his long-suffering wife, upon arriving by airplane from Wales, reportedly said, "Is the fucking man dead yet?," while his mourning admirers, such as the poet John Berryman, intoned that if Thomas died, poetry would die with him.[44]

Hapgood's 1939 memoir, *A Victorian in the Modern World*, was an apology from a person whose life of excess became the norm for a number of the twentieth century's alienated journalist-literary figures. Hapgood's career in journalism and fiction writing paralleled his life of bohemianism, "advanced" moral thinking, and profligate behavior in New York's Greenwich Village, which included an unconventional marriage to fellow journalist, Neith Boyce (the two once wrote a play together about what it is like when a husband acts as if he is not married but the wife keeps hanging on in the hopes that things will work out). From an early age, Hapgood said, he experienced a "painful consciousness" that was so "intense" that it made him fear solitude and seek out constant companionship. "The madness of joy and the turmoil of distress come to me at their most tumultuous point when alone. . . . Quiet, breathing solitude, instead of soothing, distracts and harasses me, sometimes with a sense of disturbing beauty, sometimes with a sense of terror and impending awfulness," he wrote. "In spite of myself, the Infinite torments me." Hapgood's life of hard-drinking, extramarital sexual affairs, and intense socializing occurred against the backdrop of his troubled marriage to Boyce, who tolerated his infidelities but suffered for them. Drink, Hapgood said, often spurred him to engage in "depravity, in viciousness itself," as well as "extravagant gestures of what is called immorality . . . I have been busily engaged all my life in confessing to my friends, especially my wife, and, as far as I could, the world, so I had no need either of the confessional or the psychoanalyst." With all that, Hapgood said, "this feeling of cosmic woe (has) been part of my life. . . . Now I hate to wake up early . . . when I am left alone in the universe. It is a moment of spiritual—I was going to say agony, but that is not the word. Everything seems to drop out of my life, and out of life itself, as if it were all a painful illusion. . . . I know, when I am in this condition, that in a few hours, after my morning coffee, and the resumption of the occupations of the day, that state of feeling will disappear; otherwise those early morning moments would be intolerable."[45]

Lardner's rise among the hard-drinking sportswriters of his day, and his personal collapse amid the Gatsby-like glitter of 1920s Long Island social life, can be viewed as the alcoholic's shadow side of the American dream. After the great success of his national newspaper column and his satirically vernacular short stories, Lardner moved into the Long Island social scene made famous by his friend, fellow alcoholic, and youthful neighbor, Fitzgerald (who saw his own coming fate in Lardner's but proved helpless in doing anything about it). The extravagant social whirl in *The Great Gatsby* was modeled on the parties thrown at the estate of another Lardner neighbor, Bayard Swopes, the editor of the *New York World*, and they often spilled over into Lardner's residence. A shy and modest man, Lardner, like Fitzgerald, could never decide if he was contemptuous of or fatally attracted to the lifestyle of the rich and famous. But his choice of the over-the-top 1920s high life provided little help in overcoming his crippling inferiority complex and his sense of failure (that he could not give up his various journalistic sidelines or write the novel that critics wanted him to write), or in curtailing the drinking patterns that led to his death at age forty-eight while suffering from insomnia, lung and heart disease, and a wasted liver.[46]

Charles Bukowski—as the defiant outsider who turned to self-destructive behavior as a protest against the mundane nature of American life—acknowledged that his hostility to social norms was rooted in the abusive treatment he received as a boy from a tyrannical father who beat him mercilessly for sins real and imagined. As the alcoholic poet of skid row and the literary chronicler of the world of transients and the marginalized, Bukowski took to alcohol early and in ways that can be connected to his father's punitive philosophy of child rearing. His father's contentious view of the world filtered down to his son who adopted a stone-faced posture to deal with the regular beatings he received from his father's razor strap. Bukowski's response to his father's treatment became the model for his worldview ("The oppressive factor remains like a shadow overhead. . . . There is always a father trying to press down and annihilate you") and contributed to the creation of his fictional alter ego, Henry Chinaski, whose reckless and recalcitrant behavior helped to make Bukowski a hero of the 1970s counterculture. His semiautobiographical novels—most notably *Post Office*, in which Chinaski's tribulations as a postal clerk parallel Bukowski's own employment in the post office for more than a decade—and his journalism for alternative newspapers helped him to maintain writing discipline until he could put his years of peripatetic employment behind him. When his father was long dead and he finally was able to think of himself as a success, Bukowski said, "Thank you father for my poetry and stories, for my house, for my car, for my bank account. Thank you for those beatings that taught me how to endure."[47]

Brendan Behan is another figure whose consumption of alcohol and other substances helped to set the standard for how much physical abuse a writer's body could endure before it expired. Behan's compulsive drinking, on top of a diabetic condition—which put him in and out of hospitals for emergency treatment throughout his years—began early in the Dublin slums where he grew up. Behan's youthful exposure to stress and destructive lifestyles—his father, step-grandmother, and two step-aunts were imprisoned for a time for their activities in support of the Irish Republican Army, while his paternal grandmother introduced him to drinking and encouraged him to make alcohol a part of his life before he was a teenager ("I never turned to drink," he once said, "it seemed to turn to me"; at another point, he added, "I *had* a drink problem; I couldn't get enough of it")—is often viewed as the basis for a life that sometimes seemed to be little more than a suicide mission. Whether it was in his early role as a would-be IRA terrorist bomber (for which he was arrested, beaten, and jailed in an English boy's reformatory) or his later life in which he proudly proclaimed that he would drink himself to death before he would submit to the recovery programs that his wife was pressing on him, Behan lived a frantic and self-destructive existence. Biographer Michael O'Sullivan said two traumatic issues appeared to overwhelm him—his apparently bisexual nature that conflicted with his conservative Irish Catholic cultural background and his attraction to the violence of the Irish independence movement that led to repeated run-ins with the authorities (although he never succeeded in harming people or detonating any of the explosives he carried with him). As a playwright and a longtime columnist for the *Irish Press*, Behan mixed fact with fancy in the tradition of Addison and Steele; he wrote about contemporary Irish affairs in his columns through the mouths of a series of semifictional Dublin characters who expressed in witty and colloquial ways Behan's many opinions, including about the serious and tragic issues of Irish life. He endeared himself to his Irish audience when he once appeared on a BBC show with Malcolm Muggeridge in a drunk and incoherent condition. Bellicose and abusive to his wife, Behan once said, "I am not a priest but a sinner. I am not a psychiatrist but a neurotic. My neuroses are the nails and saucepans by which I get my living." In his last days, when his binge drinking was followed with more frequent hospitalizations, he responded to his wife's threats to have him institutionalized, "If you do that, and I come out alive, that day I will drink myself to death," he said, later adding, "Alcoholics die of alcohol."[48]

In fact, the circumstances of a number of journalist-literary figures at the end of their lives proved to be a grim subtext to the drink-up-and-live-for-the-day philosophy in which so many based their existence. Thomas Paine's final years were spent as a bitter and embattled figure, plagued with a variety of ailments and tongue-lashing his enemies in print and in person. Regarding his drinking to excess, there were reports of his embarrassing behavior at social gatherings and the neglect of his hygiene, with one report even claiming that he "performed the offices of nature in his bed." Poe experienced such acute and ongoing bouts of anxiety that drinking was one of the only ways that he could find temporary relief; however, because he had a disposition that could not tolerate alcohol, drinking often propelled him into terrible spells of delirium, alcoholic hallucinations, and half-conscious behavior, which was his state when he died after a drunken binge in 1849. London's drinking and drug use contributed to his physical deterioration as a relatively young man (he suffered from obesity, rheumatism, swollen ankles, bladder problems, and even arsenic poisoning from trying to treat venereal disease). Hart Crane's raging alcoholic's life has been described as vibrating with "an explosive terror . . . elated, wretched, violent, Rabelaisian" before he threw himself off a ship on his way home from Mexico in 1932. James Thurber, too, struck a sad figure toward the end of his life: crawling from bar to bar, acting loudly and obstreperously, checking himself in and out of sanitariums, crashing into chairs and wetting himself at parties. At the end of his days, Capote was so loaded up on drugs that it was impossible to determine the exact chemical cause of his death. London, Benchley, Agee, Thurber, Behan, and Capote were all told that drinking was killing them, but they could not or did not care to wean themselves off the bottle. There is much poignancy—as well as a dim sense of the implications by all those involved—when biographers tell the story of how Benchley, who had avoided alcohol because of his perception that out-of-control drinking was a family weakness, was encouraged by his hard-drinking colleagues, Parker and Robert Sherwood, to abandon his teetotaling ways and take his first drink (an orange blossom) in a New York speakeasy (which was followed by Benchley's quick descent into a life of boozy dissipation that culminated in his death from liver disease at age fifty-six). Not many years after that first drink, Benchley quipped, "I know I'm drinking myself to a slow death, but I'm in no hurry."[49]

It was remarkable how often these addictive and psychologically compulsive behaviors tended to blow up into full-blown dysfunction when a final stimulant—artistic celebrity—was added. For many of these figures, their status as celebrated artists and high-profile journalists, their roles as important moneymakers and public figures, and their family members and friends who were willing to shield them from the consequences of their behavior meant that they were able to get away with flagrant and self-indulgent antics that otherwise might have brought them down. "You know, Norman, they would've put you in the booby hatch years ago if you didn't have your family-supported appartus," was the way Peter Manso, Mailer's one-time friend and the author of an unflattering biography about him, claimed that he had once put it to Mailer. In fact, the management (or mismanagement) of fame could be a traumatic factor for those who reached stratospheric levels of popularity in their lifetimes. "I've asked myself a thousand times: why did this happen to me?" said Capote of his drug and alcohol addictions. ". . . I think the reason is that I was famous too young. . . . Famous people sometimes become like turtles turned over on their backs. Everybody is picking at the turtles. . . . It takes an enormous effort for him to turn over."[50]

Many journalist-literary figures lived in the days before modern antidepression pharmaceuticals and mood-controlling psychotropic drugs—and many lived before the theories of Sigmund Freud and the expansion of the psychology profession made it possible to try to deal with emotional illness as a health issue. However, in whatever era they lived in, many opted for the tried-and-true methods for dealing with their problems—drink, drugs, sex, work, travel, and, of course, writing—that had served generations of journalists and literary figures before them. Few, in the end, evinced much interest in psychology beyond using it to help shape their literary themes and characters, and few ultimately looked to anything beyond their art as a means of saving themselves.

In their literature and their public lives, many journalist-literary figures were groundbreakers in trying to do away with the restrictions that cramped the human spirit by battling the rigidities of Puritanism, judgmental moral standards, and social and political oppression. But as fiercely as they fought the restrictive forces of the world outside, they also fought—and often were defeated by—their own self-destructive tendencies. That so many journalist-literary figures found themselves imprisoned in debilitating and damaging behaviors leads one to ponder the ironies of lives that were lived for the sake of freedom and fearless artistic expression but ended up so miserable for themselves and those around them.

New Challenges, New Treatments

*Trauma and the Contemporary
Journalist-Literary Figure*

"All human beings should try to learn before
they die what they are running
from, and to, and why."

—James Thurber

Sadly, the letters and correspondence of James Thurber toward the end of his career indicate that the final outcome was not always easy for the writer living with the effects of trauma, psychological stress, and behaviors that tried to compensate for the emotional disequilibrium caused by inherited proclivities and family dysfunction. Like his friend, Ernest Hemingway, Thurber suffered from a combination of early life traumatic experiences and emotional struggles that fueled his journalistic and artistic ambitions but also contributed to actions in his final years that were viewed by friends as pathetic and out-of-control. Virtually blind, cantankerous, alcoholic, and in perpetual conflict with his editors at the *New Yorker* magazine, Thurber spent much of his time attending late-night parties and drinking in the company of Hemingway, F. Scott Fitzgerald, and other friends whose self-destructive lives also were falling apart. When Thurber learned that Hemingway had ended his life with a shotgun blast at his Sun Valley home in 1961, he was devastated. "I believe that all of us, especially the men, are manic-depressed. . . . I keep fighting it, though, and I have no shotgun, Thank God," he wrote in a series of despairing letters to friends. (When Thurber died a few months later, suffering from arteriosclerosis, the effects of several small strokes, and a blood tumor, as well as the consequences of his heavy drinking, his last words to his daughter were reportedly, "God bless . . . God damn.")[1]

In contrast, Thurber's close friend and mentor, E. B. White, is one of the few examples of a journalist-literary personality who was afflicted with neurotic symptoms (he once described a "nervous crack-up" in 1943 as "a panic fear, as near as I can make out, [that] is not of death. It is an amorphous fear, lacking in form") but achieved some level of inner peace in his twilight years. Although White experienced the effects of anxiety and nervous tension throughout his life, he presented a very different picture than Thurber in his later career: producing his most celebrated art (the children's books—*Charlotte's Web*, *Stuart Little*, and *The Trumpet of the Swan*), documenting in *Charlotte's Web* the cycle of life and death that he embraced as part of the natural world, spending much of his time on a hobby farm in Maine where he observed contentedly the comings and goings of the seasons, and philosophizing in sanguine terms in his writings for the *New Yorker* and other magazines that helped his readership find sustenance in dealing with the gloomy global issues that embroiled the United States during World War II and the Cold War. "We should all do what, in the long run, gives us joy," he wrote, "even if it is only picking grapes or sorting laundry." (White—despite a late-life falling out with Thurber, who disliked White's wife, a *New Yorker* editor—nonetheless delivered the eulogy at Thurber's funeral. "When he was well and sober, there was never a kinder, nicer friend," White would come to say.)[2]

In reality, Thurber's life patterns were more the norm for the 150 journalist-literary figures who have been the focus of this study. It is not always easy to know which came first—the drunkard or the environment that encouraged the out-of-control drinker to drink, the emotionally troubled personality or the work life that brought out unhealthy responses in a journalist-literary figure. Yet, the contrast between White's and Thurber's lives raises important questions that emerge from this examination: If artistic achievement by journalist-literary figures often has seemed to grow out of pain and dysfunction, is it inevitable that great emotional suffering and fractured personal lives must be the price of artistic accomplishment? Beyond that, what should one make of the role of journalism and the impact of the journalistic environment as a precipitating factor in such tumultuous lives? Should one conclude that journalism attracts personalities who are already psychologically troubled, harbor grandiose ambitions, and look to the stimulation of journalism and art as a way to help maintain their emotional equilibrium and deal with traumatic pasts? If this is the case, are there lessons that might be taken from the lives of these figures that would be helpful to psychologists, journalists, and the researchers who study the impact of trauma, stress, and risk-taking experiences on today's journalists and their emotional well-being?

Historians and literary scholars have long recognized the many great and troubled artists who have seemed to sacrifice themselves for the sake of their art, and perhaps one should simply conclude this discussion by noting how many journalist-literary figures can be included in those ranks. However, one cannot help but see the shape of a collective diagnosis coming out of the disturbed lives of these personalities—and particularly so those who lived before the advent of modern psychology, family systems theory, substance abuse recovery programs, and stress management concepts became a prominent part of the contemporary mental health scene. One wonders what might have happened if these journalistic writers had available psychotropic and antidepression medications, mental health counseling programs, the findings of research about the effects of trauma on emotional well-being, and Alcoholics Anonymous and other support systems that would stress the importance of relying on something beyond one's own ego and artistic will for emotional recovery.

At the same time, it is hard to imagine someone such as Hemingway sitting around with a men's group trying to soften his "hairy beast" within, or attending therapy or counseling sessions as a way to come to terms with his family upbringing, or taking Prozac in lieu of the alcoholic self-medication that was his preferred method for dealing with life's traumas and challenges. But Hemingway also probably would not have found it pleasant to know how much contemporary scholars, biographers, and critics—now steeped in the psychological sciences—have taken to interpreting his life and his art by analyzing his patterns of denial, his lack of self-understanding, his "transference" of emotional distress into macho poses, and his perceived weaknesses (his drinking, his behaviors with women, his seeking out of danger, and his obsessive pursuit of manly outdoors activities) in ways that he chose to see as strengths. Like Hemingway, many journalist-literary figures—with their brilliant and insightful minds—seemed to recognize the manner in which old and unhealed emotional wounds and compulsions worked within their literary characters but all too often could not find the internal tools to apply that wisdom to their own lives.

As traditional newspapers and news organizations have staggered under powerful economic, demographic, and technological pressures and as journalistic writing migrates toward the internet, the job of the journalist is being transformed and the environment that will produce journalistic artists is evolving in ways that promise new literary formats and creative venues in the coming years. It also is clear that the traditional culture of journalism—the world of the newsroom, the activities of the professional journalist, the possibilities for an aspiring literary writer to gain an apprenticeship in journalism—is undergoing great change as blogging, digital convergence, social media, updated electronic news, and the shrinkage of the gatekeeper role of editors and news organizations have opened new opportunities for the entrepreneurial writer. However, many of these pioneers in digital journalism and digital journalistic literature to come are operating in highly stressful and sometimes relatively isolated circumstances in which the possibilities promised by digital computing have opened new vistas but also disrupted the old forms and practices of news writing. Text and writing are changing shape as digitized pathways put traditional print forms of communication in competition with video, mobile graphics, the formats of handheld electronic devices, and multimedia platforms; young people have embraced electronic convergence to such a degree that one cannot be certain what forms of writing and reading material will survive into the future. Whether this brave, new media world offers more or fewer possibilities for the probing and the comprehension of traumatic experience (beyond the trauma that mounting numbers of laid-off news workers have experienced) is an open question and one that can only be answered as the influence of technology developments and where they are taking journalism becomes clearer.

Although journalistic writing and journalistic literature in some form are virtually certain not to disappear, the life of the journalist may be carried out in lonelier, more insecure, and more stressful circumstances than in the recent past, and the support systems that have been available to journalists—such as they have been—may be even more minimal as the traditional newsroom is threatened with becoming an historical artifact. Many journalistic and newsroom friendships have encouraged unhealthy behavior (particularly in the area of drinking), but—within certain, special relationships—a journalist-literary figure has provided the companionship and emotional support for a fellow writer who would not otherwise be inclined to ask for help. Whether it was in the early days of journalistic literary history (Joseph Addison and Richard Steele, James Boswell and Samuel Johnson, Charles Lamb and Samuel Taylor Coleridge) or the middle years (Mark Twain and William Dean Howells, H. L. Mencken and Theodore Dreiser, Vera Brittain and Winifred Holtby, Dorothy Parker and Robert Benchley, Katherine Anne Porter and Eudora Welty), a troubled journalist-literary figure sometimes has received a friendly shoulder to help bolster his or her courage. However, this has almost never led to the "saving" of the friend in need—nor did it compensate for the timely seeking out of professional help (in the days when such a thing was available) that a journalist-literary figure rarely was willing to do. Regardless of whether or not such legendary journalistic friendships continue into the future, today's journalists and journalistic artists, whatever their writing circumstances, have access to greater information about the role that trauma can play within the life of the journalistic professional and the opportunity to find sympathetic surroundings for sharing with others the personal effects of traumatic experience (as anyone who has attended a journalism and trauma program or conference has witnessed)—but only if they wish to avail themselves of it.

In the years ahead, it will be interesting to see if our greater "sophistication" about mental health matters will translate into less painful personal and professional lives for journalists and journalist-literary figures to come. Sigmund Freud contended that knowledge could free humans from the traps of unexamined emotions. However, the romantics (and artists both before and since) have operated from the principle that the production of art can require great suffering, and that, without it, much creative energy is lost. Who knows if the journalistic tradition of machoism and denial will undergo a transformation in the manner of the changes that are reshaping the economic and technological side of the business, or if journalists and journalist-literary figures will continue to choose to play the role of the stoic professional or the suffering artist as the preferred method for dealing with the pain that can come from chronicling the news of the day and the psychic strain of expanding their ambitions into the fields of fiction and literature?

In particular, the availability of new psychotropic drugs that combat depression, anxiety, and other emotional disorders are playing a revolutionary role in bringing respite to personalities suffering from the internal ailments that often have been the ground out of which great written art has emerged. It is fascinating, for example, to try to imagine what might have been the impact of pharmaceutically enhanced serotonin levels on the many troubled journalist-literary figures studied here. In fact, many factors have altered the circumstances in which writers articulate the joys and the pain of the human experience—and, as human beings continue to find ways to alleviate human suffering, one has to consider the possibilities that the nature of journalistic and artistic expression may be affected. However, it is worth noting that—despite the advancements of medical science, psychological theory and practice, and the psycho-pharmaceutical industry—literary writers throughout the decades, including those who have come out of journalism, have stubbornly continued to manifest in their emotional lives and their literary themes the effects of traumatic experience, as many elements in this study demonstrate.

We—or at least, those of us who reside in advanced economies—live in a time when reductions in child mortality, improvements in treating childhood and adulthood diseases, freedom from military conscription, and recovery programs and pharmaceutical treatments for psychological illness and substance abuse have reduced our exposure to at least some of the traumatic events and their emotional impacts that were commonplace in the lives of journalist-literary figures of the past. Yet, it is unclear whether the new assaults on our psyches—threats of terrorism, video and televised violence, fear of crime, horrific military and civil violence in global hotspots, increases in divorce and broken families, illegal drug use and gang hostilities, a greater awareness of childhood sexual and spousal abuse, and the withdrawal of religious consolation in artistic, intellectual, and journalistic circles—have left us any less vulnerable to the emotional responses to trauma.

There are indications that journalists'—and the journalistic profession's—greater awareness of the impact of traumatic experience is showing up in today's literary journalism and journalistic fiction. Whether it is Ted Conover's narratives of Kenyan truck drivers, *The Routes of Man*, and Lara Santoro's novel, *Mercy*, about the impact of AIDS in Africa; the searing, on-the-ground accounts of the conflicts in Iraq and Afghanistan by Dexter Filkins, David Finkel, and Sebastian Junger; Giles Foden's novel, *The Last King of Scotland*, about the bloody regime of Ugandan leader Adi Imin; Philip Caputo's novels that probe the loss and grief to be found in global conflict zones; or Jess Walter's *The Zero* and Chris Cleaves's *Incendiary*, about the 9/11 and Al-Qaeda terrorist attacks, journalist-authors are not shying away from presenting audiences with intense and vivid accounts of trauma's influence on the mind, soul, and body and are doing it in ways that can be deeply unsettling to the reader. One can argue that today's chroniclers of trauma are asking greater things of the contemporary audience in feeling sympathy for the victims of terrible events in today's world, even to the point of risking secondary traumatization by providing disturbing details that can filter into readers' feelings and imaginations. In reading Cleaves's *Little Bee*, about a teenage woman refugee who flees the tribal violence in Nigeria's oil field regions but who loses her family, including a sister who is savagely molested and murdered in her presence, it occurred to me that the ability to keep readers moving through such trying material is a talent in today's publishing environment, and that the capacity to induce empathy in an audience rather than the impulse to simply shut the book is a literary gift. In an age when we can become numb to the accounts of the barbarities that human beings can inflict on each other, the writers who use "compassionate narrative" to open up our eyes and our emotions to the traumas of others should be thanked for finding a pathway into the collective human heart.

The power of storytelling—whether it involves fact or imagination or a combination of the two—has long been one of humankind's greatest tools for comprehending and communicating the incidents in life that can scar our spirits and darken our inner lives. Yet there are deep rewards to be found in the reading of this painful material, just as there can be in confronting the residue of trauma in our own lives. Time and again, as the journalist-literary figures in this study have demonstrated, the hold of trauma in our minds and our emotions can be eased somewhat if a story can be "written out" and shared with others. In a similar fashion, I hope that this study may help to expand our understanding of the historical context on which the contemporary study of trauma, journalism, and literature rests and to provide additional perspective about how today's and future journalistic writers, and their audiences, may hope to address the painful emotional events that invariably visit human beings in their personal and professional journeys through life.

Appendix

Table 1. Journalist-Literary Figures and Their Traumatic Experiences

	Lost parent while young*	Abandonment*/ harsh, abusive rearing#/ sexual abuse+	Raised w/ psychologically ill, alcoholic parent*/ from broken family#/ death of spouse, children, siblings while young+/ traumatic divorce, marriage, affair^	Military experience*/ war reporting#/ war trauma+/ lost child or sibling in military^	Mental health problem*	Job trauma as journalists/ writers*	Alcohol or drug problem*	Sanitorium*	Suicide*/ suicide attempt or thoughts#	Experience as minority*/ and/or gay-bisexual or dealing with rumors about#
Henry Adams			+		*	*			#	
Joseph Addison						*				
James Agee	*	*#			*	*	*		#	
Conrad Aiken	*	*	*		*	*	*		#	
Sherwood Anderson			*		*	*	*			
Maya Angelou		*+	*#		*	*	*		#	*
Gertrude Atherton		*	#+							
Djuna Barnes		*#+			*	*	*	*	#	#
James M. Barrie		*+	*+		*	*	*			
Brendan Behan			*+	*+			*			#
Robert Benchley		*#	*+	^		*	*			
Ambrose Bierce		*	+	*+	*	*	*		#	
Lillie Devereux Blake	*	*	+	#		*				
Nellie Bly	*				*	*				
James Boswell					*	*	*			
Mary Elizabeth Braddon		#	#							
Jimmy Breslin			*		*	*	*			
Vera Brittain				+^	*					
Heywood Broun				*	*	*	*			
Charles Bukowski		#			*	*	*		#	
Erskine Caldwell				#	*	*	*			
Truman Capote		*#	*#		*	*	*		#	#

Author	1	2	3	4	5	6	7	8	9
Philip Caputo							*##+	*	*
Angela Carter						*		*	*
Willa Cather	#					*		*	#
Raymond Chandler	#	*			*	*	*	*	*
Susan Cheever					*	*	*	*	*
Charles Chesnutt	*					*		#	#
G. K. Chesterton	#				*	*	*	+	#
Lydia Maria Child						*		#	*
Samuel T. Coleridge				*	*	*	*	*	*
Hart Crane	#	*		*#	*	*	*	*#	*#
Stephen Crane				*	*	*	#	+	*
Rebecca Harding Davis					*	*		+	
Richard Harding Davis	#			#	*	*	#	*	*
Dorothy Day	#				*	*		*∧	
Daniel Defoe				*	*	*		*	
Thomas De Quincey				*	*	*	+	*	*
Peter De Vries					*	*	*+	*	
Charles Dickens					*	*		*	
Joan Didion	#		*	*	*	*	#	*	
John Dos Passos	*				*	*	#	*	
Frederick Douglass	*				*	*	#	*	
Theodore Dreiser	#				*	*	#		
W. E. B. Du Bois	*				*	*	#	*	
Paul Laurence Dunbar	*				*	*	#∧	*	
Finley Peter Dunne					*	*		*	
George Eliot	*				*	*	<	*	
Gloria Emerson	*				*	*	*	*	
Emily Faithfull	#				*	*	#		*
Sui Sin Far	*				*	*	*#		

Table 1. (cont.)

	Lost parent while young*	Abandonment*/harsh, abusive rearing#/sexual abuse+	Raised w/psychologically ill, alcoholic parent*/from broken family#/death of spouse, children, siblings while young+/traumatic divorce, marriage, affair^	Military experience*/war reporting#/war trauma+/lost child or sibling in military^	Mental health problem*	Job trauma as journalists/writers*	Alcohol or drug problem*	Sanitorium*	Suicide*/suicide attempt or thoughts#	Experience as minority*/and/or gay-bisexual or dealing with rumors about#
Edna Ferber				#		*				
Fanny Fern	*	#	*+^		*	*				
Henry Fielding	*	*	*+			*	*			
E. M. Forster	*	*#				*				#
Philip Freneau	*			*+	*	*	*			
Robert Frost	*		*+	*	*	*	*		#	
Margaret Fuller		#		#	*	*				
Martha Gellhorn				#+	*	*				
Charlotte Perkins Gilman		*	#^		*	*			★	
Katharine Glasier	*		+		*	*	*			
Gail Godwin	*		*#		*	*	*			
Graham Greene		*		#	*	*	*		#	
Pete Hamill				*		*	*			
Hutchins Hapgood					*	*	*			
Joel Chandler Harris		*	#		*	*	*			
Bret Harte	*					*	*			
Eliza Haywood			^			*				
William Hazlitt			^		*	*				
Ernest Hemingway		*	*	*#+	*	*	*	★	★	
O. Henry	*	*	*		*	*	*			
Michael Herr				#+	*	*	*			

Name	1	2	3	4	5	6	7	8	9	10	11	12
John Hersey								#+				
Pauline Hopkins							*	*		*		*
Wm. Dean Howells		+				*	*	*	*			
Langston Hughes		*	#			*	*	*	*		#	*#
Leigh Hunt		*				*	*	*				
Zora Neale Hurston	*	*#+	*+			*	*	*				*
Douglas Jerrold		*	*+				*	*			#	
Samuel Johnson			*			*	*	*			#	
George Kaufman			*+			*	*	*				
Jack Kerouac		*	+			*	*	*				#
Tracy Kidder			*+			*	*				#	
Rudyard Kipling			#^			*	*					
Charles Lamb	*		*			*	*	*	*			
Ring Lardner						*	*	*	*			
Charlotte Lennox	*		*			*	*	*				
Meridel Le Sueur			#			*	*					
Sinclair Lewis	*		^			*	*	*	*			
A. J. Liebling			#			*	*	*				
Jack London		*	#			*	*	*	*			
James Russell Lowell		*				*	*	*		#		
Norman Mailer			*			*	*	*	*			
Delarivière Manley	*	<				*	*					
Harriet Martineau		*				*	*					
John Masefield	*					*	*		*			
Victoria Earle Matthews	#	#^				*	*					*
Mary McCarthy	*	*#	*^			*	*	*				
H. L. Mencken	*	+	#			*	*	*		*		
Margaret Mitchell	*					*	*	*		*		
H. H. Munro	*	*#+				*	*	*				#
Edith Nesbit	*	<				*	*					

Table 1. (cont.)

	Lost parent while young*	Abandonment*/ harsh, abusive rearing#/ sexual abuse+	Raised w/ psychologically ill, alcoholic parent*/ from broken family#/ death of spouse, children, siblings while young+/ traumatic divorce, marriage, affair^	Military experience*/ war reporting#/ war trauma+/ lost child or sibling in military^	Mental health problem*	Job trauma as journalists/ writers*	Alcohol or drug problem*	Sanitorium*	Suicide*/ suicide attempt or thoughts#	Experience as minority* and/or gay-bisexual or dealing with rumors about#
Frank Norris	*		#	#		*				
Caroline Norton			^		*	*				
Tim O'Brien		*	*	*+	*				#	
John O'Hara	*				*	*	*		#	
Eugene O'Neill			*		*		*	*	#	
Margaret Oliphant	*		^+	*+						
George Orwell		*#	+	*+	*	*	*			
Thomas Paine				*+	*	*	*			
Dorothy Parker	*	*#	^		*	*	*		#	
Edgar Allan Poe	*	*	#+		*	*	*		#	
Katherine Anne Porter	*	*	^		*	*	*		#	
J. B. Priestley				*+	*	*	*			
V. S. Pritchett		#			*	*				
Mike Royko			*	*	*	*	*			
Damon Runyon		*	*		*	*	*			
John Ruskin		#			*	*		*		
Carl Sandburg			*	*	*	*			#	
George Samuel Schuyler	*			*		*				
Agnes Smedley	*					*				
Tobias Smollett	*			*+		*				
W. T. Stead		*				*				

	1	2	3	4	5	6	7
Richard Steele	★	★			★	★	
Lincoln Steffens		★	★	★	★	★	
John Steinbeck		#	★	★	★	★	#
Wallace Stevens	★	★	★	★	★	★	
Jonathan Swift		★	★	★	★		
Ida Tarbell				★	★		
William M. Thackeray	★	★	<	★	★		
Dylan Thomas		★			★	★	
Dorothy Thompson	★#	#^	<	★	★		#
Hunter S. Thompson	★	★	★	★			★
James Thurber	★	★	★+	★	★	★	
Mark Twain	★	★+	★	★	★	★	#
Kurt Vonnegut, Jr.	#	★	★+	★	★		#
Auberon Waugh	#	★	★+	★			
Evelyn Waugh		★	#	★	★		#
H. G. Wells	★	★	★	★	★		#
Ida Wells-Barnett	★			★			
Rebecca West	★	★^	#	★	★	★	#
E. B. White				★	★		
Walt Whitman	★	★	★+	★	★		#
Elie Wiesel	★	★#	+	★	★		
Oscar Wilde			<	★	★		#
Edmund Wilson		★	★	★	★	★	
P. G. Wodehouse	★		+	★	★		
Mary Wollstonecraft	#	★^		★		★	#
Virginia Woolf	★	+		★		★	★
Richard Wright	★#	★#	★#	★	★		★

Table 2. Traumatic Experiences as Journalists and Writers

	Blocked publication of articles or sued	Publication died or told to kill publication	Fired/ quit under pressure/ lost column	Humiliating job experience, press coverage, or anonymity revealed	Jailing, held hostage or detained for writing activities or indicted or blacklisted	Mental health collapse on job	Family journalism trauma or bad affairs/ bad marriages with other journalists	Traumatic coverage on job
Henry Adams				★				
Joseph Addison		★						
James Agee	★							★
Sherwood Anderson						★		★
Djuna Barnes					★			★
J. M. Barrie			★					
Brendan Behan					★			
Robert Benchley	★		★					★
Ambrose Bierce							★	★
Lillie Devereux Blake	★							★
Nellie Bly								★
James Boswell						★		★
Mary Eliz. Braddon				★			★	
Jimmy Breslin			★					
Heywood Broun			★			★		
Erskine Caldwell	★				★		★	★
Truman Capote			★					★
Philip Caputo					★			★
Raymond Chandler			★					
Charles Chesnutt								★

Name	1	2	3	4	5	6	7	8	9
Lydia Maria Child	★								
Samuel T. Coleridge	★							★	★
Stephen Crane	★								★
Reb. Harding Davis	★								★
Rich. Harding Davis									★
Dorothy Day		★							
Daniel Defoe				★					
Thomas De Quincey			★	★					
Charles Dickens								★	★
Joan Didion			★						★
John Dos Passos									★
Frederick Douglass								★	
Theodore Dreiser				★				★	★
W. E. B. Du Bois				★	★			★	★
Paul Laurence Dunbar					★				
Peter Finley Dunne					★				
George Eliot		★			★				
Gloria Emerson					★				★
Emily Faithfull					★				
Edna Ferber			★		★				
Fanny Fern		★			★				
Henry Fielding					★				
Philip Freneau								★	
Margaret Fuller									★
Martha Gellhorn		★							★
Charlotte P. Gilman		★							
Katharine Glasier		★	★						★

Table 2. (cont.)

	Blocked publication of articles or sued	Publication died or told to kill publication	Fired/quit under pressure/lost column	Humiliating job experience, press coverage, or anonymity revealed	Jailing, held hostage or detained for writing activities or indicted or blacklisted	Mental health collapse on job	Family journalism trauma or bad affairs/bad marriages with other journalists	Traumatic coverage on job
Gail Godwin								
Graham Greene	*							*
Pete Hamill			*					
Hutchins Hapgood							*	
Bret Harte			*					*
Eliza Haywood			*	*				
William Hazlitt				*				
Ernest Hemingway			*				*	*
O. Henry					*			
Michael Herr								*
John Hersey								*
Pauline Hopkins	*		*					
William Dean Howells						*		
Langston Hughes					*			*
Leigh Hunt					*			
Zora Neale Hurston				*				
Samuel Johnson						*		
George Kaufman			*	*				
Meridel Le Sueur				*	*			*
Sinclair Lewis			*				*	

A. J. Liebling	★							
Jack London	★	★						
Delariviére Manley		★			★			★
Mary McCarthy		★			★			
H. L. Mencken						★		★
Margaret Mitchell								★
H. H. Munro	★							
Edith Nesbit		★						
Frank Norris	★	★						
Caroline Norton					★			
John O'Hara				★		★		
George Orwell	★			★				★
Thomas Paine				★		★		
Dorothy Parker		★		★		★		★
Edgar Allan Poe			★	★		★	★	
V. S. Pritchett	★			★		★		
Damon Runyon	★	★				★		
John Ruskin			★				★	
Carl Sandburg	★			★		★		
George S. Schuyler	★			★		★		
Agnes Smedley	★			★				
Tobias Smollett				★				
W. T. Stead	★			★	★			
Richard Steele				★	★		★	
Lincoln Steffens	★					★		
John Steinbeck	★			★		★		★
Jonathan Swift					★			

Table 2. (cont.)

	Blocked publication of articles or sued	Publication died or told to kill publication	Fired/ quit under pressure/ lost column	Humiliating job experience, press coverage, or anonymity revealed	Jailing, held hostage or detained for writing activities or indicted or blacklisted	Mental health collapse on job	Family journalism trauma or bad affairs/ bad marriages with other journalists	Traumatic coverage on job
Ida Tarbell								
William M. Thackeray		*	*					*
Dorothy Thompson			*				*	
Hunter S. Thompson			*					*
James Thurber			*					
Mark Twain	*		*					
Auberon Waugh			*					
Evelyn Waugh	*							
H. G. Wells							*	
Ida Wells-Barnett		*						*
Rebecca West							*	
E. B. White			*				*	
Walt Whitman								*
Elie Wiesel								*
Oscar Wilde					*			
Edmund Wilson							*	*
P. G. Wodehouse					*			*
Mary Wollstonecraft				*				
Richard Wright								*

Notes

(Many references can be found in the *Dictionary of Literary Biography* [Detroit: Gale Research, 1981–2009], and *Contemporary Authors Online* [Detroit: Gale Research, 2003–2007], http://www.gale.cengage.com.) All online sources were accessed and the URLs were verified during the week of January 17–23, 2011.

Introduction: Trauma, News, and Narrative

1. Kenneth S. Lynn, *Hemingway* (1987; repr., Cambridge, Mass.: Harvard University Press, 1996), 26; Charles A. Fenton, *The Apprenticeship of Ernest Hemingway: The Early Years* (New York: Viking, 1954), 1.

2. Kay Redfield Jamison, *Touched with Fire: Manic-Depressive Illness and the Artistic Temperament* (1993; repr., New York: Free Press, 1994), 7, 18–19, 26, 29–31, 36–37, 40–41, 43, 53–54, 60, 62–63, 67, 72, 84, 96–98, 110–111, 116–118, 120, 124, 126, 128, 162, 192–193, 200, 214, 219–236, 249–250, 255, 267–270.

3. George Becker, "The Association of Creativity and Psychopathology: Its Cultural-Historical Origins," *Creativity Research Journal* 13:1 (2000): 45–57; Felix Post, "Creativity and Psychopathology—A Study of 291 World-Famous Men," *British Journal of Psychiatry* 165 (July 1994): 22–34; Daniel Nettle, "Schizotypy and Mental Health amongst Poets, Visual Artists, and Mathematicians," *Journal of Research in Personality* 40:6 (2006): 876–890.

4. Anthony Feinstein, *Journalists under Fire: The Psychological Hazards of Covering War* (Baltimore: The Johns Hopkins University Press, 2006), 60–61, 72–73, 132–133, 182.

5. Mitchell Stephens, *A History of News: From the Drum to the Satellite* (New York: Viking, 1988), 133, 241, 263–270.

6. Doug Underwood, *Journalism and the Novel: Truth and Fiction, 1700–2000* (Cambridge: Cambridge University Press, 2008), 42–43, 99–100, 108, 123–124.

7. Ibid., 199–235. Also see Doug Underwood, "Depression, Drink, and Dissipation: The Troubled Inner World of Famous Journalist-Literary Figures and Art as the Ultimate Stimulant," *Journalism History* 32 (Winter 2007): 186–200.

8. Anthony Feinstein, John Owen, and Nancy Blair, "A Hazardous Profession: War, Journalists, and Psychopathology," *American Journal of Psychiatry* 159:9 (2002): 1570–1575; Omar Ghaffer and Anthony Feinstein, "Reporting under Fire: Understanding Psychopathology of War Journalists," *Psychiatric Times* 22 (April 2005): 31–33; Anthony Feinstein and Dawn Nicolson, "Embedded Journalists in the Iraq War: Are They at Greater Psychological Risk?" *Journal of Traumatic Stress* 18:2 (2005): 129–132; Caroline M. Pyevich, Elana Newman, and Eric Daleiden, "The Relationship among Cognitive Schemas, Job-Related Traumatic Exposure, and Post-traumatic Stress Disorder in Journalists," *Journal of Traumatic Stress* 16:4 (2003): 325–328. See also Nigel C. Hunt, *Memory, War and Trauma* (Cambridge: Cambridge University Press, 2010).

Jennifer L. Manlowe lists five characteristics of trauma that she says were taken from a conversation with Robert Lifton, who says trauma: (1) leaves an indelible imprint in the form of intense, sometimes repressed, memories that are often death related; (2) includes no time limit, and pain can endure for a lifetime; (3) potentially generates guilt or other forms of self-condemnation; (4) creates psychic numbing and diminished capacity to feel; (5) profoundly affects human relationships and surrounds them with suspicion and makes them vulnerable to disruption; (6) makes help or friendship appear to be counterfeit nurturance, as something insincere and unreliable; (7) brings on struggle with meaning at various levels; and (8) interrupts one's sense of personal continuity—one's lifeline—and there is a need to find new grounding and connectedness for the self. Jennifer Manlowe, *Faith Born of Seduction: Sexual Trauma, Body Image, and Religion* (New York: New York University Press, 1995), 6, 43.

Lifton's definition can be compared with "Post Traumatic Stress Disorder" as defined in the American Psychiatric Association's *Diagnostic Statistical Manual of Mental Health Disorders III*, developed from federal data and published in 1980 and 1987. PTSD is diagnosed when: (1) a person has experienced an event that is outside the range of usual human experience and that would be markedly distressing to almost anyone; (2) the traumatic event is persistently re-experienced through intrusive recollections of the traumatic experience, recurrent distressing dreams of the event, sudden action or feeling as if the traumatic event were recurring (flashbacks), and/or intense psychological distress at exposure to symbolic aspects of traumatic events; (3) there is persistent avoidance of stimuli associated with the trauma or numbing of general responsiveness; (4) there are persistent symptoms of increased arousal (e.g., sleep disturbance, hypervigilance, easily startled); and (5) the duration of the disturbance lasts at least one month.

9. Alice Miller, *Prisoners of Childhood* (New York: Basic, 1981); Manlowe, *Faith Born of Seduction*, 15–16.

10. Anthony Storr, *Solitude: A Return to the Self* (New York: Free Press, 1988), 113–119, 125, 128, 143.

11. Edmund Wilson, *The Wound and the Bow* (1929; repr., New York: Oxford University Press, 1947), 1–181, 214–242; David Aberbach, *Surviving Trauma: Loss, Literature and Psychoanalysis* (New Haven, Conn.: Yale University Press, 1989); Mark A. Heberle, *A Trauma Artist: Tim O'Brien and the Fiction of Vietnam* (Iowa City: University of Iowa Press, 2001); Kirby Farrell, *Post-Traumatic Culture: Injury and Interpretation in the Nineties* (Baltimore: The Johns Hopkins University Press, 1998).

12. Farrell, *Post-Traumatic Culture*, 5, 7; E. Ann Kaplan, *Trauma Culture: The Politics of Terror and Loss in Media and Literature* (New Brunswick, N.J.: Rutgers University Press, 2005), 1–2, 24–41.

13. Janice Haaken, *Pillar of Salt: Gender, Memory, and the Perils of Looking Back* (New Brunswick, N.J.: Rutgers University Press, 1998), 68.

14. Arieh Shalev notes some commonalities in the research literature about psychological and traumatic stress, including: (1) pretrauma vulnerability generally encompasses genetic and biological risk factors, as well as factors relating to one's life course, rearing environment, mental health, family history of mental disorders, and personality; (2) genetic factors can count for as much as one-third of individual vulnerability to mental health symptoms; (3) family history of psychiatric disorders (particularly involving alcohol) is a predictor of PTSD under certain combat situations; (4) prior mental disorders, childhood sexual and physical abuse, and negative experiences with parents (including separation from parents, parental poverty, and lower family educational levels) can increase the risk for developing PTSD, often with these variables working in combination with each other; (5) the intensity of a traumatic experience (combat, rape, torture, physical injury) contributes significantly to the development of PTSD. Arieh Y. Shalev, "Stress versus Traumatic Stress: From Acute Homeostatic Reactions to Chronic Psychopathology," in *Traumatic Stress: The Effects of Overwhelming Experience on Mind, Body, and Society,* edited by Bessel A. van der Kolk, Alexander C. McFarlane, Lars Weisaeth (New York: Guilford, 1996), 79, 86.

15. Jonah Lehrer, "Depression's Upside," *New York Times Magazine* (Feb. 28, 2010): 38–44; Paul W. Andrews Jr. and J. Anderson Thomson Jr., "The Bright Side of Being Blue: Depression as an Adaptation for Analyzing Complex Problems," *Psychological Review* 3 (July 2009): 620–654; Susan Nolen-Hoeksema, Blair E. Wisco, and Sonja Lyubomivsky, "Rethinking Rumination," *Perspectives on Psychological Science* 3:5 (2008): 400–424; Joseph P. Forgas, "When Sad Is Better than Happy: Negative Affect Can Improve the Quality and Effectiveness of Persuasive Messages and Social Influence Strategies," *Journal of Experimental Social Psychology* 43:4 (2007): 513–528; Peter Kramer, *Listening to Prozac* (New York: Penguin, 1997).

16. Judith Herman, *Trauma and Recovery* (New York: Basic, 1992), 13–32; Ruth Leys, *Trauma: A Genealogy* (Chicago: University of Chicago Press, 2000), 4, 18–22; Manlowe, *Faith Born of Seduction*, 11–13; Ian Hacking, *Rewriting the Soul: Multiple Personality and the Sciences of Memory* (Princeton, N.J.: Princeton University Press, 1995), 25; Kaplan, *Trauma Culture*, 29–32; Cathy Caruth, *Unclaimed Experience: Trauma, Narrative, and History* (Baltimore: The John Hopkins University Press, 1996), 57–72.

17. Leigh Gilmore, *The Limits of Autobiography: Trauma and Testimony* (Ithaca, N.Y.: Cornell University Press, 2001), 10–11, 18–19, 24; Laurie Vickroy, *Trauma and Survival in Contemporary Fiction* (Charlottesville: University Press of Virginia, 2002), xi; Hunt, *Memory, War and Trauma*, 3, 162.

18. Vickroy, *Trauma and Survival*, 12–14; Kai Erickson, "Notes on Trauma and Community," in *Trauma: Explorations in Memory*, edited by Cathy Caruth (Baltimore: The John Hopkins University Press, 1995), 184–185; Laura S. Brown, "Not Outside the Range: One Feminist Perspective on Psychic Trauma," in Caruth, *Trauma*, 101, 105, 107–111; Hacking, *Rewriting the Soul*, 13–15, 114, 187, 191–194; Leys, *Trauma*, 8, 33, 229–307; Gilmore, *Limits of Autobiography*, 26; Haaken, *Pillar of Salt*, 2–5, 60–83, 142; Kali Tal, *World of Hurt: Reading the Literatures of Trauma* (New York: Cambridge University Press, 1996), 17–22; Walter Kalaidjian, *The Edge of Modernism: American Poetry and the Traumatic Past* (Baltimore: The Johns Hopkins University Press, 2006).

19. Doug Underwood, "Trauma, Journalism, and Fiction: An Historical-Conceptual Analysis of the Impact of Traumatic Experiences in the Lives of Famous Journalist-Literary Figures." Paper delivered to Canadian Journalism Forum on Violence and Trauma. London, Ontario. February 2008.

20. Robert Jay Lifton, *Home from the War: Vietnam Veterans: Neither Victims or Executioners* (New York: Simon and Schuster, 1973), 395–398, 401; Herman, *Trauma and Recovery*; Kaplan, *Trauma Culture*, 19, 33–41.

21. Heberle, *Trauma Artist*, xv-xxi, 2, 9–10, 43, 77; Tobey C. Herzog, *Tim O'Brien* (New York: Twayne, 1997), 8–9; Don Rignalda, *Fighting and Writing the Vietnam War* (Jackson: University Press of Mississippi, 1994), 90–114; Philip D. Beidler, *Re-Writing America: Vietnam Authors in Their Generation* (Athens: The University of Georgia Press, 1991), 6–48.

22. Underwood, *Journalism and the Novel*, 46; Richard West, *Daniel Defoe: The Life and Strange, Surprising Adventures* (1998; repr., New York: Carroll and Graf, 2000), xiii.

23. Thomas De Quincey, *Confessions of an English Opium Eater* (1821; repr., New York: Oxford University Press, 1985); Herschel Baker, *William Hazlitt* (Cambridge, Mass.: Harvard University Press, 1962), 410–417; William Hazlitt, http://www.encyclopedia.com/doc/1G1-101564078.html; James Boswell, http://www.kirjasto.sci.fi/boswell.html; Samuel Johnson, htpp://www.victorianweb.org/previctorian/Johnson/rambler1.html.

24. Richard Wright, *Black Boy* (1937; repr., New York: Signet, 1963); James Agee, *A Death in the Family* (1957; repr., New York: Bantam, 1969); Theodore Dreiser, *A Book about Myself* (1922; repr., Greenwich, Conn.: Premier, 1965); Adams, http://www.enotes.com/education-henry; Doris Langley Moore, *E. Nesbit: A Biography* (Philadelphia, Pa.: Chilton, 1966), 103; Lynn, *Hemingway*, 27; Fenton, *Apprenticeship of Ernest Hemingway*, 1.

25. Hemingway, "Junior F.B.I. men" quotation, http://www.quotationsbook.com.

26. Jamison, *Touched with Fire*, 228–230; Lynn, *Hemingway*, 36, 63; Hemingway, "happiness" quotation, http://www.quotationspage.com.

27. Lynn, *Hemingway*, 27, 38, 41–43, 45; Roy Morris Jr., *Ambrose Bierce: Alone in Bad Company* (1995; repr., New York: Oxford University Press, 1998), 13.

28. Lynn, *Hemingway*, 133, 220, 253, 267, 427, 530–531, 582–593; Jamison, *Touched with Fire*, 229.

29. Carlos Baker, *Ernest Hemingway: A Life Story* (New York: Scribner's, 1969), 162–165, 168–178, 298–299, 333–334, 344–345, 351, 395, 440; Lynn, *Hemingway*, 509.

30. Baker, *Ernest Hemingway*, 44–45, 56–64; Hemingway, "world breaks" quote, www.notable-quotes.com, emphasis in original.

31. Lynn, *Hemingway*, 122, 157, 359, 525, 529–531.

32. Ibid., 106, 396, 426, 432, 436, 504, 510, 552.

33. Ibid., 50, 157, 411, 413, 570.

34. Ibid., 220; Fenton, *Apprenticeship of Ernest Hemingway*, 242, 256.

35. Bertram D. Sarason, *Hemingway and the Sun Set* (Washington, D.C.: National Cash Register Company, 1972), 6, 13, 15, 40, 43, 117–118, 134, 155, 234; Baker, *Ernest Hemingway*, 147–155.

36. Doug Underwood, *From Yahweh to Yahoo!: The Religious Roots of the Secular Press* (Urbana: University of Illinois Press, 2002), 71, 97–98; Baker, *Ernest Hemingway*, 449.

37. J. F. Kobler, *Ernest Hemingway: Journalist and Artist* (1968; repr., Ann Arbor, Mich.: UMI Research Press, 1984), 18.

38. The studies identified in each category on the Web of Science site were accessed September 21, 2010, through the Suzzallo Library, University of Washington. Categories (with search terms and the number of studies) included: trauma growing out of childhood that continued as stresses in adulthood (depression and depressed parent, 532; loss of parent and mental health, 53); adult stresses connected to lifestyle and life circumstances (divorce and mental health, 405; minorities and mental health, 498; gay and mental health, 653); work in professions with stress (employment and mental health, 2,198; job loss and mental health, 169); exposure to war and abuse (war and mental health, 1,197; violence and mental health, 3,241; abuse and mental health, 6,853); management of personal mental health and physical issues (drugs and mental health, 1,953; alcohol and mental health, 4,531; counseling and mental health, 1,342; institutionalization and mental health, 187); religious upbringing or involvement (religion and mental health, 719; spirituality and mental health, 534); connection between one or more life stresses and the susceptibility to emotional ailments (stressors and mental health, 1,343; stress and mental health, 10,343).

Chapter 1. Stories of Harm, Stories of Hazard

1. Irving Howe, *Sherwood Anderson* (Toronto: George J. McLeod, 1951), 46–49.

2. Ibid., 47–48.

3. Ibid., 31–49.

4. Ibid., 42–44, 65–75, 97–101.

5. Sherwood Anderson, *Winesburg, Ohio* (1919; repr., New York: Viking, 1974), 120, 142.

6. Ibid., 49–57, 165, 233–247.

7. West, *Daniel Defoe*, xiii, 168–169, 271–272; Maximillian Novak, *Daniel Defoe: Master of Fictions* (Oxford, U.K.: Oxford University Press, 2001), 603–607; Daniel Defoe, *A Journal of the Plague Year* (1722; repr., New York: Norton, 1992); Daniel Defoe, *Due Preparations for the Plague* (1722; repr., London: J. M. Dent, 1902).

8. Charles Dickens, *David Copperfield* (1850; repr., New York: MacMillan, 1962), 603–604.

9. Ernest Hemingway, *The Sun Also Rises* (1926; repr., New York: Scribner's, 2003), 42; Jonathan Yardley, *Ring: A Biography of Ring Lardner* (New York: Random House, 1977); Guy Szuberla, "Damon Runyon," *Dictionary of Literary Biography* (1989); Richard Marling, *Raymond Chandler* (Boston: Twayne, 1986).

10. John O'Hara, *BUtterfield 8* (1934; repr., New York: Bantam, 1961), 101, 109–115, 119, 146, 160, 162, 220, 275, 279.

11. Kate McLoughlin, *Martha Gellhorn: The War Writer in the Field and in the Text* (Manchester, U.K.: Manchester University Press, 2007), 66, 75, 154, 187–189.

12. Katherine Biers, "Djuna Barnes Makes a Specialty of Crime: Violence and the Visual in Her Early Journalism," in *Women's Experience of Modernity, 1875–1945,* edited by Ann L. Ardis and Lewis W. Lewis (Baltimore: The Johns Hopkins University Press, 2003), 237, 243–245; Barnes, "narrative" quotation, http://www.plaidder.com.

13. Truman Capote, *In Cold Blood* (1965; repr., New York: Vintage, 1994), 132; Gerald Clarke, *Capote: A Biography* (1988; repr., New York: Ballantine, 1989), 326–328.

14. Zachary Leader, "Coleridge and the Uses of Journalism," in *Grub Street and the Ivory Tower: Literary Journalism and Literary Scholarship from Fielding to the Internet,* edited by Jeremy Treglown and Bridget Bennett (New York: Clarendon-Oxford University Press, 1998), 28; Rosemary Ashton, *The Life of Samuel Taylor Coleridge: A Critical Biography* (Oxford, U.K.: Blackwell, 1996), 334–338; Peter Martin, *A Life of Boswell* (1999; repr., London: Phoenix Press, 2000), 394–397; John Dixon Hunt, *The Wider Sea: A Life of John Ruskin* (London: J. M. Dent, 1982), 317, 370–371; Brian Maidment, "Readers Fair and Foul: John Ruskin and the Periodical Press," in *The Victorian Periodical Press: Samplings and Soundings,* edited by Joanne Shattock and Michael Wolff (Toronto: University of Toronto Press, 1982), 56; Michael D. Marcaccio, *The Hapgoods: Three Earnest Brothers* (Charlottesville: University Press of Virginia, 1977), 160–161, 220; William McKeen, *Hunter S. Thompson* (Boston: Twayne, 1991), 15.

15. Underwood, "Depression, Drink, and Dissipation," 186–200.

16. Lehrer, "Depression's Upside," 38–44; Andrews and Thomson, "The Bright Side of Being Blue," 620–654.

17. Victoria Glendinning, *Jonathan Swift* (London: Hutchinson, 1998), 1–15, 23, 48, 121–126, 179–180, 245–246, 262–275; A. L. Rowse, *Jonathan Swift* (New York: Scribner's, 1975), 11–13, 85–86, 231; J. A. Downie, *Jonathan Swift: Political Writer* (London: Routledge, 1984), 183–184, 202–203, 215–220, 330, 337–340.

18. Donald Greene, *Samuel Johnson* (New York: Twayne, 1970), 158; Donald Greene,

"Samuel Johnson, Journalist," in *Newsletters to Newspapers: Eighteenth-Century Journalism*, edited by Donovan H. Bond and W. Reynolds McLeod (Morgantown: The School of Journalism, West Virginia University, 1977), 91; W. Jackson Bate, *Samuel Johnson* (New York: Harcourt Brace Jovanovich, 1975), 202–205; Robert Spector, *Samuel Johnson and the Essay* (Westport, Conn.: Greenwood, 1997), 8.

19. West, *Daniel Defoe*, xiii, 278–303; Novak, *Daniel Defoe*, 8–9.

20. Winifred F. Courtney, *Young Charles Lamb 1775–1802* (London: Macmillan, 1982), 109, 114–116, 235–236, 270.

21. David S. Reynolds, *Walt Whitman's America: A Cultural Biography* (1995; repr., New York: Vintage, 1996), 23, 27–28, 69–73, 198–200, 391–403.

22. Edwin H. Cady, *The Road to Realism: The Early Years 1837–1885 of William Dean Howells* (Syracuse, N.Y.: Syracuse University Press, 1956), 23, 55–56, 66, 243–244; Susan Goodman and Carl Dawson, *William Dean Howells: A Writer's Life* (Berkeley: University of California Press, 2005), 26–33.

23. Gary Scharnhorst, *Bret Harte: Opening the American Literary West* (Norman: University of Oklahoma Press, 2000), 13–14; Richard O'Connor, *Bret Harte: A Biography* (Boston: Little, Brown, 1966), 41–47, 230–231.

24. Kathryn Hughes, *George Eliot: The Last Victorian* (New York: Farrar Straus Giroux, 1998), 26–28, 35, 83–86, 98–101, 107–108, 120, 131–132, 144–145, 176.

25. West, *Daniel Defoe*, 84, 240–41; Novak, *Daniel Defoe*, 699; Defoe, *Plague Year*, 50, 54–58; Underwood, *Journalism and the Novel*, 45–53.

26. Bate, *Samuel Johnson*, 372–373, 407–412; Chester F. Chapin, *The Religious Thought of Samuel Johnson* (Ann Arbor: University of Michigan Press, 1968), 86–87; Martin, *Life of Boswell*, 24, 51–52, 121–123, 238–240, 247–248; Underwood, *Yahweh to Yahoo!*, 54–56; Underwood, *Journalism and the Novel*, 57–65.

27. Hughes, *George Eliot*, 27–35, 70–71, 279–280.

28. Mark Twain, *The Adventures of Huckleberry Finn* (1884; repr., New York: Laurel, 1971), 27, 264; Mark Twain, *Letters from the Earth* (1938; repr., New York: Harper and Row, 1974), 20, 42; Justin Kaplan, *Mr. Clemens and Mark Twain: A Biography* (New York: Simon and Schuster, 1966), 14.

29. Dreiser, *Book about Myself*, 69–70, 457–459; Theodore Dreiser, *Dawn: An Autobiography of Early Youth* (1931; repr., Santa Rosa, Calif.: Black Sparrow Press, 1998), 551–553; Underwood, *Journalism and the Novel*, 113–114.

30. Peter De Vries, *The Blood of the Lamb* (Boston: Little, Brown, 1961), 25, 207–208, 236–238.

31. Nancy L. Roberts, *Dorothy Day and the Catholic Worker* (Albany: State University of New York Press, 1984), 18–19, 23–27, 87; James H. Forest, *Love Is the Measure* (New York: Paulist Press, 1986) 4, 11, 50; Michael Coren, *Gilbert, The Man Who Was G. K. Chesterton* (New York: Paragon, 1990), 44–52, 58–64; Selina Hastings, *Evelyn Waugh: A Biography* (Boston: Houghton Mifflin, 1994), 507–508; Douglas Lane Patey, *The Life of Evelyn Waugh: A Critical Biography* (1998; repr., Malden, Mass.: Blackwell, 2001), 36–37; Michael Shelden, *Graham Greene: The Enemy Within* (New York: Random House, 1994), 105–109, 287.

32. A. C. Goodson, "Samuel Taylor Coleridge," and James C. McKusick, "Samuel Taylor Coleridge," *Dictionary of Literary Biography* (1990, 1991).

33. Underwood, *Journalism and the Novel*, 42–43, 65–68; Fred Kaplan, *Dickens: A Biography* (Baltimore: The Johns Hopkins University Press, 1988), 354–355, 380–381; Twain, *Huckleberry Finn*, 51; Coleridge, "youth" quotation, http://www.bartleby.com.

34. Underwood, *Journalism and the Novel*, 73–77; Kenneth Silverman, *Edgar A. Poe: Mournful and Never-Ending Remembrance* (1991; repr., New York: Harper Perennial, 1992), 1, 3, 7–8, 110, 112, 152, 183–184, 191, 199–200, 209, 408, 423–424, 427.

35. David S. Reynolds, *Beneath the American Renaissance: The Subversive Imagination in the Age of Emerson and Melville* (Cambridge, Mass.: Harvard University Press, 1989), 231–232, 238–239, 243, 246–247.

36. Susan M. Levin, *The Romantic Art of Confession: De Quincey, Musset, Sand, Lamb, Hogg, Frémy, Soulié, Janin* (Columbia, S.C.: Camden House, 1998), 19–20, 28–29, 31, 93.

37. Maidment, "Readers Fair and Foul," 46; Hunt, *Life of John Ruskin*, 370–372, 383, 385, 395, 397–398, 405; Tim Hilton, *John Ruskin: The Later Years* (New Haven, Conn.: Yale University Press, 2000), 344, 408–409; Andrew Leng, "Letters to Workmen? *Fors Clavigera*, Whistler vs. Ruskin, and Sage Criticism in Crisis," *Prose Studies* 24:1 (April 2001): 63–92.

38. Andrew Birkin, *J. M. Barrie and the Lost Boys* (London: Constable, 1979), 1–2, 13–14, 37, 59, 85; Janet Dunbar, *J. M. Barrie: The Man behind the Image* (Boston: Houghton Mifflin, 1970), 149, 152–153, 175–176, 244.

39. John Seelye, *War Games: Richard Harding Davis and the New Imperialism* (Amherst: University of Massachusetts Press, 2003), 12, 18; Gerald Langford, *The Richard Harding Davis Years: A Biography of a Mother and Son* (New York: Holt, Rinehart and Winston, 1961), 66, 72, 97, 148–149, 159, 168, 208, 211, 270, 285; Janice Milner Lasseter, "Rebecca Harding Davis," *Dictionary of Literary Biography* (2001).

40. Laurence Bergreen, *James Agee: A Life* (1984; repr., New York: Penguin, 1985), 298; Scott Elledge, *E. B. White: A Biography* (1984; repr., New York: Norton, 1986), 269; Marion Meade, *Dorothy Parker: What Fresh Hell Is This?* (1987; repr., New York: Penguin, 1989), 161; Jeremy Treglown, *V. S. Pritchett: A Working Life* (New York: Random House, 2004), 191; Richard O'Connor, *Heywood Broun: A Biography* (New York: Putnam's, 1975), 192; Marion K. Sanders, *Dorothy Thompson: A Legend in Her Time* (Boston: Houghton Mifflin, 1973), 99–100; Thurber, "psychiatrist" quotation, http://www.quotationspage.com.

41. Shelden, *Graham Greene*, 11–12, 27–28, 45–52, 215–229, 316, 327, 331, 388–395.

42. Graham Greene, *The Heart of the Matter* (1948; repr., New York: Viking, 1963), 306; Shelden, *Graham Greene*, 15, 105–109, 287, 316; Hastings, *Evelyn Waugh*, 546.

43. James Woodress, *Willa Cather: A Literary Life* (1987; repr., Lincoln: University of Nebraska Press, 1989), 69–70, 110, 125–126, 131, 142–143, 337–338; Janis P. Stout, "Willa Cather's Early Journalism: Gender, Performance, and the 'Manly Battle Yarn,'" *Arizona Quarterly* 55:3 (1999): 72–74, 76–77; Carolyn Kitch, "The Work that

Came before the Art: Willa Cather as Journalist, 1893–1912," *American Journalism* 14:3/4 (1997): 430–431, 436, 439; The Willa Cather Archive at cather.unl.edu.

44. Joan Acocella, *Willa Cather and the Politics of Criticism* (New York: Vintage, 2000), 45–65; Woodress, *Willa Cather*, 127, 141–142, 245; Hermione Lee, *Willa Cather: A Life Saved Up* (1989; repr., New York: Virago, 2000), 4, 10–17, 57–59, 70–73, 105–118.

45. Scott Meredith, *George S. Kaufman and His Friends* (Garden City, N.Y.: Doubleday, 1974), 19–25, 37, 49, 255, 257–258; Miller, *Prisoners of Childhood*, ix, 6, 8–9, 11–12, 24–25, 35, 38–39, 44–45, 56, 85–86; Lee, *Willa Cather*, 28–29.

46. Burton Bernstein, *Thurber: A Biography* (1975; repr., New York: Ballantine, 1976), 24–26, 37–39, 163, 279, 298, 300, 566, 568–571; Thurber, "laughter of man" quotation, http://www.brainyquote.com.

47. J. J. Wilson, "Virginia Woolf," Linda Mills Woolsey, "Thomas De Quincey," Stephen R. Whited, "John Masefield," and Wanda H. Giles, "Gail Godwin," *Dictionary of Literary Biography* (1985, 1991, 1995, 2009); Bergreen, *James Agee*, 14–19, 33, 306–307; Jamison, *Touched with Fire*, 225–227.

48. Billy Altman, *Laughter's Gentle Soul: The Life of Robert Benchley* (New York: Norton, 1997), 26; Gerald Nicosia, *Memory Babe: A Critical Biography of Jack Kerouac* (Berkeley: University of California Press, 1994), 24, 27.

49. Paul M. Cousins, *Joel Chandler Harris: A Biography* (Baton Rouge: Louisiana State University Press, 1968), 19–49; Joan Givner, *Katherine Anne Porter: A Life* (New York: Touchstone, 1982), 38–43; Linden Peach, *Angela Carter* (New York: St. Martin's, 1998), 16–17.

50. Szuberla, "Damon Runyon," Carolyn Garrett Cline, "William Sydney Porter," *Dictionary of Literary Biography* (1989); O'Connor, *Bret Harte*, 100, 103–104, 116–117.

51. Elie Wiesel, *Night* (1958; repr., New York: Hill and Wang, 2006), xi–xxii, 45; Jack Kolbert, "Elie Wiesel," and Simon P. Sibelman, "Elie Wiesel," *Dictionary of Literary Biography* (1989, 2004); Ted L. Estess, *Elie Wiesel* (New York: Ungar, 1980), 2, 8–9, 17–19, 24, 30.

52. Frances Kiernan, *Seeing Mary Plain: A Life of Mary McCarthy* (New York: Norton, 2000), 29–33; Richard Lingeman, *Sinclair Lewis: Rebel from Main Street* (New York: Random House, 2002), 313.

53. Geneviève Moreau, *The Restless Journey of James Agee* (New York: Morrow, 1977), 35; Bergreen, *James Agee*, 16, 168–169, 298.

54. Mary McCarthy, *Memories of a Catholic Girlhood* (New York: Harcourt, Brace, 1946), 3–4, 13, 15, 17, 37–38, 44–45, 49–50.

55. Agee, *Death in the Family*, 241–243, 249, 265.

56. Ibid., 315; McCarthy, *Memories*, 72–86.

57. Edward Butscher, *Conrad Aiken: Poet of White Horse Veil* (Athens: University of Georgia Press, 1988), 38, 41–48, 227; Peter J. Reed, "Kurt Vonnegut Jr.," *Dictionary of Literary Biography* (1995); Stacey Peebles, "Fighting to Understand: Violence, Form, and Truth-Claims in Lesly, Vonnegut, and Herr," *Philological Quarterly* 84:4 (2005): 479–496.

58. Meade, *Dorothy Parker*, 12–16, 21.

59. Joan Didion, *The Year of Magical Thinking* (2006; repr., New York: Vintage International, 2007), 15, 27, 170, 188, 198.

60. D. J. Taylor, *Thackeray: The Life of a Literary Man* (1999; repr., New York: Carroll and Graf, 2001), 22–24.

61. Andrew Sinclair, *Jack: A Biography of Jack London* (1977; repr., New York: Pocket, 1979), 2–9, 12–13, 25–26, 33, 36–37.

62. Townsend Ludington, *John Dos Passos: A Twentieth Century Odyssey* (New York: Dutton, 1980), 2–3, 7, 52.

63. Maya Angelou, *I Know Why the Caged Bird Sings* (New York: Random House, 1969), 76–78, 82–83, 85; Lynn Z. Bloom, "Maya Angelou," *Dictionary of Literary Biography* (1985).

64. Clarke, *Capote*, 6, 11, 13–14, 23–25, 400–401.

65. Ibid., 45, 62–63; Paul Mariani, *The Broken Tower: A Life of Hart Crane* (1999; repr., New York: Norton, 2000), 301, 324, 338.

66. Neil McKenna, *The Secret Life of Oscar Wilde* (New York: Basic, 2005), 330–335, 465–475, 480–481, 514, 548; Dominic Hibberd's essay on H. H. Munro in the *Oxford Dictionary of National Biography* (New York: Oxford University Press, 2004).

67. Jamison, *Touched with Fire*, 267–269; Hastings, *Evelyn Waugh*, 17, 22–29; Cline, "William Sydney Porter," Luther S. Luedtke and Keith Lawrence, "William Sydney Porter," and Merritt Moseley, "Auberon Waugh," *Dictionary of Literary Biography* (1989, 1998); Richard O'Connor, *O. Henry: The Legendary Life of William S. Porter* (Garden City, N.Y.: Doubleday, 1970), 7; Carol Gelderman, *Mary McCarthy: A Life* (New York: St. Martin's, 1988), 10–12, 107; Kiernan, *Seeing Mary Plain*, 146–147, 151, 153.

68. Szuberla, "Damon Runyon," and Michael J. Dillon, "James Breslin," *Dictionary of Literary Biography* (1997); Jimmy Breslin, *Damon Runyon* (New York: Ticknor and Fields, 1991), 6, 58, 60, 138, 285, 382, 388; Breslin, "marvelous personality" quotation, www.cityroom.blogs.nytimes.com; www.thoughts.forbes.com.

69. Susan Cheever, *Home before Dark: A Biographical Memoir of John Cheever by His Daughter* (Boston: Houghton Mifflin, 1984), 77, 164–165, 181–183, 205, 209, 213–216.

70. Auberon Waugh, *Will This Do?: The First Fifty Years of Auberon Waugh, An Autobiography* (1991; repr., London: Arrow, 1992), 29–31, 36–37, 43, 45, 54, 67, 124–125, 185–187.

Chapter 2. Trafficking in Trauma

1. Robert E. Hemenway, *Zora Neale Hurston: A Literary Biography* (Urbana: University of Illinois Press, 1977), 17, 42, 69–70, 90, 220–221, 329–334, 346; Deborah G. Plant, *Zora Neale Hurston: A Biography of the Spirit* (Westport, Conn.: Praeger, 2007), 21–22.

2. George Orwell, *Down and out in Paris and London* (1933; repr., San Diego, Calif.: Harvest, 1961), 16, 37; Michael Shelden, *Orwell: The Authorized Biography* (New York: HarperCollins, 1991), 120–121, 126, 131, 166.

3. Sally Ledger, *Dickens and the Popular Radical Imagination* (Cambridge: Cambridge University Press, 2007), 3, 66, 102–103, 119, 133–135, 219, 225; Robert L. Patten, "Dickens as Serial Author: A Case of Multiple Identities," in *Nineteenth-Century Media and the Construction of Identities,* edited by Laurel Brake, Bill Bell, and David Finkelstein (New York: Palgrave, 2000), 146.

4. Hughes, *George Eliot,* 83, 98–101, 107–108, 118–120, 140–142, 163–164; Gordon S. Haight, *George Eliot and John Chapman* (New Haven, Conn.: Yale University Press, 1940), 100–102; Elaine Showalter, *A Literature of Their Own: British Women Novelists from Bronte to Lessing* (Princeton, N.J.: Princeton University Press, 1977), 95; Underwood, *Journalism and the Novel,* 77–79.

5. Anne Edwards, *Road to Tara: The Life of Margaret Mitchell* (New Haven, Conn.: Ticknor and Fields, 1983), 101–102, 109, 115; Patrick Allen, ed., *Margaret Mitchell Reporter* (Athens, Ga.: Hill Street Press, 2000), v, xiii.

6. Wright, *Black Boy,* 84, 271–272; Underwood, *Journalism and the Novel,* 150, 174, 176.

7. Showalter, *Literature of Their Own,* 80; Margaret Beetham, *A Magazine of Her Own?: Domesticity and Desire in the Woman's Magazine 1800–1914* (London: Routledge, 1996), 129–130; Joanne Shattock, "Women's Work: Victorian Women Writers and the Press," *Gaskell Society Journal* 14 (2000): 23–25; Nancy Armstrong, *Desire and Domestic Fiction: A Political History of the Novel* (New York: Oxford University Press, 1987), 20–21, 48; Ellen Moers, *Literary Women* (Garden City, N.Y.: Doubleday, 1976), 47, 119; Dallas Liddle, *The Dynamics of Genre: Journalism and the Practice of Literature in Mid-Victorian Britain* (Charlottesville: University Press of Virginia, 2009), 9; Alexis Easley, *First Person Anonymous: Women Writers and Victorian Print Media, 1830–1870* (Aldershot, U.K.: Ashgate, 2004), 41; Carolyn L. Karcher, "Lydia Maria Child and the *Juvenile Miscellany*: The Creation of an American Children's Literature," in *Periodical Literature in Nineteenth-Century America,* edited by Kenneth M. Price and Susan Belasco Smith (Charlottesville: University Press of Virginia, 1995), 107–108.

8. Showalter, *Literature of Their Own,* 21, 25, 29–30, 79, 97, 154; Hilary Fraser, Stephanie Green, and Judith Johnson, *Gender and the Victorian Periodical* (Cambridge: Cambridge University Press, 2003), 28–29; Catherine C. Mitchell, ed., *Margaret Fuller's New York Journalism* (Knoxville: The University of Tennessee Press, 1995), 35–36.

9. Gary Scharnhorst, *Charlotte Perkins Gilman* (Boston: Twayne, 1985), 5–8, 10; Lawrence J. Oliver and Gary Scharnhorst, "Charlotte Perkins versus Ambrose Bierce: The Literary Politics of Gender in Fin-de-Siecle California," in *Charlotte Perkins Gilman and Her Contemporaries,* edited by Cynthia J. Davis and Denise D. Knight (Tuscaloosa: The University of Alabama Press, 2004), 36–39; Morris, *Ambrose Bierce,* 146, 154–155, 165–166.

10. Carolyn Kitch, "'The Courage to Call Things by Their Right Names': Fanny Fern, Feminine Sympathy, and Feminist Issues in Nineteenth-Century American Journalism," *American Journalism* 13:3 (1996): 286–303; Joyce Warren, "Uncommon

Discourse: Fanny Fern and the *New York Ledger*," in Price and Smith, *Periodical Literature*, 52, 54, 61; Elizabethada A. Wright, "Open-Ended Oratory: Fanny Fern's Use of the Periodical as a Rhetorical Platform," *American Journalism* 18:2 (2001): 64–82.

11. Fanny Fern, *Ruth Hall and Other Writings* (1854; repr., New Brunswick, N.J.: Rutgers University Press, 1986), 116; Joyce W. Warren, *Fanny Fern: An Independent Woman* (New Brunswick, N.J.: Rutgers University Press, 1992), 54–70, 72–97, 104–142.

12. Charlotte S. McClure, "Gertrude Atherton," Lois Josephs Fowler, "Caroline Norton," and Winifred Hughes, "Mary Elizabeth Braddon," *Dictionary of Literary Biography* (1981, 1983, 1983); "Emily Faithfull," http://www.gerald-massey.org.uk/faithfull.

13. Thomas Grant, "Dorothy Parker," Margaret McDowell, "Rebecca West," Judith Barisonzi, "Edith Nesbit," Jeff Berglund, "Meridel Le Sueur," and Erika Rothwell, "Katharine Bruce Glasier," *Dictionary of Literary Biography* (1982, 1985, 1995, 1998, 2005); Julia Briggs, *A Woman of Passion: The Life of Edith Nesbit, 1854–1924* (London: Hutchinson, 1987), 57–58; "Agnes Smedley," *Contemporary Authors Online* (2003).

14. W. A. Swanberg, *Dreiser* (New York: Scribner's, 1965), 320; Shelden, *Graham Greene*, 306–307; Daniel R. Schwarz, *Broadway Boogie Woogie: Damon Runyon and the Making of New York City Culture* (New York: Palgrave Macmillan, 2003), 9; Patricia Ward D'Itri, *Damon Runyon* (Boston: Twayne, 1982), 17, 42–46, 62, 112–113; Breslin, *Damon Runyon*, 20–26, 41–45, 64–65, 68–69, 72–73, 177, 179–180, 227–229, 258–260, 305–307; O'Connor, *Bret Harte*, 231–234, 256–257, 261–265, 279–280; Kaplan, *Dickens*, 367–396; Dan B. Miller, *Erskine Caldwell: The Journey from Tobacco Road* (New York: Knopf, 1994), 93, 182–184; Michael Foot, *H. G.: The History of Mr. Wells* (London: Doubleday, 1995), 86; Altman, *Laughter's Gentle Soul*, 215, 218–219; Meade, *Dorothy Parker*, 135, 215–216.

15. Meade, *Dorothy Parker*, 103–107. Quotes can be found at http://www.goodreads.com ("He'll be cross . . ."); http: womenshistory.about.com ("keeping all my eggs . . ."), ("Scratch a lover . . ."), ("nobility in women . . .").

16. Frederick Douglass, *My Bondage and My Freedom* (1855; repr., New York: Modern Library, 2003), 10, 13; William S. McFeely, *Frederick Douglass* (New York: Norton, 1991), 6, 10, 147; David T. Z. Mindich, "Understanding Frederick Douglass: Toward a New Synthesis Approach to the Birth of Modern Journalism," *Journalism History* 26:1 (2000): 15–22.

17. W. E. B. Du Bois, *The Souls of Black Folks: Up from Slavery*, reprinted in *Three Negro Classics* (New York: Avon, 1965), 214–215; Addison Gayle Jr., "W. E. B. Du Bois," Doris Lucas Laryea, "Paul Laurence Dunbar," Norma R. Jones, "George Samuel Schuyler," and Shirley Wilson Logan, "Victoria Earle Matthews," *Dictionary of Literary Biography* (1986, 1986, 1987, 2000); Hanna Wallinger, "Pauline E. Hopkins as Editor and Journalist," in Price and Smith, *Periodical Literature*, 153, 162–163, 165; C. K. Doreski, "Inherited Rhetoric and Authentic History: Pauline Hopkins at the *Colored American Magazine*," in *The Unruly Voice: Rediscovering Pauline Hopkins,* edited by John Cullen Gruesser (Urbana: University of Illinois Press, 1996), 75, 80–81, 90.

18. Charles W. Chesnutt, *The Marrow of Tradition* (1901; repr., Ann Arbor: The

University of Michigan Press/Ann Arbor Paperbacks, 1990), 274–275; Dolen Perkins, "'White Heat' in Wilmington: The Dialogue between Journalism and Literature in *The Marrow of Tradition*," *North Carolina Literary Review* 11 (2002): 38–47; Kenneth M. Price, "Charles Chesnutt, the *Atlantic Monthly*, and the Intersection of African-American Fiction and Elite Culture," in Price and Smith, *Periodical Literature*, 261, 263, 267; William L. Andrews, "Charles Chesnutt," Sylvia Lyons Render, "Charles Chesnutt," and Stephanie Athey, "Ida Wells-Barnett," *Dictionary of Literary Biography* (1986, 1989, 2000).

19. Richard Wright, *Native Son* (1940; repr., New York: Harper and Row, 1989), 316–317, 319, 336; Wright, *Black Boy*, 111–112.

20. Mary Helen Washington, "Foreword," and Henry Louis Gates Jr., "Afterword," in Zora Neale Hurston, *Their Eyes Were Watching God* (1937; repr., New York: Perennial, 1998), ix–xvii, 195–205; Laura M. Zaidman, "Zora Neale Hurston," *Dictionary of Literary Biography* (1989).

21. Sui Sin Far, *Mrs. Spring Fragrance and Other Writings* (1912; repr., Urbana: University of Illinois Press, 1995), 60, 83; Maria N. Ng, "Chop Suey Writing: Sui Sin Far, Wayson Choy, and Judy Fong Bates," *Essays on Canadian Writing* 65 (Fall 1998): 171–186; Nicole Tonkovich, "Edith Maude Eaton," and Diana Birchall, "Edith Maude Eaton," *Dictionary of Literary Biography* (2000, 2005).

22. "William Thomas Stead," *Contemporary Authors Online* (2003).

23. Theodore Dreiser, "Nigger Jeff," in *Free and Other Stories* (New York: Boni and Liveright, 1918), 111; Dreiser, *Book about Myself*, 397; Underwood, *Yahweh to Yahoo!*, 113–114, 123–126.

24. Underwood, *Journalism and the Novel*, 132–134.

25. Sinclair, *Jack*, 48–49, 134–135, 169; Wikipedia, "Jack London," 8.

26. Underwood, *Journalism and the Novel*, 129–131.

27. Miller, *Erskine Caldwell*, 203–205, 213–222, 261–269.

28. Jackson J. Benson, *John Steinbeck, Writer: A Biography* (1984; repr., New York: Penguin, 1990), 346, 355, 370–371; Jan Whitt, "'To Do Some Good and No Harm': The Literary Journalism of John Steinbeck," *Steinbeck Review* 3:2 (2006): 43, 60; Paul Bailey, "Researching Tom Joad: John Steinbeck, Journalist, 1936," *Chronicles of Oklahoma* 83:1 (2005): 72–75.

29. Bergreen, *James Agee*, 162–165, 172, 174, 177, 179, 181, 213–214, 218, 235, 260–261; Moreau, *Journey of James Agee*, 278; Dennis Russell, "Documentary Journalism of the 1930's: Pursuing the Social Fact," *Popular Culture Review* 8:2 (1997): 17–34; David Madden, "The Test of a First-Rate Intelligence: Agee and the Cruel Radiance of What Is," in *James Agee: Reconsiderations,* edited by Michael A. Lofaro (Knoxville: The University of Tennessee Press, 1992), 35.

30. Howe, *Sherwood Anderson*, 215–230.

31. Moreau, *Journey of James Agee*, 142, 185–199; Bergreen, *James Agee*, 179–180; Shelden, *Graham Greene*, 324–327; Elana Newman, "Occupational Health and Journalists," and Patrice Keats, "Secondary Traumatization in First Responders: A Critical Ethnographic Study of Photojournalists and Journalists." Presentations to Ca-

nadian Journalism Forum on Trauma and Violence. London, Ontario. February 10, 2008.

32. Swanberg, *Dreiser*, 94–105, 375; Underwood, *Journalism and the Novel*, 125–126; Dreiser, *Book about Myself*, 390–391, 414; Dreiser, *Dawn*, 209–210.

33. Shelden, *Orwell*, 25–33, 92, 106, 108, 178, 337–349, 351.

34. Altman, *Laughter's Gentle Soul*, 131–135.

35. Jan Whitt, *Women in American Journalism: A New History* (Urbana: University of Illinois Press, 2008), 92–99; Katherine Anne Porter, "The Art of Fiction No. 29," http://www.theparisreview.org/interviews/4569/the-art-of-fiction-no-29-katherine -anne-porter.

36. Ron Powers, *Mark Twain: A Life* (2005; repr., New York: Free Press, 2006), 9, 14, 41–44, 476–477.

37. Shelden, *Orwell*, 219.

Chapter 3: Trauma in War, Trauma in Life

1. Linda H. Davis, *Badge of Courage: The Life of Stephen Crane* (Boston: Houghton Mifflin, 1998), 264–266; R. W. Stallman, *Stephen Crane: A Biography* (New York: Braziller, 1968), 393–394.

2. Christopher Benfey, *The Double Life of Stephen Crane* (New York: Knopf, 1992), 15, 229–230; Davis, *Badge of Courage*, 274; Underwood, *Journalism and the Novel*, 128–129.

3. Morris, *Ambrose Bierce*, 2, 91–92, 132, 233.

4. Ibid., 234, 249–268.

5. Susan F. Beegel, "The Critical Reputation of Ernest Hemingway," in *The Cambridge Companion to Hemingway*, edited by Scott Donaldson (Cambridge: Cambridge University Press, 1996), 275. See also Neil K. Moran, *Kipling and Afghanistan: A Study of the Young Author as Journalist Writing on the Afghan Border Crisis of 1884–1885* (Jefferson, N.C.: McFarland, 2005); Richard Keeble, "Orwell as War Correspondent: A Reassessment," *Journalism Studies* 2:3 (2001): 393–406; Michael B. Salwen, "Evelyn Waugh's *Scoop*: The Facts behind the Fiction," *Journalism and Mass Communication Quarterly* 78 (Spring 2001): 150–171; Michael B. Salwen, "Evelyn in Ethiopia: The Novelist as War Correspondent and Journalism Critic," *Journalism Studies* 2:1 (2001): 5–25; Michael S. Sweeney, "'Delays and Vexation': Jack London and the Russo-Japanese War," *Journalism and Mass Communication Quarterly* 75 (Autumn 1998): 548–559; Patrick B. Sharp, "The Great White 'Race Adventure': Jack London and the Yellow Peril," in *Crossing Oceans: Reconfiguring American Literary Studies in the Pacific Rim*, edited by Noelle Brada-Williams and Karen Chow (Hong Kong: Hong Kong University Press, 2004); John C. Bromley, "Richard Harding Davis and the Boer War," *American Journalism* 7:1 (1990): 12–22; Donald Vanouse, "Stephen Crane in Cuba: From Jingoism to Criticism," *Stephen Crane Studies* 11:2 (2002): 23–32; William Crisman, "'Distributing the News': War Journalism as Metaphor for Language in Stephen Crane's Fiction," *Studies in American Fiction* 30 (Fall 2002): 207–227; John Dudley, "Crane's Dispatches from

Cuba: The Dynamics of Race, Class, and Professionalism in 'The Correspondents' War,'" *Stephen Crane Studies* 11:2 (2002): 11–22; John Dudley, "Inside and Outside the Ring: Manhood, Race, and Art in American Literary Naturalism," *College Literature* 29:1 (2002): 53–82; Jesse S. Crisler, "The College Man in South Africa: A New Article by Frank Norris," *Frank Norris Studies* 3 (2003): 5–7; Christopher C. Sullivan, "John Steinbeck, War Reporter: Fiction, Journalism, and Types of Truth," *Journalism History* 23:1 (1997): 16–23; Mimi Riesel Gladstein, "Mr. Novelist Goes to War: Hemingway and Steinbeck as Front-Line Correspondents," *War, Literature, and the Arts* 15:1/2 (2003): 258–266; William E. Coté, "Correspondent or Warrior? Hemingway's Murky World War II 'Combat' Experience," *Hemingway Review* 22:1 (2002): 88–104; William E. Coté, "Hemingway's Spanish Civil War Dispatches: Literary Journalism, Fiction, or Propaganda?" *North Dakota Quarterly* 60:2 (1992): 193–293; William E. Diebler, "Dateline: D-Day: Ernest Hemingway Reported on Ernest Hemingway: Martha Gellhorn Reported on the War: Both Were Searching for the Truth," *North Dakota Quarterly* 68:2/3 (2001): 295–302; Amitava Banerjee, "Tragedian on the Scene: Hemingway as a War Correspondent," *Indian Journal of American Studies* 26:1 (1996): 31–38.

6. Anthony Feinstein, "The Emotional Health of Journalists." Address to Canadian Journalism Forum on Violence and Trauma, February 10, 2008, London, Ontario.

7. Ibid.; Donald J. Ringnalda, "Michael Herr," *Dictionary of Literary Biography* (1997).

8. Feinstein, Owen, and Blair, "Hazardous Profession," 1570–1575; Feinstein, *Journalists under Fire*, 60–61, 72–73, 132–133, 182; Michael Robertson, *Stephen Crane, Journalism, and the Making of Modern American Literature* (New York: Columbia University Press, 1997), 111; Davis, *Badge of Courage*, 192–195, 261–262; Sinclair, *Jack*, 172, 178, 180, 182, 190–191, 198, 202, 210–211, 213, 225, 240–241; Lynn, *Hemingway*, 509; Vincent Brome, *J. B. Priestley* (London: Hamish Hamilton, 1988), 57, 181–182, 213–214, 295, 329, 345, 360, 386, 430; Shelden, *Graham Greene*, 75, 230, 246–247, 310, 322, 324, 353, 355–356; Benson, *John Steinbeck*, 121, 355, 536–537, 998; Hastings, *Evelyn Waugh*, 97, 337, 601, 621.

9. Feinstein, "Emotional Health of Journalists."

10. Hunt, *Memory, War and Trauma*, 140–160; Heberle, *Trauma Artist*, 75–80, 231.

11. Michael Schudson, *Discovering the News: A Social History of American Newspapers* (New York: Basic, 1978), 61–65.

12. Morris, *Ambrose Bierce*, 21–39, 60, 63, 65–74, 83–86, 88–89, 230–234.

13. Robertson, *Stephen Crane*, 139, 144–145, 151–152, 163–164; Dudley, "Crane's Dispatches from Cuba," 11–22; McLoughlin, *Martha Gellhorn*, 12.

14. Morris, *Ambrose Bierce*, 21–39, 60, 63, 65–74, 83–86, 88–89, 231; Richard O'Connor, *Ambrose Bierce: A Biography* (Boston: Little, Brown, 1967), 22–23, 41–42.

15. John Richetti, Introduction to Daniel Defoe, *Robinson Crusoe* (1719; repr., London: Penguin, 2001), xxviii.

16. Philip Young, *Ernest Hemingway: A Reconsideration* (University Park: Pennsylvania State University Press, 1966), 163–171; Joseph De Falco, *The Hero in Hemingway's Short Stories* (Pittsburgh, Pa.: University of Pittsburgh Press, 1963); Delbert E.

Wylder, *Hemingway's Heroes* (Albuquerque: University of New Mexico Press, 1969); Leo Gurko, *Ernest Hemingway and the Pursuit of Heroism* (New York: Crowell, 1968); Thomas Myers, "Tim O'Brien," *Dictionary of Literary Biography* (1995).

17. Robert Spector, *Tobias George Smollett* (Boston: Twayne, 1989), 39–46; James Glen Stovall, "Philip Freneau," and Richard D. Fulton, "Douglas Jerrold," *Dictionary of Literary Biography* (1985, 1996); Jacob Axelrad, *Philip Freneau, Champion of Democracy* (Austin: University of Texas Press, 1967), 109, 112, 328; Underwood, *Journalism and the Novel*, 56–57.

18. Walt Whitman, *Specimen Days*, in *Specimen Days, Democratic Vistas, and Other Prose*, edited by Louise Pound (1892; repr., Garden City, N.Y.: Doubleday, Doran, 1935), 43; Reynolds, *Walt Whitman's America*, 411, 426–431.

19. Whitman, *Specimen Days*, 29–30, 39–40, 46.

20. Ambrose Bierce, *Tales of Soldiers and Civilians and Other Stories* (New York: Penguin, 2000), 23, 25, 37, 41, 59–62; Russell Duncan and David J. Klooster, eds., *Phantoms of a Blood-Stained Period: The Complete Civil War Writings of Ambrose Bierce* (Amherst: University of Massachusetts Press, 2002), 8–9, 11, 15–16, 19–21, 26, 28; Bierce, "little battle-yarns" quotation in review of David M. Owens, *The Devil's Topographer: Ambrose Bierce and the American War Story* (Knoxville: University of Tennessee Press, 2006), http://www.ambrosebierce.org.

21. Ambrose Bierce, "What I Saw at Shiloh" and "An Affair of Outposts," in Duncan and Klooster, *Phantoms of a Blood-Stained Period*, 103–104, 123, 126, 183; Bierce, *Tales of Soldiers*, 74, 76–77.

22. Ambrose Bierce, *Skepticism and Dissent: Selected Journalism from 1898–1901*, edited by Lawrence I. Berkove (Ann Arbor, Mich.: Delmas, 1980), 116, 139, 149; Duncan and Klooster, *Phantoms of a Blood-Stained Period*, 27–28.

23. John Dos Passos, *Three Soldiers* (1921; repr., New York: Modern Library, 1932), 157, 207–208, 259; Ludington, *John Dos Passos*, 129–130, 134, 138.

24. Vera Brittain, *Wartime Chronicle: Diary 1939–1945* (London: Gollancz, 1989), 18; Deborah Gorham, *Vera Brittain: A Feminist Life* (Oxford, U.K.: Blackwell, 1996), 1–2, 81.

25. Gorham, *Vera Brittain*, 81, 107–108, 113, 127–128, 144–145.

26. David Sanders, "John Hersey," *Dictionary of Literary Biography* (2003).

27. John Hersey, *Hiroshima* (1946; repr., New York; Bantam, 1986), 25, 51–52, 104–105.

28. Kurt Vonnegut, *Slaughterhouse-Five* (1969; repr., New York: Dell, 1991), 4, 22–27, 177–178, 191, 210, 214.

29. Ibid., 5, 8–10; Laura M. White, "P. G. Wodehouse," *Dictionary of Literary Biography* (2009).

30. Michael Herr, *Dispatches* (1977; repr., New York: Vintage, 1991), 63.

31. Ibid., 20; Peebles, "Fighting to Understand," 479–496; Marc Weingarten, *The Gang That Wouldn't Write Straight: Wolfe, Thompson, Didion, and the New Journalism Revolution* (New York: Crown, 2006), 173–174.

32. David Bennett, "Tracy Kidder," *Dictionary of Literary Biography* (1997); "Gloria Emerson," *Contemporary Authors Online* (2007); Philip Caputo, *A Rumor of War* (1977; repr., New York: Ballantine, 1986), 191, 219, 297, 323; Philip Caputo, *DelCorso's Gallery* (1983; repr., New York: Harper Perennial, 1991), 28, 176.

33. A. J. Langguth, *Saki: A Life of Hector Hugh Munro* (New York: Simon and Schuster, 1981), 254, 258–259, 266, 277; Maureen Modlish, "H. H. Munro," and Alexander Malcolm Forbes, "H. H. Munro," *Dictionary of Literary Biography* (1984, 1996).

34. Schudson, *Discovering the News*, 61–65.

35. Phillip Knightley, *The First Casualty, from the Crimea to Vietnam: The War Correspondent as Hero, Propagandist, and Myth-Maker* (New York: Harcourt Brace Jovanovich, 1975), 43–44.

36. George Orwell, "Rudyard Kipling," in *Kipling and the Critics*, edited by Elliott Gilbert (New York: New York University Press, 1965), 74.

37. Langguth, *Saki*, 251; Franklin Walker, *Frank Norris: A Biography* (1932; repr., New York: Russell and Russell, 1963), 176; Rena Sanderson, "Hemingway's Literary Sisters: The Author through the Eyes of Women Writers," in *Hemingway and Women: Female Critics and the Female Voice*, edited by Lawrence R. Broer and Gloria Holland (Tuscaloosa: The University of Alabama Press, 2002), 280; Paine, "glow of hope" quotation, http://www.positive.atheism.org.

38. H. Wayne Morgan, *Writers in Transition: Seven Americans* (New York: Hill and Wang, 1963), 1–22. Crane's conception of the hero's code is discussed extensively in Morgan. An analysis of Hemingway's version can be found in Young, *Ernest Hemingway*, 56–78. Kipling's version of the hero's code is expressed in the character Mowgli and in the "law of the jungle" from *The Jungle Book* and *The Second Jungle Book*. It is summarized in the poem "The Law of the Jungle," http:/www.poetryloverspage .com. It also is expressed in the characters of Gunga Din, in Kipling's poem of the same name, and Kimball O'Hara, the protagonist of Kipling's novel *Kim*.

39. Robert W. Schneider, *Five Novelists of the Progressive Era* (New York: Columbia University Press, 1965), 94–111; Stallman, *Stephen Crane*, 5, 54–56; Benfey, *Double Life of Stephen Crane*, 15, 229–230; Davis, *Badge of Courage*, 264–266.

40. Stallman, *Stephen Crane*, 362, 364, 368–369, 371–372, 377, 393; W. L. Swanberg, *Citizen Hearst: A Biography of William Randolph Hearst* (1961; repr., New York: Collier, 1986), 187–191; Peter Manso, *Mailer: His Life and Times* (1985; repr., New York: Washington Square, 2008), 89.

41. Stephen Crane, *Stephen Crane: Uncollected Writings*, edited by Olov W. Fryckstedt (Uppsala, Sweden: Studia Anglistica Upsaliensia, 1963), 257–259, 261, 269, 348, 351, 360–362; Stallman, *Stephen Crane*, 354, 359.

42. Stephen Crane, *Wounds in the Rain and Other Impressions of War* (1900; repr., New York: Knopf, 1926), 130–131, 236, 238.

43. Stephen Crane, *Active Service*, in *Collected Works* (1899; repr., Secaucus, N.J.: Castle, 1986), 293, 300; Underwood, *Journalism and the Novel*, 172.

44. Philip Mason, *Kipling: The Glass, the Shadow and the Fire* (New York: Harper

and Row, 1975), 133, 199, 300; Charles Carrington, *Rudyard Kipling: His Life and Work* (1955; repr., New York: Penguin, 1986), 394, 397; Lord Birkenhead, *Rudyard Kipling* (London: Weidenfeld and Nicolson, 1978), 216–217, 222, 224; Martin Seymour-Smith, *Rudyard Kipling* (London: Macdonald, 1989), 111–112.

45. Birkenhead, *Rudyard Kipling*, 210–212; Mason, *Kipling*, 91, 93–94; Seymour-Smith, *Rudyard Kipling*, 172–173.

46. Carrington, *Rudyard Kipling*, 367; Birkenhead, *Rudyard Kipling*, 210–212; *Sea to Sea*, chap. 36, ebooks.adelaide.edu.au.

47. Rudyard Kipling, *The Light That Failed* (1891; repr., London: House of Stratus, 2003), 220–221, 226–227.

48. Sinclair, *Jack*, 78–79, 109–111; Sweeney, "Delays and Vexations," 548–559.

49. Stallman, *Stephen Crane*, 368, 393–394; Sinclair, *Jack*, 109, 111, 135; John C. Bromley, "Richard Harding Davis," *Dictionary of Literary Biography* (1989).

50. Walker, *Frank Norris*, 83, 89, 109, 119–120, 189, 199; Crisler, "College Man in South Africa," 5–7.

51. Lynn, *Hemingway*, 502–504, 509–510, 512–522; Coté, "Correspondent or Warrior?," 88–104; Gladstein, "Mr. Novelist Goes to War," 258–266.

52. Lynn, *Hemingway*, 80–92.

53. Ernest Hemingway, *A Farewell to Arms* (1929; repr., New York: Scribners, 1957), 11, 27, 92, 131–132, 338.

54. Hemingway, *The Sun Also Rises*, 39.

55. Ernest Hemingway, *By-Line: Ernest Hemingway* (1968; repr., New York: Penguin, 1980), 323–324, 336–338.

56. Carl Rollyson, *Nothing Ever Happens to the Brave: The Story of Martha Gellhorn* (New York: St. Martin's, 1990), 105–108; Diebler, "Date-line: D-Day," 295–302; Sanderson, "Hemingway's Literary Sisters," 280.

57. Giovanna Dell'Orto, "'Memory and Imagination are the Great Deterrents': Martha Gellhorn at War as Correspondent and Literary Author," *Journal of American Culture* 27:3 (2004): 303–314; Martha Gellhorn, *A Stricken Field* (1940; repr., London: Virago, 1986).

58. Faith Berry, *Langston Hughes: Before and beyond Harlem* (Westport, Conn.: Lawrence Hill, 1983), 260–269.

59. Benson, *John Steinbeck*, 496, 504–505, 529–533, 997–1000, 1004, 1009–1014; Sullivan, "John Steinbeck, War Reporter," 16–23; Gladstein, "Mr. Novelist Goes to War," 258–266.

60. Shelden, *Orwell*, 267–271, 276–277, 284; Orwell, "dreamed incessantly of Spain" quotation, http://www.h-net.org.

61. George Orwell, *Homage to Catalonia* (1938; repr., London: Secker & Warburg, 1997), 137–139, 141, 143, 145–146, 184–185.

62. Shelden, *Orwell*, 318, 326, 333, 437; Orwell, "life is suffering" quotation, http://www.classiclit.about.com.

63. Shelden, *Graham Greene*, 23–27, 33–34, 324–339.

64. Moseley, "Auberon Waugh," *Dictionary of Literary Biography*; Hastings, *Evelyn Waugh*, 528, 578.

65. Paula Reed, "Edna Ferber," Jo R. Mengedoht, "Dorothy Thompson," Grace Farrell, "Lillie Devereux Blake," Eric Purchase, "Sarah Margaret (Fuller marchesa d') Ossoli," and Angela Courtney, "Edna Ferber," *Dictionary of Literary Biography* (1981, 1984, 1999, 2001, 2003).

66. Hilary Mills, *Mailer: A Biography* (New York: Empire, 1982), 83, 215–232, 257; Mary V. Dearborn, *Mailer: A Biography* (Boston: Houghton Mifflin, 1999), 26, 39–40; Manso, *Mailer*, 76, 81.

67. Filkins, comments, http://www.bookbrowse.com; Finkel, comments, http://www.thebookstudio.com; Dexter Filkins, *The Forever War* (2008; repr., New York: Vintage, 2009), 340.

68. Bernstein, *Thurber*, 384–385.

Chapter 4. Depression, Drink, and Dissipation

1. Lynn, *Hemingway*, 336–337, 576–579.

2. Ibid., 530–531, 582–593; Rena Sanderson, "Hemingway and Gender History," in Donaldson, *Cambridge Companion to Hemingway*, 184.

3. Storr, *Solitude*, 123; "Virginia Woolf," *Contemporary Authors Online* (2004).

4. Ben Hecht and Charles MacArthur, *The Front Page: From Theatre to Reality* (1928; repr., Hanover, N.H.: Smith and Kraus, 2002), 80, 85–86, 144, 187.

5. Underwood, "Depression, Drink, and Dissipation," 187. Dunne quote, http://www.quotes.dictionary.com.

6. Pete Hamill, *A Drinking Life: A Memoir* (Boston: Little Brown, 1994), 183–185, 212, 229–230.

7. Eberhard H. Uhlenhuth, Harriet De Wit, Mitchell B. Balter, Chris E. Johanson, and Glen D. Mellinger, "Risks and Benefits of Long-Term Benzodiazepine Use," *Journal of Clinical Psychopharmacology* 8:3 (1988): 161–167; Carl Salzman, "Issues and Controversies Regarding Benzodiazepine Use," *NIDA Res Monograph* 131 (1993): 68–88; Lorne B. Warneke, "Benzodiazepines: Abuse and New Use," *Canadian Journal of Psychiatry* 36:3 (1991): 194–205; August Piper Jr., "Addiction to Benzodiazepines-How Common?" *Archives of Family Medicine* 4 (November 1995): 968.

8. Robert Lichter, Stanley Rothman, and Linda S. Lichter, *The Media Elite: America's New Powerbrokers* (Bethesda, Md.: Adler and Adler, 1986), 93–131; Justin Kaplan, *Lincoln Steffens: A Biography* (New York: Simon and Schuster, 1974), 278–279; Mary E. Tomkins, "Ida M. Tarbell," *Dictionary of Literary Biography* (1986).

9. Doug Underwood and Dana Bagwell, "Journalists with Literary Ambitions No Less Satisfied with Their Jobs," *Newspaper Research Journal* 27 (Spring 2006): 75–83; Doug Underwood and Dana Bagwell, "Newspapers as Launching Pads for Literary Careers: A Study of How Today's Literary-Aspirants in the Newsroom Feel about Daily Journalism's Role in Developing Literary Talent." Association for Education in Journalism and Mass Communication, San Francisco, Calif., August 2006; Doug Underwood, *When MBAs Rule the Newsroom: How the Marketers and Managers Are Reshaping Today's Media* (New York: Columbia University Press, 1993), 26–37,

219–222; Keith Stamm and Doug Underwood, "The Relationship of Job Satisfaction to Newsroom Policy Changes," *Journalism Quarterly* 70 (Fall 1993): 528–541.

10. Feinstein, Owen, and Blair, "Hazardous Profession," 1570–1575; Ghaffer and Feinstein, "Reporting under Fire," 31–33; Feinstein and Nicolson, "Embedded Journalists in the Iraq War," 129–132; Pyevich, Newman, and Daleiden, "Relationship among Cognitive Schemas," 325–328; Roger Simpson and James Boggs, "An Exploratory Study of Traumatic Stress among Newspaper Journalists," *Journalism Communication Monographs* 1:1 (1999): 1–24.

11. In the mental health area, I looked for evidence that a journalist-literary figure suffered from depression, anxiety, manic-depressive tendencies, or other forms of emotional imbalance without necessarily trying to judge whether this might be deemed a fully diagnosable condition. With substance abuse, the task was a bit trickier because most artists drink at least somewhat, and it required some judgment to determine when a drinking pattern could be viewed as a drinking problem. However, note that this method may underestimate how many journalist-literary figures suffered from mental health or substance abuse problems because contemporary journalist-literary figures often have not had biographies written about them beyond short online accounts that often do not discuss their personal lives in great detail.

12. Again, this figure may underestimate the percentage of journalist-literary figures who suffered from mental health issues. Contemporary journalist-literary figures that have not had in-depth biographies written about them were included in the total number of journalist-literary figures studied. For mental health issues in the general public, see http://www.surgeongeneral.gov./library/mentalhealth/chapter1. Also see Underwood, "Depression, Drink, and Dissipation," 197–198 (n. 51) for biographical references about mental and emotional troubles for many of the figures cited in the appendix. Information about the mental health of the following figures also can be found in Gale's online biographies for Angelou, Braddon, Caputo, Cheever, Rebecca H. Davis, Herr, Hurston, Kidder, Masefield, Nesbit, Norton, Vonnegut, Wiesel, and Wollstonecraft. In addition, other references to mental health issues include: Barnes (Phillip F. Herring, *Djuna: The Life and Work of Djuna Barnes* [New York: Viking, 1950], 233, 246, 295–296); Barrie (Lisa Chaney, *Hide-and-Seek with the Angels: A Life of J. M. Barrie* [London: Hutchinson, 2005], 18–21, 46, 62–63, 65, 68, 99, 277; Dunbar, *J. M. Barrie*, 380, 385–387); Bly (Brooke Kroeger, *Nellie Bly: Daredevil, Reporter, Feminist* [New York: Times Books, 1994], 136, 188–190, 192, 369); Broun (O'Connor, *Heywood Broun*, 112, 176–177, 192); Carter (Peach, *Angela Carter*, 16–17; Sarah Gamble, *Angela Carter: A Literary Life* [New York: Palgrave Macmillan, 2006], 52–53); Chesterton (Coren, *Gilbert*, 44–52, 58–62); Defoe (Novak, *Daniel Defoe*, 468, 671–672, 701–702); Dickens (Jamison, *Touched with Fire*, 268; Kaplan, *Dickens*, 30, 59, 69, 508, 535); Fern (Warren, *Fanny Fern*, 228; Nancy A. Walker, *Fanny Fern* [New York: Twayne, 1993], 11); Frost (Jay Parini, *Robert Frost: A Life* [New York: Henry Holt, 1999], 61, 64); Godwin (history.com/this-day-in-history); Hapgood (Marcaccio,

Hapgoods, 160–162, 194–198, 219–220); Harte (Axel Nissen, *Bret Harte: Prince and Pauper* [Jackson: University Press of Mississippi, 2000], 49); Kaufman (Meredith, *George S. Kaufman*, 6–8); Kipling (Wilson, *Wound and the Bow*, 166–168); Liebling (Raymond Sokolov, *Wayward Reporter: The Life of A. J. Liebling* [New York: Harper and Row, 1980], 131, 195, 231, 233); Lowell (Edward Wagenknecht, *James Russell Lowell: Portrait of a Many-Sided Man* [New York: Oxford University Press, 1971], 48–51); O'Brien (Heberle, *Trauma Artist*, xv, 289, 293); Porter (Givner, *Katherine Anne Porter*, 445–446); Pritchett (Treglown, *V. S. Pritchett*, 119, 191); Ruskin (Hunt, *Life of John Ruskin*, 370–371); Steffens (Kaplan, *Lincoln Steffens*, 175–176); Dorothy Thompson (Sanders, *Dorothy Thompson*, 99–100, 107); Hunter Thompson (William McKeen, *Outlaw Journalist: The Life and Times of Hunter S. Thompson* [New York: Norton, 2008], 264–265, 344, 347–351, 355–356; McKeen, *Hunter S. Thompson*, 1, 14–15, 51–61); Twain (James Caron, *Mark Twain: Unsanctified Newspaper Reporter* [Columbia: University of Missouri Press, 2008], 167); Vonnegut (Stanley Schatt, *Kurt Vonnegut, Jr.* [Boston: Twayne, 1976], 108–109); and Wilde (Annie Marie Donahue, "Ken's Oscar," http://www.bostonphoenix.com). Quindlen, "diagnosis" quotation, http://www.quotegarden.com.

13. E. B. White, *Letters of E. B. White,* rev. ed., edited by Dorothy Lobrano Guth and Martha White (New York: Harper Perennial, 2007), xvii; Taylor, *Thackeray*, 396–397; Swanberg, *Dreiser*, 94–108; O'Connor, *Heywood Broun*, 112; Herring, *Djuna*, 295; Kalaidjian, *Edge of Modernism*, 162–165; Thackeray, "despair" quotation, http://www.quotationsbook.com.

14. James Boswell, *The Hypochondriack*, vol. 1 (1777–1783; repr., Stanford University, Calif.: Stanford University Press, 1928), 108–109, 138, 203; James Boswell, *The Hypochondriack*, vol. 2 (1777–1783; repr., Stanford University, Calif.: Stanford University Press, 1928), 2, 41–46, 157.

15. Silverman, *Edgar A. Poe*, 114–115, 151.

16. Charlotte Perkins Gilman, *The Yellow Wallpaper* (1899; repr., New York: The Feminist Press, 1973), 10, 15–16, 36, 41, 46–48.

17. Sari Edelstein, "Charlotte Perkins Gilman and the Yellow Newspaper," *Legacy* 24:1 (2007): 72–92; Denise K. Knight, "Charlotte Perkins Gilman, William Randolph Hearst, and the Practice of Ethical Journalism," in Davis and Knight, *Charlotte Gilman Perkins and Her Contemporaries*, 48; Oliver and Scharnhorst, "Charlotte Perkins versus Ambrose Bierce," 32, 36, 39; Shelley Fisher Fishkin, "'Making a Change': Strategies of Subversion in Gilman's Journalism and Short Fiction," in *Critical Essays on Charlotte Perkins Gilman*, edited by Joanne B. Karpinski (New York: G. K. Hall, 1992), 236, 244, 246.

18. Jean Marie Lutes, "Into the Madhouse with Nellie Bly: Girl Stunt Reporting in Late Nineteenth-Century America," *American Quarterly* 54:2 (2002): 217–253.

19. Ibid., 217, 224, 230–231, 244; Karen Roggenkamp, "To Turn a Fiction into Fact: Nellie Bly, Jules Verne, and Trips Around the World," *Journal of the American Studies Association of Texas* 31 (October 2000): 19–46; Nancy Bombaci, "'Well, of Course. I

Used to Be Absolutely Gorgeous Dear': The Female Interviewer as Subject/Object in Djuna Barnes's Journalism," *Criticism* 44:2 (2002): 161–185; Roberts, *Dorothy Day*, 24.

20. Chaney, *Hide-and-Seek with Angels*, 18–21; Birkin, *J. M. Barrie*, 26–28; Donna R. White, "J. M. Barrie," *Dictionary of Literary Biography* (1994); Wagenknecht, *James Russell Lowell*, 11, 41.

21. Norman and Jeanne MacKenzie, *The Life of H. G. Wells: The Time Traveller* (1973; repr., London: Hogarth, 1987), 30, 48, 72, 94, 120, 133, 137, 150, 207, 227, 278, 289, 329–331, 335–336, 339–343; Foot, *H. G.*, 55, 77, 80–82, 86, 112, 143.

22. G. K. Chesterton, *The Autobiography of G. K. Chesterton* (New York: Sheed & Ward, 1936), 29, 75–76, 89–91, 98, 100, 159, 179, 189.

23. Clarke, *Capote*, 397–398, 400–401, 498–499, 533, 542, 546.

24. Bernard Weinraub, "Mailer Tells a Lot. Not All, but a Lot," *New York Times* (October 4, 2000): partnersnytimescom; Manso, *Mailer*, 313–335; Dearborn, *Mailer*, 163–170; Vonnegut, *Slaughterhouse-Five*, 206.

25. Joan Didion, *The White Album* (1979; repr., New York: Pocket, 1980), 14–15; Katherine Usher Henderson, *Joan Didion* (New York: Frederick Ungar, 1981), 4, 10–14.

26. Lehrer, "Depression's Upside," 38–44.

27. "Module 1: Epidemiology of Alcohol Problems in the United States," National Institute on Alcohol Abuse and Alcoholism of the National Institutes of Health, http://www.pubs.nica.nih.gov. The full extent of substance abuse problems could not always be evaluated by biographical accounts in which some biographers may have shied away from assessing or fully discussing the drinking and drug-taking of their subjects. This was particularly the case for contemporary journalist-literary figures that have not had major biographies written about them. See Underwood, "Depression, Drink, and Dissipation," 198–199 (n. 53) for biographical references about substance abuse for many of the figures cited in the appendix. Substance abuse information for the following figures also can be found in Gale online biographies for Angelou, Breslin, Dunbar, Hamill, Herr, and Thomas. In addition, other references to substance abuse issues include: Barnes (Herring, *Djuna*, 233, 248–249); Barrie (Chaney, *Hide-and-Seek-with-the-Angels*, 348–349, 373, 386–387); Behan (Ted Eugene Boyle, *Brendan Behan* [New York: Twayne, 1969], 22–23); Bierce (Morris, *Ambrose Bierce*, 146, 155, 187, 198, 229); Broun (O'Connor, *Heywood Broun*, 176); Chesterton (Coren, *Gilbert*, 71–72, 134, 138–139); Hapgood (Marcaccio, *Hapgoods*, 160, 218); Lowell (Wagenknecht, *James Russell Lowell*, 29–34); Royko (John Kass, *The World of Mike Royko* [Madison: University of Wisconsin Press, 1999], 73, 94); Twain (Caron, *Mark Twain*, 129–131). Also note that Donald W. Goodwin found that bartenders and writers died of cirrhosis of the liver more than people in any other occupation. Goodwin, *Alcohol and the Writer*, 2, 4–5.

28. Howard Good, *Acquainted with the Night: The Image of Journalists in American Fiction, 1890–1930* (Metuchen, N.J.: Scarecrow Press, 1986), 77. See also Thomas Berry, *The Newspaper in the American Novel 1900–1969* (Metuchen, N.J.: Scarecrow Press, 1970).

29. Loren Ghiglione, "The American Journalist: Fiction versus Fact," in John B. Hench, ed., *Three Hundred Years of the American Newspaper* (Worchester, Mass.: American Antiquarian Society, 1991).

30. Butscher, *Aiken*, 431; Marcaccio, *Hapgoods*, 160, 220; Goodwin, *Alcohol and the Writer*, 123, 130–131.

31. Taylor, *Thackeray*, 89, 438; Morris, *Ambrose Bierce*, 154–155, 165; Yardley, *Ring*, 99, 282; Meade, *Dorothy Parker*, 346; Altman, *Laughter's Gentle Soul*, 356; Swanberg, *Dreiser*, 355, 469, 505; Hastings, *Evelyn Waugh*, 622, 624; Patey, *Life of Evelyn Waugh*, 318, 324–325; Waugh, *Will This Do?*, 30; http://www.proz.com.

32. Arthur and Barbara Gelb, *O'Neill: Life with Monte Cristo* (2000; repr., New York: Applause, 2002), 32, 74–75, 113, 129, 173–175; Giles, "Gail Godwin," *Dictionary of Literary Biography*.

33. Giles, "Gail Godwin," *Dictionary of Literary Biography*.

34. Bergreen, *James Agee*, 12–13, 17–18; Agee, *Death in the Family*, 65, 67, 69, 71–72.

35. Walt Whitman, *Franklin Evans* (1842; repr., Durham, N.C.: Duke University Press, 2007), 27–28, 50, 68, 71; Jerome Loving, *Walt Whitman: The Song of Himself* (1999; repr., Berkeley: University of California Press, 2000), 124; Justin Kaplan, *Walt Whitman: A Life* (New York: Simon and Schuster, 1980), 104–105.

36. Charles Lamb, "Confessions of a Drunkard," in *The Complete Works of Charles Lamb* (New York: Modern Library, 1935), 223–224, 226–228.

37. De Quincey, *Confessions of an English Opium-Eater*, 2, 6, 16–17, 37–41, 48–49, 53, 55, 63, 67–68, 78–79.

38. Graham Greene, *The Power and the Glory* (1940; repr., New York: Time, 1962), 30, 70, 77, 87, 92, 250.

39. Jack London, *John Barleycorn*, in *Jack London: Novels and Social Writings* (1913; repr., New York: Literary Classics of the United States, 1982), 936–938, 942, 955, 973, 982, 993–995, 997–998; Morris, *Ambrose Bierce*, 155.

40. Hunter S. Thompson, *The Rum Diary: A Novel* (New York: Simon & Schuster, 1998), 2–4, 22; Hunter S. Thompson, "What Lured Hemingway to Ketchum?," in *The Great Shark Hunt, Gonzo Papers, Volume 1: Strange Tales from a Strange Time* (1979; repr., New York: Simon & Schuster, 2003), 369–373; Paul Perry, *Fear and Loathing: The Strange and Terrible Saga of Hunter S. Thompson* (New York: Thunder's Mouth Press, 1992), 62–64, 86, 88–89, 242–244; McKeen, *Hunter S. Thompson*, 15; Thompson, "advocate drugs" quotation, http://www.brainyquote.com; Hemingway, "as necessary" quotation, www.eatdrinkpaint.blogspot.com.

41. Hamill, *A Drinking Life*, 183–185, 240.

42. Ann Waldron, "Writers and Alcohol," *The Washington Post* (March 14, 1989), 13–15; Upton Sinclair, *The Cup of Fury* (Great Neck, N.Y.: Channel Press, 1956), 13, 48, 68–69, 76, 98, 144. Sinclair also discusses Hart Crane, Stephen Crane, Dreiser, London, O. Henry, McCarthy, and O'Neill.

43. Mark Schorer, *Sinclair Lewis: An American Life* (New York: McGraw-Hill, 1961), 370–371, 423–424, 521, 536, 604, 674.

44. Andrew Lycett, *Dylan Thomas: A New Life* (Woodstock, N.Y.: Overlook Press, 2004), 53–57, 364, 368–369, 372–374.

45. Hutchins Hapgood, *A Victorian in the Modern World* (1939; repr., Seattle: University of Washington Press, 1972), 17–18, 53–54, 383–384; Marcaccio, *Hapgoods*, 160, 220.

46. Yardley, *Ring*, 239.

47. Neeli Cherkovski, *Bukowski: A Life* (1991; repr., South Royalton, Vt.: Steerforth, 1997), 16, 19, 33–34, 42, 225–227, 315.

48. Michael O'Sullivan, *Brendan Behan: A Life* (Dublin: Blackwater Press, 1997), xii, 11, 38, 40, 43, 47, 70, 139, 173, 188, 209–211, 258–261, 269, 288–289, 296, 299.

49. Jack Fruchtman, *Thomas Paine: Apostle of Freedom* (New York: Four Walls Eight Windows, 1994), 415–434; Silverman, *Edgar A. Poe*, 183–184, 416–419, 427, 433–436; Sinclair, *Jack*, 154–157, 172, 176–177, 180, 198, 202, 225, 240–242, 244–245, 248–250; Bernstein, *Thurber*, 335, 677–681; Altman, *Laughter's Gentle Soul*, 221–224, 357–360; Moreau, *Journey of James Agee*, 244–246; Boyle, *Brendan Behan*, 22–23; Clarke, *Capote*, 542, 545–546; Sinclair, *Cup of Fury*, 140; Benchley, "drinking myself to slow death" quotation, http://www.brainyquote.com.

50. Manso, *Mailer*, 699; Clarke, *Capote*, 499.

Epilogue: New Challenges, New Treatments

1. Bernstein, *Thurber*, 296, 660–661, 677, 688–689.

2. Elledge, *E. B. White*, 337; White, *Letters of E. B. White*, xvii, 236, 249, 408, 451, 679; White, "picking grapes" quotation, http://www.brainyquote.com.

Index

DOUG UNDERWOOD is a professor of communication at the University of Washington. He is the author of four books, including *From Yahweh to Yahoo!: The Religious Roots of the Secular Press.*

THE HISTORY OF COMMUNICATION

The University of Illinois Press
is a founding member of the
Association of American University Presses.

―――――――――――――――――――――

Composed in 10.5/13 Minion Pro
with Frutiger display
by Celia Shapland
at the University of Illinois Press
Manufactured by Sheridan Books, Inc.

University of Illinois Press
1325 South Oak Street
Champaign, IL 61820-6903
www.press.uillinois.edu